Mastering Jakarta Struts

James Goodwill

Wiley Publishing, Inc.

Publisher: Robert Ipsen
Editor: Robert M. Elliott
Managing Editor: John Atkins
Book Packaging: Ryan Publishing Group, Inc.

Copyeditor: Elizabeth Welch
Proofreader: Nancy Sixsmith
Compositor: Gina Rexrode
Technical Editor: Avery Regier

This book is printed on acid-free paper. ∞

Published by Wiley Publishing, Inc., Indianapolis, Indiana

Published simultaneously in Canada.

Library of Congress Cataloging-in-Publication Data:

ISBN: 0-471-21302-0

Printed in the United States of America

10 9 8 7 6 5 4 3 2

To my girls, Christy, Abby, and Emma

CONTENTS

Acknowledgments — ix

About the Author — xi

Introduction — xiii

Part I JXTA Overview

Chapter 1 Introducing the Jakarta Struts Project and Its Supporting Components — 1

The Jakarta Struts Project 1
- Understanding the MVC Design Pattern 2
- The Struts Implementation of the MVC 3

Web Applications 5
- The Directory Structure 5
- The Web Application Deployment Descriptor 6
- Packaging a Web Application 8

The Tomcat JSP/Servlet Container 8
- Installing and Configuring Tomcat 9
- Testing Your Tomcat Installation 10

Summary 12

Chapter 2 An Overview of the Java Servlet and JavaServer Pages Architectures — 13

The Java Servlet Architecture 13
- The GenericServlet and HttpServlet Classes 14
- The Life Cycle of a Servlet 16
- Building a Servlet 17
- The ServletContext 21
- Using Servlets to Retrieve HTTP Data 27

What Are JavaServer Pages? 32
- The Components of a JavaServer Page 34

Summary

Chapter 3 Getting Started with Struts — 59

Obtaining and Installing the Jakarta Struts Project 59

Creating Your First Struts Application 61
- Creating the Views 62
- Walking through the wileystruts Web Application 73

Summary 76

Part II Core Struts

Chapter 4 The Controller — 77

The ActionServlet Class 77
- Extending the ActionServlet 79
- Configuring the ActionServlet 80

The Action Class 82
The execute() Method 82
Extending the Action Class 83
Configuring the Action Class 84
Struts Plugins 87
init() 87
destroy() 87
Creating a Plugin 87
Configuring a Plugin 89
The RequestProcessor 90
Creating a New RequestProcessor 90
Configuring an Extended RequestProcessor 93
Summary 93

Chapter 5 The Views 95

Building a Struts View 95
Deploying JSPs to a Struts Application 96
JSPs that Gather Data 97
Summary 103

Chapter 6 Internationalizing Your Struts Applications 105

I18N Components of a Struts Application 105
The Controller 106
The View 108
Internationalizing the wileystruts Application 109
Summary 114

Chapter 7 Managing Errors 115

Struts Error Management 115
ActionError 115
ActionErrors 117
Adding Error Handling to the wileystruts Application 118
The ActionForm.validate() Method 119
<html:errors /> 121
Error Management in the Action.perform() Method 123
Summary 128

Chapter 8 Creating Custom ActionMappings 129

What Is an ActionMapping? 129
Creating a Custom ActionMapping 131
Creating an ActionMapping Extension for the wileystruts Application 132
Deploying the wiley.WileyActionMapping Extension 133
Using the wiley.WileyActionMapping Extension in the wileystruts Application 134
Summary 137

Chapter 9 The Struts JDBC Connection Pool 139

What Is a DataSource? 139
Using a DataSource in Your Struts Application 140
Creating a Sample Database 140

Using a DataSource in a Struts Application 142
Summary 147

Chapter 10 **Debugging Struts Applications** **149**

Embedding Tomcat into a Java Application 149
Debugging a Struts Application 158
Setting Up the Debug Environment 158
Debugging the wileystruts Application 162
Summary 164

Chapter 11 **Developing a Complete Struts Application** **165**

The Employees Application Definition 165
Preparing the Employees Application 165
Creating the Employees Model 172
Building the Employees Application 179
Walkthrough 229
Summary 233

Part III **Struts Reference**

Chapter 12 **The struts-config.xml File** **235**

The Struts Subelements 236
The <icon /> Subelement 236
The <display-name /> Subelement 237
The <description /> Subelement 237
The <set-property /> Subelement 238
Adding a Struts DataSource 238
Adding FormBean Definitions 240
Adding Global Forwards 241
Adding Actions 243
Adding a RequestProcessor 245
Adding Message Resources 246
Adding a Plug-in 247

Chapter 13 **The Bean Tag Library** **249**

Installing the Bean Tags 249
<bean:cookie /> 250
<bean:define /> 251
<bean:header /> 252
<bean:include /> 253
<bean:message /> 254
<bean:page /> 255
<bean:parameter /> 256
<bean:resource /> 256
<bean:size /> 257
<bean:struts /> 258
<bean:write /> 259

Chapter 14 **The HTML Tag Library** 261

Installing the HTML Tags 261
<html:base /> 262
<html:button /> 262
<html:cancel /> 264
<html:checkbox /> 267
<html:errors /> 269
<html:form /> 270
<html:hidden /> 272
<html:html /> 273
<html:image /> 274
<html:img /> 276
<html:link /> 279
<html:multibox /> 282
<html:select /> 285
<html:option /> 288
<html:options /> 290
<html:password /> 292
<html:radio /> 294
<html:reset /> 297
<html:rewrite /> 299
<html:submit /> 300
<html:text /> 302
<html:textarea /> 305

Chapter 15 **The Logic Tag Library** 309

Installing the Logic Tags 309
<logic:empty /> 310
<logic:notEmpty /> 310
<logic:equal /> 311
<logic:notEqual /> 312
<logic:forward /> 313
<logic:redirect /> 313
<logic:greaterEqual /> 315
<logic:greaterThan /> 316
<logic:iterate /> 316
<logic:lessEqual /> 318
<logic:lessThan /> 319
<logic:match /> 320
<logic:notMatch /> 321
<logic:present /> 322
<logic:notPresent /> 323

Chapter 16 **The Template Tag Library** 325

Installing the Template Tags 325
<template:get /> 326
<template:insert /> 327
<template:put /> 328

Index 329

ACKNOWLEDGMENTS

I would like to begin this text by thanking the people who made this book what it is today. They are the people who took my words and shaped them into something that I hope will help you use and develop Jakarta Struts applications. Of these people, I would like to especially thank Tim Ryan, Avery Regier, and Liz Welch. They all contributed considerably to what I hope is a successful book.

On a closer note, I would like to thank everyone at my company, Virtuas Solutions, LLC, for their support while I was completing this text. The entire "UNREAL" staff contributed by picking up my assignments when my plate was too full.

Finally, the most important contributors to this book are my wife, Christy, and our daughters, Abby and Emma. They are the ones who really sacrificed during the development of this text, and they are the ones who deserve the credit for this book. Without their support, this text would be a collection of words that made very little sense.

ABOUT THE AUTHOR

James Goodwill is the co-founder and chief technology officer at Virtuas Solutions, LLC, located in Denver, Colorado. With over 10 years of experience, James leads Virtuas' Senior Internet Architects in the development of cutting-edge tools designed for J2EE e-business acceleration.

In addition to his professional experience, James is a member of the JSP 2.0 Expert Group (JSR-152.) He is the author of the best-selling Java titles *Developing Java Servlets*, *Pure JavaServer Pages*, *Apache Jakarta Tomcat*, and *Mastering JSP Custom Tags and Tag Libraries*. James is also a regular columnist on the Java community Web site, OnJava.com.

More information about James, his work, and his previous publications can be found at his company's Web site, www.virtuas.com.

Introduction

Throughout my experiences in server-side development, I have assembled many applications using many different technology combinations. Of all of these, I am most impressed with the Java server-side technologies, including servlets, EJBs, JSPs, and JSP custom tags.

This text focuses on a particular server-side Java framework, known as the Jakarta Struts project, or simply enough Struts. Struts combines two of the most popular server-side Java technologies—JSPs and servlets—into a server-side implementation of the Model-View-Controller design pattern. It was conceived by Craig McClanahan in May of 2000, and has been under the watchful eye of the Apache Jakarta open source community since that time.

The remarkable thing about the Struts project is its early adoption, which is obviously a testament to both its quality and utility. The Java community, both commercial and private, has really gotten behind Struts. It is currently supported by all of the major application servers including BEA, Sun, HP, and (of course) Apache's Jakarta-Tomcat. The Tomcat group has even gone so far as to use a Struts application, in its most recent release 4.0.4, for managing Web applications hosted by the container.

This book covers everything you need to know about the Struts project and its supporting technologies, including JSPs, servlets, Web applications, and the Jakarta-Tomcat JSP/servlet container. The goal of this text is to provide you with the foundation you need to design, build, and deploy Jakarta Struts applications.

As I have stated with most of my book projects, there will be topics that I have not discussed, but that are of interest to individual readers. If you run across such an issue or just have a question, please feel free to contact me at books@virtuas.com. In these e-mails, please be sure to place the text "Jakarta-Struts" in the subject line.

Thanks and good luck,

James Goodwill III

The Organization of the Book

The book you are about to begin is formatted as a tutorial describing the Jakarta Struts project. It is divided into 16 distinct chapters, beginning with an introduction of Struts and continuing with discussions about each of the major Struts components:

Chapter 1: Introducing the Jakarta Struts Project and Its Supporting Components lays the groundwork for the complete text. We introduce the Jakarta Struts project, and discuss the Model-View-Controller (MVC) design pattern that it's based on. We also define Java Web applications, and explain how to construct and use them. In addition, we examine the Jakarta-Tomcat Web application container, the container used for all our examples.

Chapter 2: An Overview of the Java Servlet and JavaServer Pages Architectures contains a JSP and servlet primer. It is aimed at the Java developer who is not yet familiar with these two technologies. These topics are the foundation of Jakarta Struts projects, and you must understand them before continuing with the text.

Chapter 3: Getting Started with Struts is where we first encounter actual Struts code. This chapter covers the step-by-step process of building a Struts application by taking you through the development of a simple Struts application.

Chapter 4: The Controller begins our first detailed discussions of an individual group of Struts components. In this chapter, we look at four distinct Struts Controller components: the ActionServlet class, the Action class, Plugins, and the RequestProcesser.

Chapter 5: The Views discusses the Struts implementation of the View component of the MVC design pattern. This chapter covers everything you need to know when connecting JSPs to a Struts Controller. We also briefly discuss some of the tag libraries provided by the Struts framework.

Chapter 6: Internationalizing Your Struts Applications describes the Struts mechanisms for internationalized application development. Here, we examine each of the components used and provide an example of internationalizing a Struts application.

Chapter 7: Managing Errors looks at some of the methods available to you when you're managing errors in a Struts application. We begin by looking at the different error classes provided by the Struts framework, and we show how errors can be managed in both the Controller and Views of a Struts application by adding error handling to a sample application.

Chapter 8: Creating Custom ActionMappings discusses the org.apache.struts.action.ActionMapping class, which provides the information that the ActionServlet needs to know about the mapping of a request to a particular instance of an action class. After describing the default ActionMapping, we go on to explain how you can extend the ActionMapping class to provide specialized mapping information to the ActionServlet.

Chapter 9: The Struts JDBC Connection Pool discusses how you can leverage the built-in Struts functionality to manage a DataSource connected to a sample database.

Chapter 10: Debugging Struts Applications takes you through the process of creating an embedded version of the Tomcat container. We then describe the steps for adding the new container and a sample Struts application to an IDE for debugging.

Chapter 11: Developing a Complete Struts Application takes you through the development of an entire Struts application. The purpose of this chapter is to tie all of the previous discussions together by creating a practical Struts application.

Chapter 12: The struts-config.xml File describes the struts-config.xml file, the Struts deployment descriptor. We tell you how you can add and configure each major Struts component in this file.

Chapters 13–16: The Struts Custom Tag Libraries describe the Struts framework's tag libraries. In these chapters, we examine each of the Struts tag libraries, including the Bean, HTML, Logic, and Template tag libraries. We describe the custom tags in the library, look at their attributes, and provide examples of how they can be used.

CHAPTER 1

Introducing the Jakarta Struts Project and Its Supporting Components

In this chapter, we lay the foundation for all our further discussions. We start by providing a high-level description of the Jakarta Struts project. We then describe Java Web applications, which act as the packaging mechanism for all Struts applications. We conclude this chapter with a discussion of the Jakarta Tomcat JSP/servlet container, which we use to host all of our examples throughout the remainder of this text.

At the end of this chapter, you should have an understanding of what the Struts project is, be familiar with its packaging mechanism, and have an installed JSP/servlet container to run your Struts applications.

The Jakarta Struts Project

The Jakarta Struts project, an open-source project sponsored by the Apache Software Foundation, is a server-side Java implementation of the Model-View-Controller (MVC) design pattern. The Struts project was originally created by Craig McClanahan in May 2000, but since that time it has been taken over by the open-source community.

The Struts project was designed with the intention of providing an open-source framework for creating Web applications that easily separate the presentation layer and allow it to be abstracted from the transaction/data layers. Since its inception, Struts has received quite a bit of developer support, and is quickly becoming a dominant factor in the open-source community.

NOTE

There is a small debate going on in the development community as to the type of design pattern that the Struts project most closely resembles. According to the documentation provided by the actual developers of the Struts project, it is patterned after the MVC, but some folks insist that it more closely resembles the Front Controller design pattern described by Sun's J2EE Blueprints Program. The truth is that it does very much resemble the Front Controller pattern, but for the purpose of our discussions, I am sticking with the developers. If you would like to examine the Front Controller yourself, you can find a good article on this topic at the Java Developer Connection site: http://developer.java.sun.com/developer/technicalArticles/J2EE/despat/.

Understanding the MVC Design Pattern

To gain a solid understanding of the Struts Framework, you must have a fundamental understanding of the MVC design pattern, which it is based on. The MVC design pattern, which originated from Smalltalk, consists of three components: a Model, a View, and a Controller. Table 1.1 defines each of these components.

Table 1.1 The Three Components of the MVC

COMPONENT	DESCRIPTION
Model	Represents the data objects. The Model is what is being manipulated and presented to the user.
View	Serves as the screen representation of the Model. It is the object that presents the current state of the data objects.
Controller	Defines the way the user interface reacts to the user's input. The Controller component is the object that manipulates the Model, or data object.

We will discuss each of these components in more detail throughout this chapter. Some of the major benefits of using the MVC include:

Reliability: The presentation and transaction layers have clear separation, which allows you to change the look and feel of an application without recompiling Model or Controller code.

High reuse and adaptability: The MVC lets you use multiple types of views, all accessing the same server-side code. This includes anything from Web browsers (HTTP) to wireless browsers (WAP).

Very low development and life-cycle costs: The MVC makes it possible to have lower-level programmers develop and maintain the user interfaces.

Rapid deployment: Development time can be significantly reduced because Controller programmers (Java developers) focus solely on transactions, and View programmers (HTML and JSP developers) focus solely on presentation.

Maintainability: The separation of presentation and business logic also makes it easier to maintain and modify a Struts-based Web application.

The Struts Implementation of the MVC

The Struts Framework models its server-side implementation of the MVC using a combination of JSPs, custom JSP tags, and Java servlets. In this section, we briefly describe how the Struts Framework maps to each component of the MVC. When we have completed this discussion, we will have drawn a portrait similar to Figure 1.1.

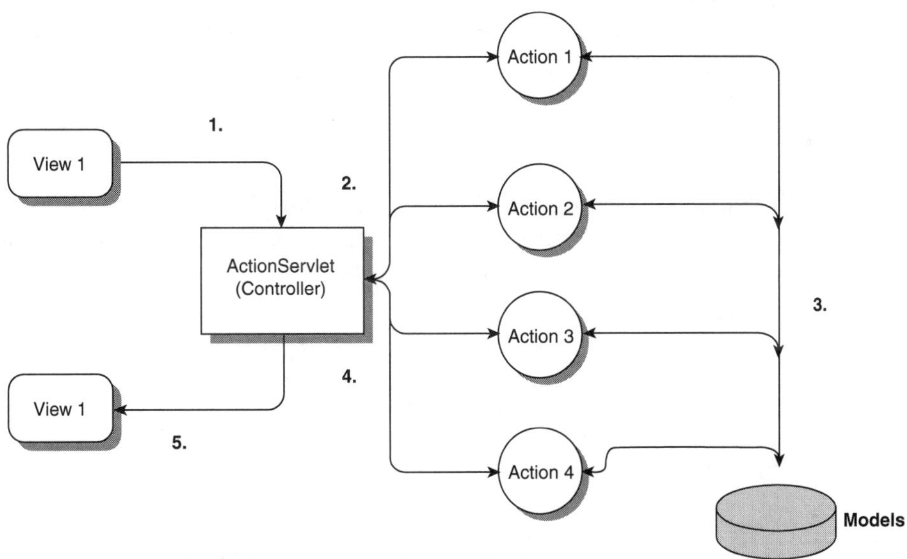

Figure 1.1 The Struts implementation of the MVC.

Figure 1.1 depicts the route that most Struts application requests follow. This process can be broken down into five basic steps. Following these steps is a description of the ActionServlet and Action classes.

1. A request is made from a previously displayed View.
2. The request is received by the ActionServlet, which acts as the Controller, and the ActionServlet looks up the requested URI in an XML file (described in Chapter 3, "Getting Started with Struts"), and determines the name of the Action class that will perform the necessary business logic.
3. The Action class performs its logic on the Model components associated with the application.
4. Once the Action has completed its processing, it returns control to the ActionServlet. As part of the return, the Action class provides a key that indicates the results of its processing. The ActionServlet uses this key to determine where the results should be forwarded for presentation.
5. The request is complete when the ActionServlet responds by forwarding the request to the View that was linked to the returned key, and this View presents the results of the Action.

The Model

The Struts Framework does not provide any specialized Model components; therefore, we will not dedicate an entire chapter to the Model component. Instead, we will reference Model components as they fit into each example.

The View

Each View component in the Struts Framework is mapped to a single JSP that can contain any combination of Struts custom tags. The following code snippet contains a sample Struts View:

```
<%@page language="java">
<%@taglib uri="/WEB-INF/struts-html.tld" prefix="html">

<html:form action="loginAction.do"
  name="loginForm"
  type="com.wiley.loginForm" >

  User Id: <html:text property="username"><br/>
  Password: <html:password property="password"><br/>
  <html:submit />
</html:form>
```

As you can see, several JSP custom tags are being leveraged in this JSP. These tags are defined by the Struts Framework, and provide a loose coupling to the Controller of a Struts application. We build a working Struts View in Chapter 3; and in Chapter 5, "The Views," we examine the Struts Views in more detail.

The Controller

The Controller component of the Struts Framework is the backbone of all Struts Web applications. It is implemented using a servlet named org.apache.struts.action.ActionServlet. This servlet receives all requests from clients, and delegates control of each request to a user-defined org.apache.struts.action.Action class. The ActionServlet delegates control based on the URI of the incoming request. Once the Action class has completed its processing, it returns a key to the ActionServlet, which is then used by the ActionServlet to determine the View that will present the results of the Action's processing. The ActionServlet is similar to a factory that creates Action objects to perform the actual business logic of the application.

The Controller of the Struts Framework is the most important component of the Struts MVC. We will discuss this component in Chapter 3, and in even greater detail in Chapter 4, "The Controller."

Web Applications

All Struts applications are packaged using the Java Web application format. Therefore, before we continue, let's take a brief look at Java Web applications.

Java Web applications are best described by the Java Servlet Specification 2.2, which introduced the idea using the following terms: "A Web Application is a collection of servlets, HTML pages, classes, and other resources that can be bundled and run on multiple containers from multiple vendors." In simpler terms, a Java Web application is a collection of one or more Web components that have been packaged together for the purpose of creating a complete application to be executed in the Web layer of an enterprise application. Here is a list of the common components that can be packaged in a Web application:

- Servlets
- JavaServer Pages (JSPs)
- JSP custom tag libraries
- Utility classes and application classes
- Static documents, including HTML, images, JavaScript, etc.
- Metainformation describing the Web application

The Directory Structure

All Web applications are packed into a common directory structure, and this directory structure is the container that holds the components of a Web application. The first step in creating a Web application is to create this structure. Table 1.2 describes a sample Web application named wileyapp, and lists the contents of each of its directories. Each one of these directories will be created from the *<SERVER_ROOT>* of the Servlet/JSP container.

Table 1.2 The Web Application Directory Structure

DIRECTORY	CONTAINS
/wileyapp	This is the root directory of the Web application. All JSP and HTML files are stored here.
/wileyapp/WEB-INF	This directory contains all resources related to the application that are not in the document root of the application. This is where your Web application deployment descriptor is located. You should note that the WEB-INF directory is not part of the public document. No files contained in this directory can be served directly to a client.
/ wileyapp/WEB-INF/classes	This directory is where servlet and utility classes are located.
/ wileyapp/WEB-INF/lib	This directory contains Java Archive (JAR) files that the Web application is dependent on.

If you're using Tomcat as your container, the default root directory is *<CATALINA_HOME>*/webapps/. Figure 1.2 shows the wileyapp as it would be hosted by a Tomcat container.

NOTE

Web applications allow compiled classes to be stored in both the /WEB-INF/classes and /WEB-INF/lib directories. Of these two directories, the class loader will load classes from the /classes directory first, followed by the JARs in the /lib directory. If you have duplicate classes in both the /classes and /lib directories, the classes in the /classes directory will take precedence.

The Web Application Deployment Descriptor

The backbone of all Web applications is its deployment descriptor. The Web application deployment descriptor is an XML file named web.xml that is located in the /*<SERVER_ROOT>*/*applicationname*/WEB-INF/ directory. The web.xml file describes all of the components in the Web application. If we use the previous Web application name, wileyapp, then the web.xml file would be located in the /<*SERVER_ROOT*>/wileyapp /WEB-INF/ directory. The information that can be described in the deployment descriptor includes the following elements:

- ServletContext init parameters
- Localized content
- Session configuration
- Servlet/JSP definitions
- Servlet/JSP mappings
- Tag library references
- MIME type mappings
- Welcome file list
- Error pages
- Security information

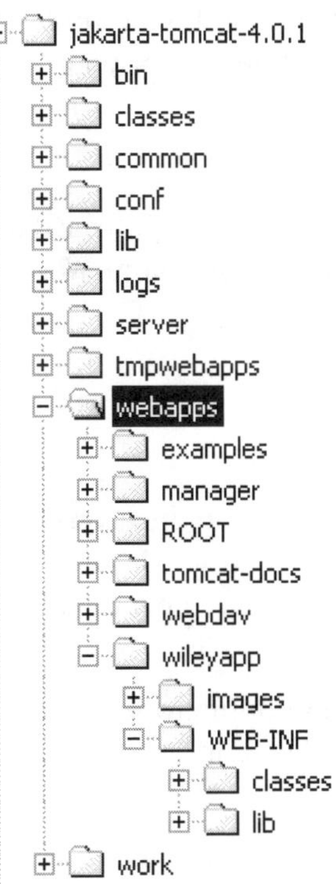

Figure 1.2 The wileyapp Web application hosted by Tomcat.

This code snippet contains a sample deployment descriptor that defines a single servlet. We examine the web.xml file in much more detail later in this text.

```
<?xml version="1.0" encoding="ISO-8859-1"?>

<!DOCTYPE web-app PUBLIC
  '-//Sun Microsystems, Inc.//DTD Web Application 2.3//EN'
  'http://java.sun.com/dtd/web-app_2_3.dtd'>

<servlet>
  <servlet-name>SimpleServlet</servlet-name>
  <servlet-class>com.wiley.SimpleServlet</servlet-class>
</servlet>

</web-app>
```

Packaging a Web Application

The standard packaging format for a Web application is a Web Archive file (WAR). A WAR file is simply a JAR file with the extension .war, as opposed to .jar. You can create a WAR file by using jar, Java's archiving tool. To create a WAR file, you simply need to change to the root directory of your Web application and type the following command:

```
jar cvf wileyapp.war .
```

This command will produce an archive file named wileyapp.war that contains the entire wileyapp Web application. Now you can deploy your Web application by simply distributing this file.

The Tomcat JSP/Servlet Container

The Tomcat server is an open-source Java-based Web application container created to run servlet and JavaServer Page Web applications. It has become Sun's reference implementation for both the Servlet and JSP specifications. We will use Tomcat for all of our examples in this book.

Before we get started with the installation and configuration of Tomcat, you need to make sure you have acquired the items listed in Table 1.3.

Table 1.3 Tomcat Installation Requirements

COMPONENT	LOCATION
Jakarta-Tomcat 4	http://jakarta.apache.org/
JDK 1.3 Standard Edition	http://java.sun.com/j2se/1.3/

Installing and Configuring Tomcat

For our purposes, we will install Tomcat as a stand-alone server on a Windows NT/2000 operating system (OS). To do this, you need to install the JDK; be sure to follow the installation instructions included with the JDK archive. For our example, we will install the JDK to drive D, which means our JAVA_HOME directory is D:\jdk1.3.

Now we need to extract the Tomcat server to a temporary directory. The default Tomcat archive does not contain an installation program; therefore, extracting the Tomcat archive is equivalent to installation. Again, we are installing to drive D, which will make the TOMCAT_HOME directory D:\ jakarta-tomcat-4.0.x.

After we have extracted Tomcat, the next step is to set the JAVA_HOME and TOMCAT_HOME environment variables. These variables are used to compile JSPs and run Tomcat, respectively. To do this under NT/2000, perform these steps:

1. Open the NT/2000 Control Panel.
2. Start the NT/2000 System Application and then select the Advanced tab.
3. Click the Environment Variables button. You will see a screen similar to Figure 1.3.
4. Click the New button in the System Variables section of the Environment Variables dialog box. Add a Variable named *JAVA_HOME*, and set its value to the location of your JDK installation. Figure 1.4 shows the settings associated with our installation.

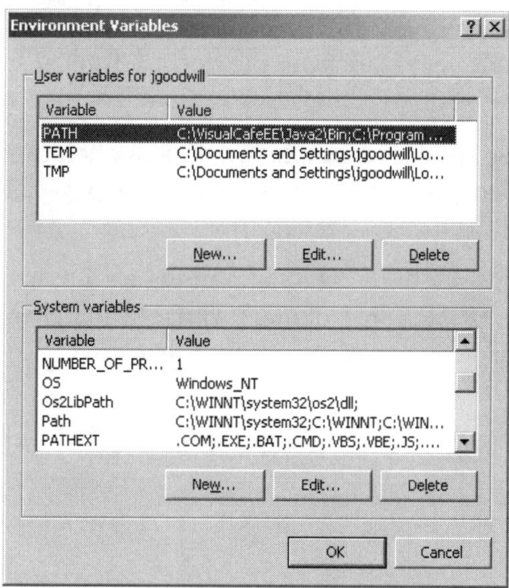

Figure 1.3 The Windows NT/2000 Environment Variables dialog box.

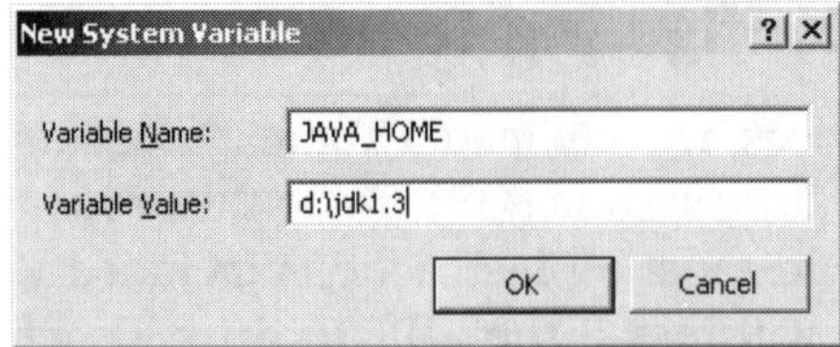

Figure 1.4 The JAVA_HOME environment settings for our installation.

5. Your final step should be to repeat Step 4, using *CATALINA_HOME* for the variable name and the location of your Tomcat installation as the value. For my installation, I set the value to *D:\jakarta-tomcat-4.0.1*.

That's all there is to it. You can now move on to the next section, in which we test our Tomcat installation.

Testing Your Tomcat Installation

Before continuing, we need to test the steps that we have just completed. To begin, first start the Tomcat server by typing the following command (be sure to replace *<CATALINA_HOME>* with the location of your Tomcat installation):

```
<CATALINA_HOME>\bin\startup.bat
```

Once Tomcat has started, open your browser to the following URL:

```
http://localhost:8080
```

You should see the default Tomcat home page, which is displayed in Figure 1.5.

The next step is to verify the installation of our JDK. The best way to do this is to execute one of the JSP examples provided with the Tomcat server. To execute a sample JSP, start from the default Tomcat home page, shown in Figure 1.5, and choose JSP Examples. You should see a page similar to Figure 1.6.

Now choose the JSP example Snoop and click the Execute link. If everything was installed properly, you should see a page similar to the one shown in Figure 1.7.

If you do not see the page shown in Figure 1.6, make sure that the location of your JAVA_HOME environment variable matches the location of your JDK installation.

Figure 1.5 The default Tomcat home page.

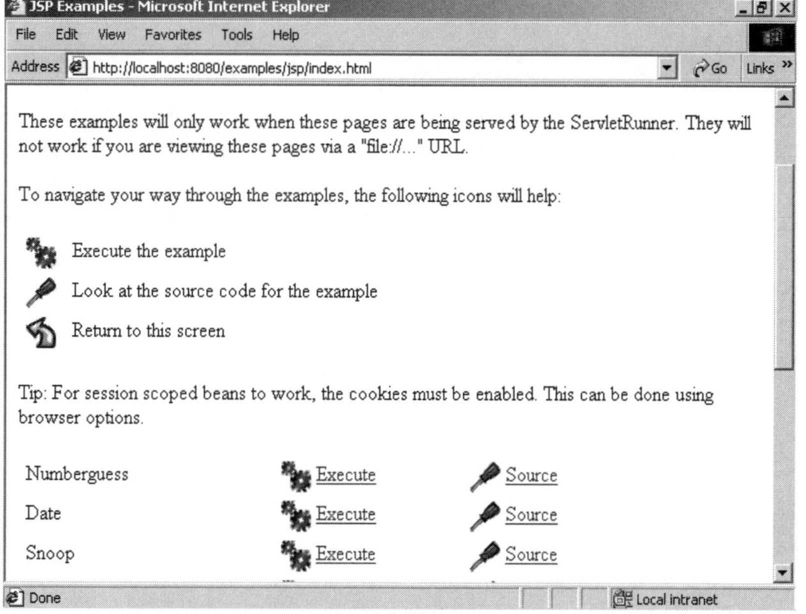

Figure 1.6 The JSP Examples page.

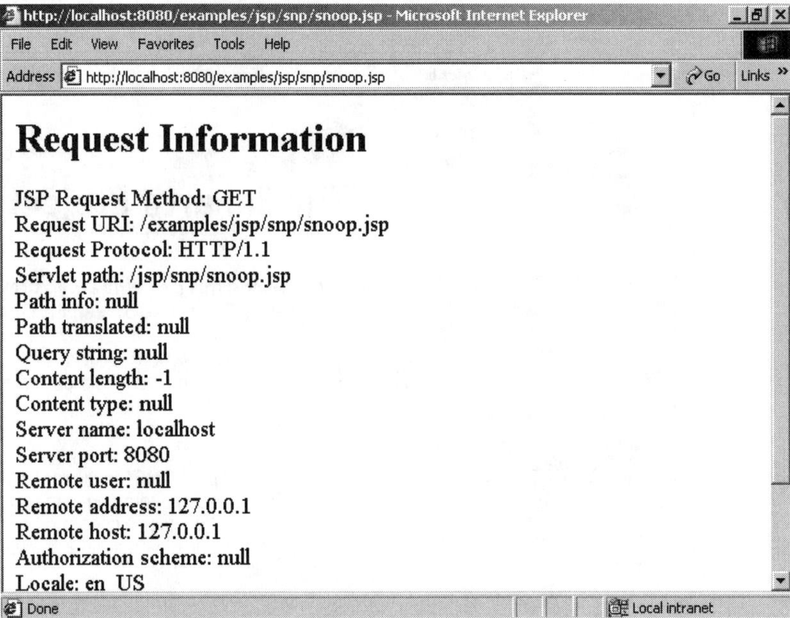

Figure 1.7 The results of the Snoop JSP execution.

Summary

Our next chapter is devoted to a brief tutorial of JSPs and servlets. The goal of this chapter will be to provide you with the foundational technologies that you will leverage throughout the remainder of this book. If you are already familiar with both of these technologies, you may want to skip to Chapter 3.

CHAPTER 2

An Overview of the Java Servlet and JavaServer Pages Architectures

In this chapter, we discuss the two technologies that the Struts framework is based on: Java servlets and JavaServer Pages (JSPs). We begin by describing the servlet architecture, including the servlet life cycle; the relationship between the ServletContext and a Web application; and how you can retrieve form data using servlets.

Once we have a solid understanding of servlets, we move on to discussing JSPs, which act as the View component in the Struts framework. In our JSP discussions, we define JSPs and describe their components.

The goal of this chapter is to provide you with a brief introduction to the servlet and JSP technologies. At the end of this chapter, you will have a clear understanding of both servlets and JSPs, and where they fit into Java Web application development.

The Java Servlet Architecture

A *Java servlet* is a platform-independent Web application component that is hosted in a JSP/servlet container. Servlets cooperate with Web clients by means of a request/response model managed by a JSP/servlet container. Figure 2.1 depicts the execution of a Java servlet.

Two packages make up the servlet architecture: javax.servlet and javax.servlet.http. The first of these, the javax.servlet package, contains the generic interfaces and classes that are implemented and extended by all servlets. The

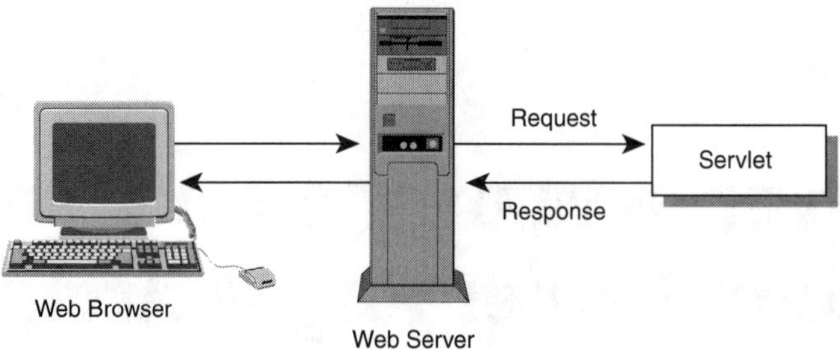

Figure 2.1 The execution of a Java servlet.

second, the javax.servlet.http package, contains all servlet classes that are HTTP protocol-specific. An example of this would be a simple servlet that responds using HTML.

At the heart of this architecture is the interface javax.servlet.Servlet. It is the base class interface for all servlets. The Servlet interface defines five methods. The three most important of these methods are the

- init() method, which initializes a servlet
- service() method, which receives and responds to client requests
- destroy() method, which performs cleanup

These are the servlet life-cycle methods. We will describe these methods in a subsequent section. All servlets must implement the Servlet interface, either directly or through inheritance. Figure 2.2 is an object model that gives you a very high-level view of the servlet framework.

The GenericServlet and HttpServlet Classes

The two main classes in the servlet architecture are the GenericServlet and HttpServlet classes. The HttpServlet class is extended from GenericServlet, which in turn implements the Servlet interface. When developing your own servlets, you will most likely extend one of these two classes.

When extending the GenericServlet class, you must implement the service() method. The GenericServlet.service() method has been defined as an abstract method in order to force you to follow this framework. The service() method prototype is defined as follows:

```
public abstract void service(ServletRequest request,
  ServletResponse response) throws ServletException, IOException;
```

The two parameters that are passed to the service() method are the ServletRequest and ServletResponse objects. The ServletRequest object holds

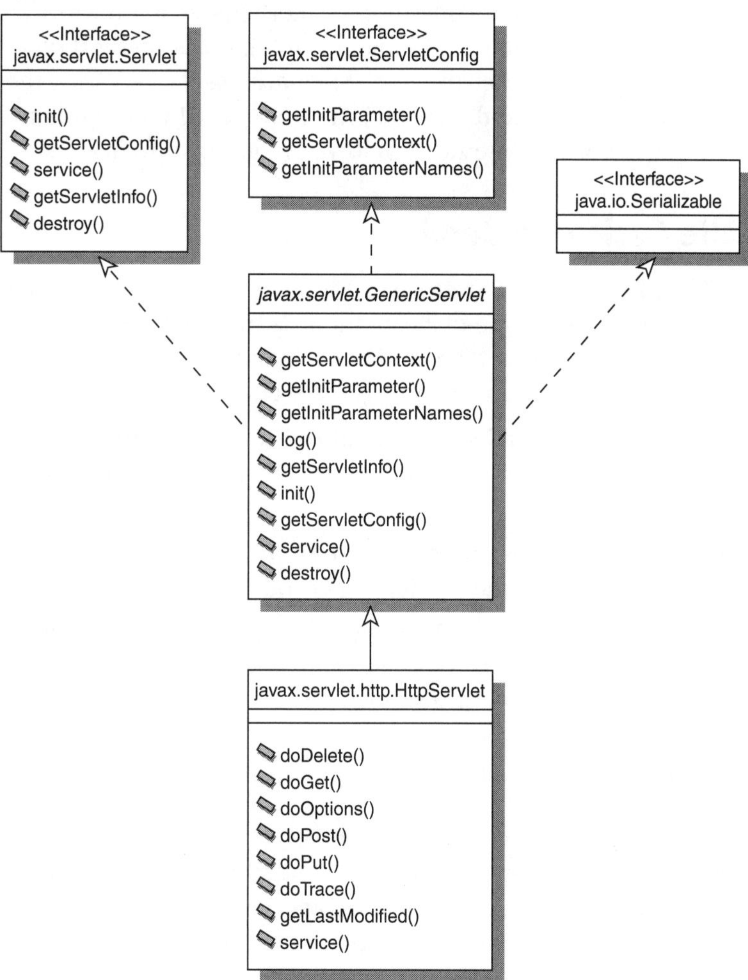

Figure 2.2 A simple object model showing the servlet framework.

the information that is being sent to the servlet, and the ServletResponse object is where you place the data you want to send back to the client.

In contrast to the GenericServlet, when you extend HttpServlet you don't usually implement the service() method; the HttpServlet class has already implemented the service() method for you. The following prototype contains the HttpServlet.service() method signature:

```
protected void service(HttpServletRequest request,
  HttpServletResponse response)
  throws ServletException, IOException;
```

When the HttpServlet.service() method is invoked, it reads the method type stored in the request and determines which HTTP-specific methods to invoke based on this value. These are the methods that you will want to override. If the method type is GET, it will call doGet(). If the method type is POST, it will call doPost(). Five other method types are associated with the service() method, but the doGet() and doPost() methods are the methods used most often, and are therefore the methods that we are going to focus on.

The Life Cycle of a Servlet

The life cycle of a Java servlet follows a very logical sequence. The interface that declares the life-cycle methods is the javax.servlet.Servlet interface. These methods are the init(), the service(), and the destroy() methods. This sequence can be described in a simple three-step process:

1. A servlet is loaded and initialized using the init() method. This method will be called when a servlet is preloaded or upon the first request to this servlet.
2. The servlet then services zero or more requests. The servlet services each request using the service() method.
3. The servlet is then destroyed and garbage collected when the Web application containing the servlet shuts down. The method that is called upon shutdown is the destroy() method.

init() Method

The init() method is where the servlet begins its life. This method is called immediately after the servlet is instantiated. It is called only once. The init() method should be used to create and initialize the resources that it will be using while handling requests. The init() method's signature is defined as follows:

```
public void init(ServletConfig config) throws ServletException;
```

The init() method takes a ServletConfig object as a parameter. This reference should be stored in a member variable so that it can be used later. A common way of doing this is to have the init() method call super.init() and pass it the ServletConfig object.

The init() method also declares that it can throw a ServletException. If for some reason the servlet cannot initialize the resources necessary to handle requests, it should throw a ServletException with an error message signifying the problem.

service() Method

The service() method services all requests received from a client using a simple request/response pattern. The service() method's signature is shown here:

```
public void service(ServletRequest req, ServletResponse res)
  throws ServletException, IOException;
```

The service() method takes two parameters:

- A ServletRequest object, which contains information about the service request and encapsulates information provided by the client
- A ServletResponse object, which contains the information returned to the client

You will not usually implement this method directly, unless you extend the GenericServlet abstract class. The most common implementation of the service() method is in the HttpServlet class. The HttpServlet class implements the Servlet interface by extending GenericServlet. Its service() method supports standard HTTP/1.1 requests by determining the request type and calling the appropriate method.

destroy() Method

This method signifies the end of a servlet's life. When a Web application is shut down, the servlet's destroy() method is called. This is where all resources that were created in the init() method should be cleaned up. The following code snippet contains the signature of the destroy() method:

```
public void destroy();
```

Building a Servlet

Now that we have a basic understanding of what a servlet is and how it works, we are going to build a very simple servlet of our own. Its purpose will be to service a request and respond by outputting the address of the client. After we have examined the source for this servlet, we will take a look at the steps involved in compiling and installing it. Listing 2.1 contains the source code for this example.

```
package chapter2;

import javax.servlet.*;
import javax.servlet.http.*;
import java.io.*;
import java.util.*;

public class SimpleServlet extends HttpServlet {
```

Listing 2.1 SimpleServlet.java. (continues)

```
  public void init(ServletConfig config)
    throws ServletException {

    // Always pass the ServletConfig object to the super class
    super.init(config);
  }

  //Process the HTTP Get request
  public void doGet(HttpServletRequest request,
    HttpServletResponse response)
    throws ServletException, IOException {

    doPost(request, response);
  }

  //Process the HTTP Post request
  public void doPost(HttpServletRequest request,
    HttpServletResponse response)
    throws ServletException, IOException {

    response.setContentType("text/html");
    PrintWriter out = response.getWriter();

    out.println("<html>");
    out.println("<head><title>Simple Servlet</title></head>");
    out.println("<body>");

    // Outputs the address of the calling client
    out.println("Your address is " + request.getRemoteAddr()
      + "\n");

    out.println("</body></html>");
    out.close();
  }
}
```

Listing 2.1 SimpleServlet.java. (continued)

Now that you have had a chance to look over the source of the SimpleServlet, let's take a closer look at each of its integral parts. We will examine where the servlet fits into the Java Servlet Development Kit (JSDK) framework, the methods that the servlet implements, and the objects being used by the servlet. The following three methods are overridden in the SimpleServlet:

- init()
- doGet()
- doPost()

Let's take a look at each of these methods in more detail.

init() Method

The SimpleServlet first defines a very straightforward implementation of the init() method. It takes the ServletConfig object that it is passed and then passes it to its parent's init() method, which stores the object for later use. The code that performs this action is as follows:

```
super.init(config);
```

NOTE

The SimpleServlet's parent that actually holds on to the ServletConfig object is the GenericServlet.

You should also notice that this implementation of the init() method does not create any resources. This is why the SimpleServlet does not implement a destroy() method.

doGet() and doPost() Methods

The SimpleServlet's doGet() and doPost() methods are where all of the business logic is truly performed, and in this case, the doGet() method simply calls the doPost() method. The only time that the doGet() method will be executed is when a GET request is sent to the container. If a POST request is received, then the doPost() method will service the request.

Both the doGet() and the doPost() methods receive HttpServletRequest and HttpServletResponse objects as parameters. The HttpServletRequest contains information sent from the client, and the HttpServletResponse contains the information that will be sent back to the client.

The first executed line of the doPost() method sets the content type of the response that will be sent back to the client. This is done using the following code snippet:

```
response.setContentType("text/html");
```

This method sets the content type for the response. You can set this response property only once, and it must be set prior to writing to a Writer or an OutputStream. In our example, we are setting the response type to text/html.

The next thing we do is get a PrintWriter. This is accomplished by calling the ServletResponse's getWriter() method. The PrintWriter will let us write to the stream that will be sent in the client response. Everything written to the PrintWriter will be displayed in the client browser. This step is completed in the following line of code:

```
PrintWriter out = response.getWriter();
```

Once we have a reference to an object that will allow us to write text back to the client, we are going to use this object to write a message to the client. This message will include the HTML that will format this response for presentation in the client's browser. The next few lines of code show how this is done:

```
out.println("<html>");
out.println("<head><title>Simple Servlet</title></head>");
out.println("<body>");

// Outputs the address of the calling client
out.println("Your address is " + request.getRemoteAddr()
  + "\n");
```

The SimpleServlet uses a very clear-cut method of sending HTML to a client. It simply passes to the PrintWriter's println() method the HTML text we want included in the response, and closes the stream. The only thing that you may have a question about is the following few lines:

```
// Outputs the address of the calling client
out.println("Your address is " + request.getRemoteAddr()
  + "\n");
```

This section of code takes advantage of information sent by the client. It calls the HttpServletRequest's getRemoteAddr() method, which returns the IP address of the calling client. The HttpServletRequest object holds a great deal of HTTP protocol-specific information about the client. If you would like to learn more about the HttpServletRequest or HttpServletResponse objects, you can find additional information at the Sun Web site:

```
http://java.sun.com/products/servlet/
```

Building and Deploying a Servlet

To see the SimpleServlet in action, we need to first create a Web application that will host the servlet, and then we need to compile and deploy this servlet to the Web application. These steps are described below:

1. Create a Web application named wileyapp, using the directory described in Chapter 1.
2. Add the servlet.jar file to your classpath. This file should be in the <*CATALINA_HOME*>/common/lib/ directory.
3. Compile the source for the SimpleServlet.
4. Copy the resulting class file to the <*CATALINA_HOME*>/webapps/wileyapp/WEB-INF/classes/chapter2/ directory. The /chapter2 reference is appended because of the package name.

Once you have completed these steps, you can execute the SimpleServlet and see the results. To do this, start Tomcat, and open your browser to the following URL:

```
http://localhost:8080/wileyapp/servlet/chapter2.SimpleServlet
```

You should see an image similar to Figure 2.3.

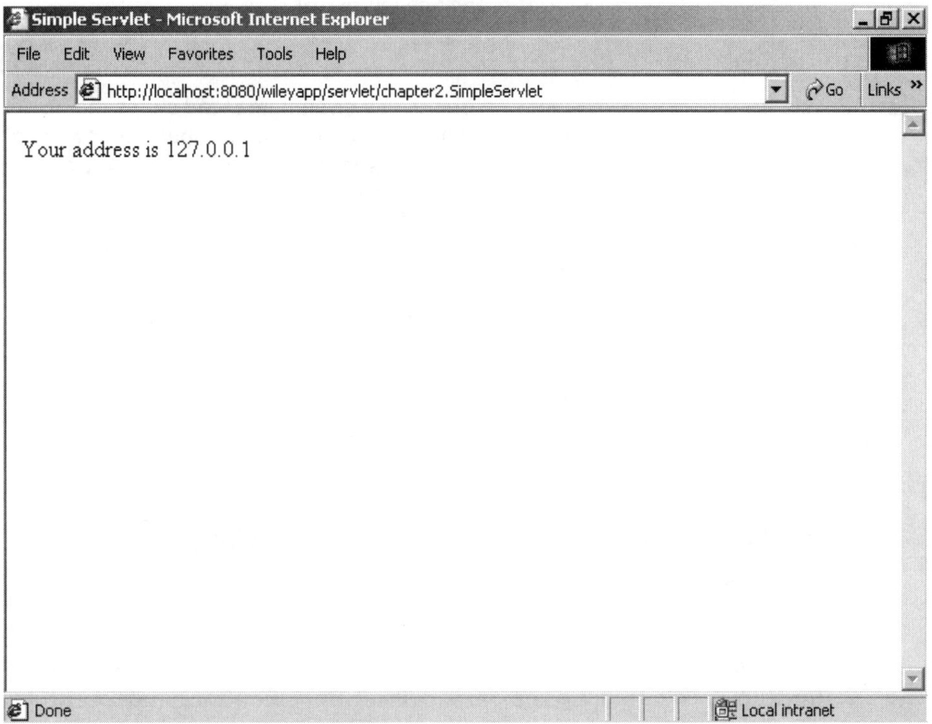

Figure 2.3 The output of the SimpleServlet.

NOTE

You will notice that the URL to access the SimpleServlet includes the string *`/servlet`* immediately preceding the reference to the actual servlet name. This text tells the container that you are referencing a servlet.

The ServletContext

A *ServletContext* is an object that is defined in the javax.servlet package. It defines a set of methods that are used by server-side components of a Web application to communicate with the servlet container.

The ServletContext is most frequently used as a storage area for objects that need to be available to all of the server-side components in a Web application.

You can think of the ServletContext as a shared memory segment for Web applications. When an object is placed in the ServletContext, it exists for the life of a Web application, unless it is explicitly removed or replaced. Four methods defined by the ServletContext are leveraged to provide this shared memory functionality. Table 2.1 describes each of these methods.

Table 2.1 The Shared Memory Methods of the ServletContext

METHOD	DESCRIPTION
setAttribute()	Binds an object to a given name, and stores the object in the current ServletContext. If the name specified is already in use, this method will remove the old object binding and bind the name to the new object.
getAttribute()	Returns the object referenced by the given name, or returns null if there is no attribute bind to the given key.
removeAttribute()	Removes the attribute with the given name from the ServletContext.
getAttributeNames()	Returns an enumeration of strings containing the object names stored in the current ServletContext.

The Relationship between a Web Application and the ServletContext

The ServletContext acts as the container for a given Web application. For every Web application, there can be only one instance of a ServletContext. This relationship is required by the Java Servlet Specification, and is enforced by all servlet containers.

To see how this relationship affects Web components, we are going to use a servlet and a JSP. The first Web component we will see is a servlet that stores an object in the ServletContext, with the purpose of making this object available to all server-side components in this Web application. Listing 2.2 shows the source code for this servlet.

```
package chapter2;

import javax.servlet.*;
import javax.servlet.http.*;
import java.io.*;
```

Listing 2.2 ContextServlet.java. (continues)

```
import java.util.*;

public class ContextServlet extends HttpServlet {

  private static final String CONTENT_TYPE = "text/html";


  public void doGet(HttpServletRequest request,
    HttpServletResponse response)
    throws ServletException, IOException {

    doPost(request, response);
  }

  public void doPost(HttpServletRequest request,
    HttpServletResponse response)
    throws ServletException, IOException {

    // Get a reference to the ServletContext
    ServletContext context = getServletContext();

    // Get the userName attribute from the ServletContext
    String userName = (String)context.getAttribute("USERNAME");

    // If there was no attribute USERNAME, then create
    // one and add it to the ServletContext
    if ( userName == null ) {

      userName = new String("Bob Roberts");
      context.setAttribute("USERNAME", userName);
    }

    response.setContentType(CONTENT_TYPE);
    PrintWriter out = response.getWriter();
    out.println("<html>");
    out.println("<head><title>Context Servlet</title></head>");
    out.println("<body>");

    // Output the current value of the attribute USERNAME
    out.println("<p>The current User is : " + userName +
      ".</p>");
    out.println("</body></html>");
  }

  public void destroy() {
  }
}
```

Listing 2.2 ContextServlet.java. (continued)

As you look over the ContextServlet, you will notice that it performs the following steps:

1. It first gets a reference to the ServletContext, using the getServletContext() method:

   ```
   ServletContext context = getServletContext();
   ```

2. Once it has a reference to the ServletContext, it gets a reference to the object bound to the name USERNAME from the ServletContext, using the getAttribute() method:

   ```
   String userName =
     (String)context.getAttribute("USERNAME");
   ```

3. It then checks to see if the reference returned was valid. If getAttribute() returned null, then there was no object bound to the name USERNAME. If the attribute was not found, it is created and added to the ServletContext, bound to the name USERNAME, using the setAttribute() method:

   ```
   // If there was no attribute USERNAME, then create
   // one and add it to the ServletContext
   if ( userName == null ) {

     userName = new String("Bob Roberts");
     context.setAttribute("USERNAME", userName);
   }
   ```

4. The value of this reference is then printed to the output stream, using an instance of the PrintWriter.println() method:

   ```
   // Output the current value of the attribute USERNAME
   out.println("<p>The current User is : " +
     userName + ".</p>");
   ```

After you have looked over this servlet, you should compile it and move the class file into the <*CATALINA_HOME*>/webapps/wileyapp/WEB-INF/classes/chapter2/ directory. This servlet is now deployed to the Web application wileyapp.

The JSP that we will be using is much like the servlet above; however, there are two differences:

- The code to access the ServletContext is in a JSP scriptlet, which we will discuss later in this chapter.
- If the JSP cannot find a reference to the USERNAME attribute, then it does not add a new one.

Otherwise, the code performs essentially the same actions, but it does them in a JSP. You can see the source for the JSP in Listing 2.3.

```
<HTML>
<HEAD>
<TITLE>
Context
</TITLE>
</HEAD>
<BODY>
<%
  // Try to get the USERNAME attribute from the ServletContext
  String userName = (String)application.getAttribute("USERNAME");

  // If there was no attribute USERNAME, then create
  // one and add it to the ServletContext
  if ( userName == null ) {

    // Don't try to add it just, say that you can't find it
    out.println("<b>Attribute USERNAME not found");
  }
  else {

    out.println("<b>The current User is : " + userName +
      "</b>");
  }
%>
</BODY>
</HTML>
```

Listing 2.3 Context.jsp.

NOTE

In the Context.jsp, we are using two JSP implicit objects: the application object, which references the ServletContext, and the out object, which references an output stream to the client. We will discuss each of these later in this chapter.

Now, copy Context.jsp to the <*CATALINA_HOME*>/webapps/wileyapp/directory, restart Tomcat, and open your browser first to the following URL:

```
http://localhost:8080/wileyapp/Context.jsp
```

You should see a page similar to Figure 2.4.

You should notice that the Context.jsp cannot find a reference to the attribute USERNAME. It will not be able to find this reference until the reference is placed there by the ContextServlet. To do this, open your browser to the following URL:

```
http://localhost:8080/wileyapp/servlet/chapter2.ContextServlet
```

You should see output similar to Figure 2.5.

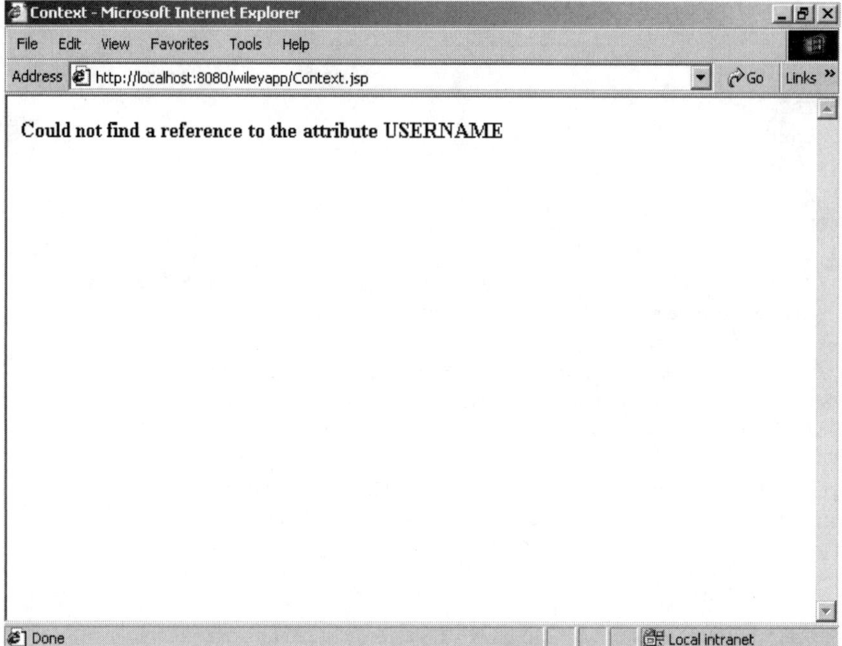

Figure 2.4 The output of the Context.jsp prior to the execution of the servlet ContextServlet.

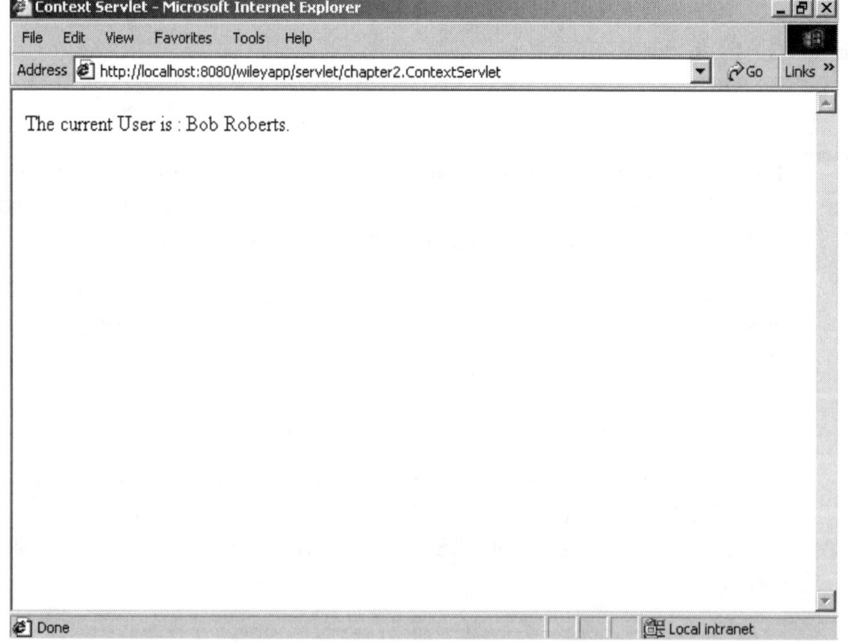

Figure 2.5 The output of the ContextServlet.

After running this servlet, the wileyapp Web application has an object bound to the name USERNAME stored in its ServletContext. To see how this affects another Web component in the wileyapp Web application, open the previous URL that references the Context.jsp, and look at the change in output. The JSP can now find the USERNAME, and it prints this value to the response.

NOTE

To remove an object from the ServletContext, you can restart the JSP/servlet container or use the ServletContext.removeAttribute() method.

Using Servlets to Retrieve HTTP Data

In this (our final) section on servlets, we are going to examine how servlets can be used to retrieve information from the client. Three methods can be used to retrieve request parameters: the ServletRequest's getParameter(), getParameterValues(), and getParameterNames() methods. Each method signature is listed here:

```
public String ServletRequest.getParameter(String name);
public String[] ServletRequest.getParameterValues(String name);
public Enumeration ServletRequest.getParameterNames ();
```

The first method in this list, getParameter(), returns a string containing the single value of the named parameter, or returns null if the parameter is not in the request. You should use this method only if you are sure the request contains only one value for the parameter. If the parameter has multiple values, you should use the getParameterValues() method.

The next method, getParameterValues(), returns the values of the specified parameter as an array of java.lang.Strings, or returns null if the named parameter is not in the request.

The last method, getParameterNames(), returns the parameter names contained in the request as an enumeration of strings, or an empty enumeration if there are no parameters. This method is used as a supporting method to both getParameter() and getParameterValues(). The enumerated list of parameter names returned from this method can be iterated over by calling getParameter() or getParameterValues() with each name in the list.

To see how we can use these methods to retrieve form data, let's look at a servlet that services POST requests: it retrieves the parameters sent to it and returns the parameters and their values back to the client. The servlet is shown in Listing 2.4.

```
package chapter2;

import javax.servlet.*;
import javax.servlet.http.*;
import java.io.*;
import java.util.*;

public class ParameterServlet extends HttpServlet {

  public void init(ServletConfig config)
    throws ServletException {

    // Always pass the ServletConfig object to the super class
    super.init(config);
  }

  // Process the HTTP GET request
  public void doGet(HttpServletRequest request,
    HttpServletResponse response)
    throws ServletException, IOException {

    doPost(request, response);
  }

  // Process the HTTP POST request
  public void doPost(HttpServletRequest request,
    HttpServletResponse response)
    throws ServletException, IOException {

    response.setContentType("text/html");
    PrintWriter out = response.getWriter();

    out.println("<html>");
    out.println("<head>");
    out.println("<title>Parameter Servlet</title>");
    out.println("</head>");
    out.println("<body>");

    // Get an enumeration of the parameter names
    Enumeration parameters = request.getParameterNames();

    String param = null;

    // Iterate over the paramater names,
    // getting the parameters values
    while ( parameters.hasMoreElements() ) {
```

Listing 2.4 ParameterServlet.java. (continues)

```
        param = (String)parameters.nextElement();
        out.println(param + " : " +
          request.getParameter(param) +
          "<BR>");
      }

      out.println("</body></html>");
      out.close();
    }
  }
```

Listing 2.4 ParameterServlet.java. (continued)

The first notable action performed by this servlet is to get all of the parameter names passed in on the request. It does this using the getParameterNames() method. Once it has this list, it performs a while loop, retrieving and printing all of the parameter values associated with the matching parameter names, using the getParameter() method. You can invoke the ParameterServlet by encoding a URL string with parameters and values, or simply by using the HTML form found in Listing 2.5.

```
<HTML>
<HEAD>
<TITLE>
Parameter Servlet Form
</TITLE>
</HEAD>
<BODY>

<form
 action="servlet/chapter2.ParameterServlet"
 method=POST>
  <table width="400" border="0" cellspacing="0">
    <tr>
      <td>Name: </td>
      <td>
        <input type="text"
               name="name"
               size="20"
               maxlength="20">
      </td>
      <td>SSN:</td>
      <td>
        <input type="text" name="ssn" size="11" maxlength="11">
```

Listing 2.5 Form.html. (continues)

```
      </td>
    </tr>
    <tr>
      <td>Age:</td>
      <td>
        <input type="text" name="age" size="3" maxlength="3">
      </td>
      <td>email:</td>
      <td>
        <input type="text"
               name="email"
               size="30"
               maxlength="30">
      </td>
    </tr>
    <tr>
      <td> </td>
      <td>  </td>
      <td>  </td>
      <td>
        <input type="submit" name="Submit" value="Submit">
        <input type="reset" name="Reset" value="Reset">
      </td>
    </tr>
  </table>
</FORM>

</BODY>
</HTML>
```

Listing 2.5 Form.html. (continued)

This HTML document contains a simple HTML form that can be used to pass data to the ParameterServlet. To see this example in action, compile the servlet, and move the class file to the <*CATALINA_HOME*>/webapps/wileyapp/WEB-INF/classes/chapter2 directory and the HTML file to the <*CATALINA_HOME*>/webapps/wileyapp/ directory. Now open your browser to the following URL:

```
http://localhost:8080/wileyapp/Form.html
```

Go ahead and populate the form (similar to what I've done in Figure 2.6), and then click the Submit button.

The response you receive will, of course, depend on your entries, but it should resemble Figure 2.7.

This example shows just how easy it is to retrieve request parameters in a servlet. While the ParameterServlet works well for most requests, it does

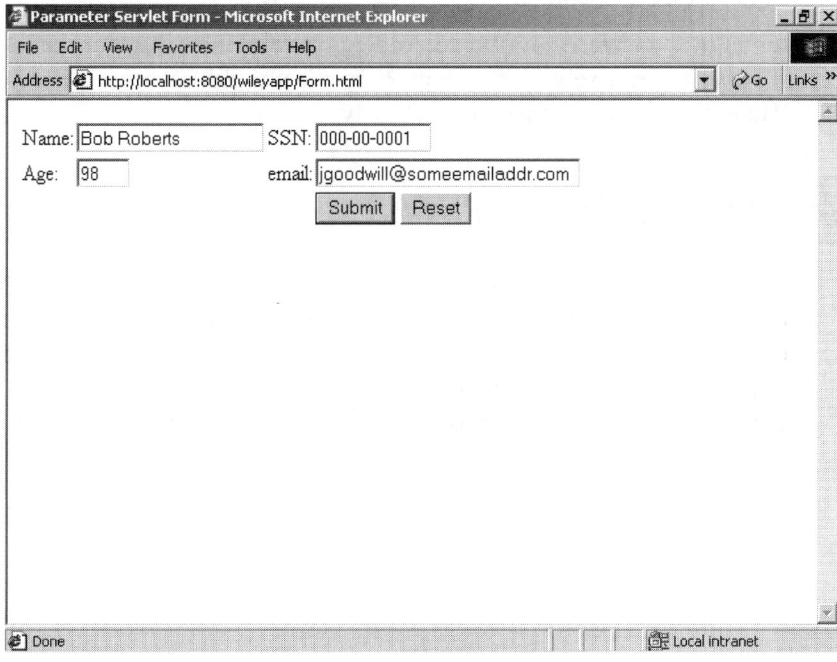

Figure 2.6 Output from Form.html.

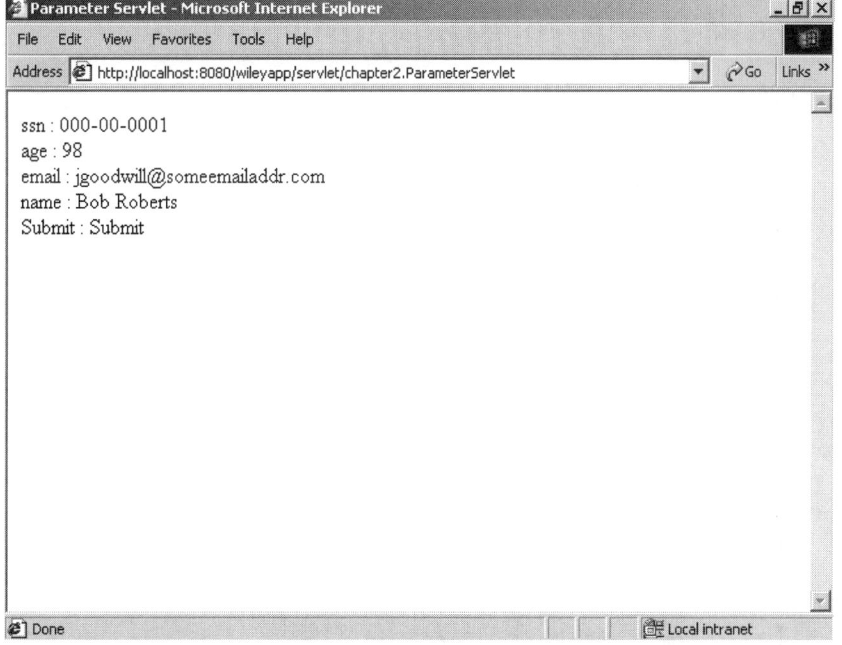

Figure 2.7 The response of the ParameterServlet.

contain an error. When we chose to use getParameter() to retrieve the parameter values, we were counting on receiving only one value per request parameter. If we could not rely on this fact, then we should have used the getParameterValues() method discussed previously.

What Are JavaServer Pages?

JavaServer Pages, or JSPs, are a simple but powerful technology used most often to generate dynamic HTML on the server side. JSPs are a direct extension of Java servlets designed to let the developer embed Java logic directly into a requested document. A JSP document must end with the extension .jsp. The following code snippet contains a simple example of a JSP file; its output is shown in Figure 2.8.

```
<HTML>
<BODY>

<% out.println("HELLO JSP READER"); %>

</BODY>
</HTML>
```

Figure 2.8 The output of the JSP example.

This document looks like any other HTML document, with some added tags containing Java code. The source code is stored in a file called hello.jsp, and should be copied to the document directory of the Web application to which this JSP will be deployed. When a request is made for this document, the server recognizes the .jsp extension and realizes that special handling is required. The JSP is then passed to the JSP engine (which is just another servlet mapped to the extension .jsp) for processing.

The first time the file is requested, it is translated into a servlet and then compiled into an object that is loaded into resident memory. The generated servlet then services the request, and the output is sent back to the requesting client. On all subsequent requests, the server will check to see whether the original JSP source file has changed. If it has not changed, the server invokes the previously compiled servlet object. If the source has changed, the JSP engine will reparse the JSP source. Figure 2.9 shows these steps.

NOTE

It's essential to remember that JSPs are just servlets created from a combination of HTML and Java source. Therefore, they have the resources and functionality of a servlet.

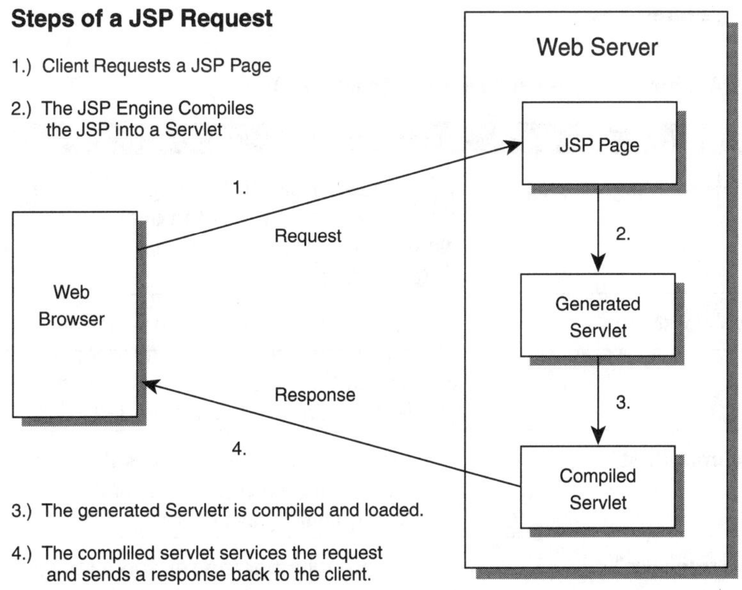

Figure 2.9 The steps of a JSP request.

The Components of a JavaServer Page

This section discusses the components of a JSP, including directives, scripting, implicit objects, and standard actions.

JSP Directives

JSP directives are JSP elements that provide global information about a JSP page. An example would be a directive that included a list of Java classes to be imported into a JSP. The syntax of a JSP directive follows:

```
<%@ directive {attribute="value"} %>
```

Three possible directives are currently defined by the JSP specification v1.2: page, include, and taglib. These directives are defined in the following sections.

The page Directive

The page directive defines information that will globally affect the JSP containing the directive. The syntax of a JSP page directive is

```
<%@ page {attribute="value"} %>
```

Table 2.2 defines the attributes for the page directive.

NOTE

Because all mandatory attributes are defaulted, you are not required to specify any page directives.

Table 2.2 Attributes for the page Directive (continues)

ATTRIBUTE	DEFINITION
language="scriptingLanguage"	Tells the server which language will be used to compile the JSP file. Java is currently the only available JSP language, but we hope there will be other language support in the not-too-distant future.
extends="className"	Defines the parent class from which the JSP will extend. While you can extend JSP from other servlets, doing so will limit the optimizations performed by the JSP/servlet engine and is therefore not recommended.
import="importList"	Defines the list of Java packages that will be imported into this JSP. It will be a comma-separated list of package names and fully qualified Java classes.
session="true|false"	Determines whether the session data will be available to this page. The default is true. If your JSP is not planning on using the session, then this attribute should be set to false for better performance.

Table 2.2 Attributes for the page Directive (continued)

ATTRIBUTE	DEFINITION
buffer="none|size in kb"	Determines whether the output stream is buffered. The default value is 8KB.
autoFlush="true|false"	Determines whether the output buffer will be flushed automatically, or whether it will throw an exception when the buffer is full. The default is true.
isThreadSafe="true|false"	Tells the JSP engine that this page can service multiple requests at one time. By default, this value is true. If this attribute is set to false, the SingleThreadModel is used.
info="text"	Represents information about the JSP page that can be accessed by invoking the page's Servlet.getServletInfo() method.
errorPage="error_url"	Represents the relative URL to a JSP that will handle JSP exceptions.
isErrorPage="true|false"	States whether the JSP is an errorPage. The default is false.
contentType="ctinfo"	Represents the MIME type and character set of the response sent to the client.

The following code snippet includes a page directive that imports the java.util package:

```
<%@ page import="java.util.*" %>
```

The include Directive

The include directive is used to insert text and/or code at JSP translation time. The syntax of the include directive is shown in the following code snippet:

```
<%@ include file="relativeURLspec" %>
```

The file attribute can reference a normal text HTML file or a JSP file, which will be evaluated at translation time. This resource referenced by the file attribute must be local to the Web application that contains the include directive. Here's a sample include directive:

```
<%@ include file="header.jsp" %>
```

NOTE

Because the include directive is evaluated at translation time, this included text will be evaluated only once. Thus, if the included resource changes, these changes will not be reflected until the JSP/servlet container is restarted or the modification date of the JSP that includes that file is changed.

The taglib Directive

The taglib directive states that the including page uses a custom tag library, uniquely identified by a URI and associated with a prefix that will distinguish each set of custom tags to be used in the page.

NOTE

If you are not familiar with JSP custom tags, you can learn what they are and how they are used in my book "Mastering JSP Custom Tags and Tag Libraries," also published by Wiley.

The syntax of the taglib directive is as follows:

```
<%@ taglib uri="tagLibraryURI" prefix="tagPrefix" %>
```

The taglib attributes are described in Table 2.3.

Table 2.3 Attributes for the taglib Directive

ATTRIBUTE	DEFINITION
uri	A URI that uniquely names a custom tag library
prefix	The prefix string used to distinguish a custom tag instance

The following code snippet includes an example of how the taglib directive is used:

```
<%@ taglib
  uri="http://jakarta.apache.org/taglibs/random-1.0"
  prefix="rand" %>
```

JSP Scripting

Scripting is a JSP mechanism for directly embedding Java code fragments into an HTML page. Three scripting language components are involved in JSP scripting. Each component has its appropriate location in the generated servlet. This section examines these components.

Declarations

JSP declarations are used to define Java variables and methods in a JSP. A JSP declaration must be a complete declarative statement.

JSP declarations are initialized when the JSP page is first loaded. After the declarations have been initialized, they are available to other declarations, expressions, and scriptlets within the same JSP. The syntax for a JSP declaration is as follows:

```
<%! declaration %>
```

A sample variable declaration using this syntax is shown here:

```
<%! String name = new String("BOB"); %>
```

A sample method declaration using the same syntax is as follows:

```
<%! public String getName() { return name; } %>
```

To get a better understanding of declarations, let's take the previous string declaration and embed it into a JSP document. The sample document would look similar to the following code snippet:

```
<HTML>
<BODY>

<%! String name = new String("BOB"); %>

</BODY>
</HTML>
```

When this document is initially loaded, the JSP code is converted to servlet code and the name declaration is placed in the declaration section of the generated servlet. It is now available to all other JSP components in the JSP.

NOTE

It should be noted that all JSP declarations are defined at the class level, in the servlet generated from the JSP, and will therefore be evaluated prior to all JSP expressions and scriptlet code.

Expressions

JSP expressions are JSP components whose text, upon evaluation by the container, is replaced with the resulting value of the container evaluation. JSP expressions are evaluated at request time, and the result is inserted at the expression's referenced position in the JSP file. If the resulting expression cannot be converted to a string, then a translation-time error will occur. If the conversion to a string cannot be detected during translation, a ClassCastException will be thrown at request time.

The syntax of a JSP expression is as follows:

```
<%= expression %>
```

A code snippet containing a JSP expression is shown here:

```
Hello <B><%= getName() %></B>
```

Here is a sample JSP document containing a JSP expression:

```
<HTML>
<BODY>

<%! public String getName() { return "Bob"; } %>
```

```
Hello <B><%= getName() %></B>

</BODY>
</HTML>
```

Scriptlets

Scriptlets are the JSP components that bring all the JSP elements together. They can contain almost any coding statements that are valid for the language referenced in the language directive. They are executed at request time, and they can make use of all the JSP components. The syntax for a scriptlet is as follows:

```
<% scriptlet source %>
```

When JSP scriptlet code is converted into servlet code, it is placed into the generated servlet's service() method. The following code snippet contains a simple JSP that uses a scripting element to print the text "Hello Bob" to the requesting client:

```
<HTML>
<BODY>

<% out.println("Hello Bob"); %>

</BODY>
</HTML>
```

You should note that while JSP scriplet code can be very powerful, composing all your JSP logic using scriptlet code can make your application difficult to manage. This problem led to the creation of custom tag libraries.

JSP Error Handling

Like all development methods, JSPs need a robust mechanism for handling errors. The JSP architecture provides an error-handling solution through the use of JSPs that are written exclusively to handle JSP errors.

The errors that occur most frequently are runtime errors that can arise either in the body of the JSP page or in some other object that is called from the body of the JSP page. Request-time errors that result in an exception being thrown can be caught and handled in the body of the calling JSP, which signals the end of the error. Exceptions that are not handled in the calling JSP result in the forwarding of the client request, including the uncaught exception, to an error page specified by the offending JSP.

Creating a JSP Error Page

Creating a JSP error page is a simple process: create a basic JSP and then tell the JSP engine that the page is an error page. You do so by setting the JSP's page directive attribute, isErrorPage, to true. Listing 2.6 contains a sample error page.

```
<html>

<%@ page isErrorPage="true" %>

Error: <%= exception.getMessage() %> has been reported.

</body>
</html>
```

Listing 2.6 Creating a JSP error page: errorpage.jsp.

The first JSP-related line in this page tells the JSP compiler that this JSP is an error page. This code snippet is

```
<%@ page isErrorPage="true" %>
```

The second JSP-related section uses the implicit exception object that is part of all JSP error pages to output the error message contained in the unhandled exception that was thrown in the offending JSP.

Using a JSP Error Page

To see how an error page works, let's create a simple JSP that throws an uncaught exception. The JSP shown in Listing 2.7 uses the error page created in the previous section.

```
<%@ page errorPage="errorpage.jsp" %>

<%

  if ( true ) {

    // Just throw an exception
    throw new Exception("An uncaught Exception");
  }

%>
```

Listing 2.7 Using a JSP error page: testerror.jsp.

Notice in this listing that the first line of code sets errorPage equal to errorpage.jsp, which is the name of the error page. To make a JSP aware of an error

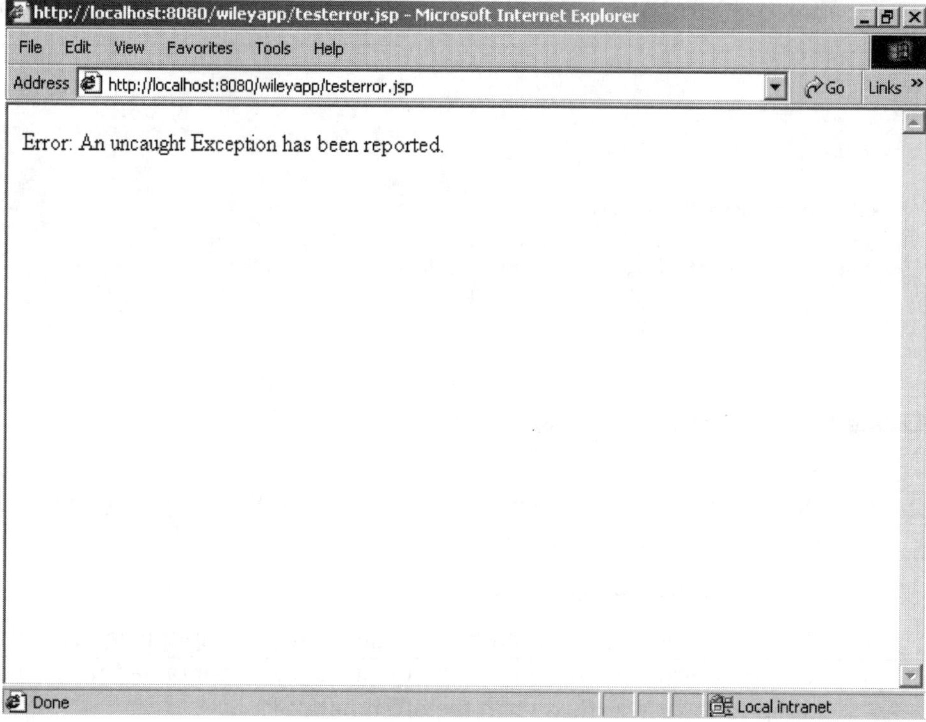

Figure 2.10 The output of the testerror.jsp example.

page, you simply need to add the errorPage attribute to the page directive and set its value equal to the location of your JSP error page. The rest of the example simply throws an exception that will not be caught. To see this example in action, copy both JSPs to the <*CATALINA_HOME*>/webapps/wileyapp/ directory, and open the testerror.jsp page in your browser. You will see a page similar to Figure 2.10.

Implicit Objects

As a JSP author, you have implicit access to certain objects that are available for use in all JSP documents. These objects are parsed by the JSP engine and inserted into the generated servlet as if you defined them yourself.

out

The implicit out object represents a JspWriter (derived from a java.io.Writer) that provides a stream back to the requesting client. The most common method of this object is out.println(), which prints text that will be displayed in the client's browser. Listing 2.8 provides an example using the implicit out object.

```
<%@ page errorPage="errorpage.jsp" %>

<html>
  <head>
    <title>Use Out</title>
  </head>
  <body>
    <%
      // Print a simple message using the implicit out object.
      out.println("<center><b>Hello Wiley" +
        " Reader!</b></center>");
    %>
  </body>
</html>
```

Listing 2.8 Using the out object: out.jsp.

To execute this example, copy this file to the <*CATALINA_HOME*>/webapps/wileyapp/ directory and then open your browser to the following URL:

```
http://localhost:8080/wileyapp/out.jsp
```

You should see a page similar to Figure 2.11.

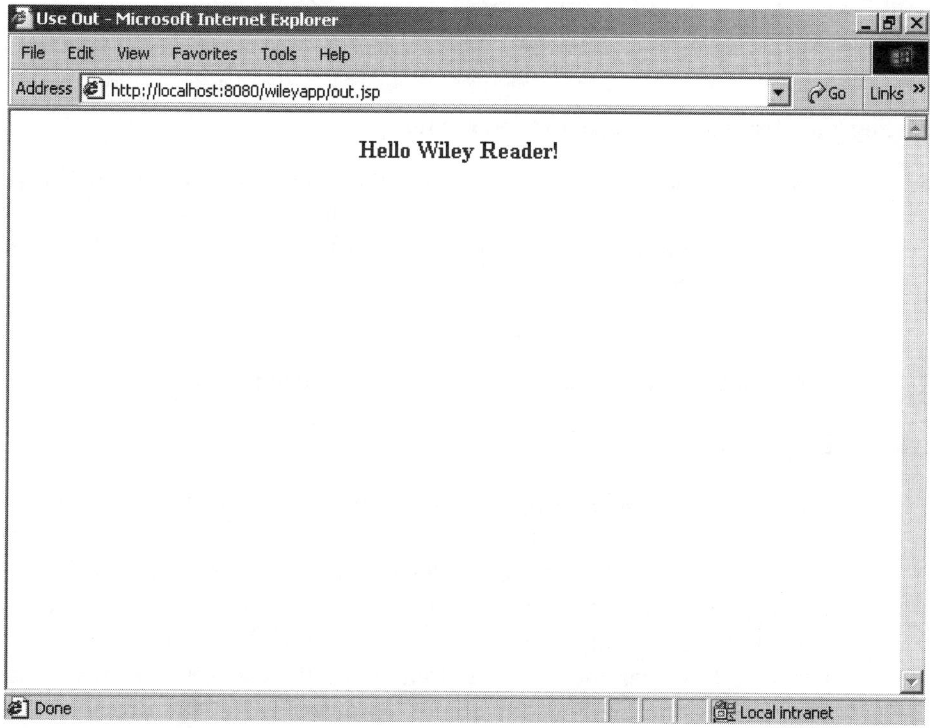

Figure 2.11 The output of out.jsp.

request

The implicit request object represents the javax.servlet.http.HttpServletRequest interface, discussed later in this chapter. The request object is associated with every HTTP request.

One of the more common uses for the request object is to access request parameters. You can do this by calling the request object's getParameter() method with the parameter name you are seeking. It will return a string with the value matching the named parameter. An example using the implicit request object appears in Listing 2.9.

```
<%@ page errorPage="errorpage.jsp" %>

<html>
  <head>
    <title>UseRequest</title>
  </head>
  <body>
    <%
      out.println("<b>Welcome: " +
        request.getParameter("user") + "</b>");
    %>
  </body>
</html>
```

Listing 2.9 Using the request object: request.jsp.

This JSP calls the request.getParameter() method, passing it the parameter *user*. This method looks for the key user in the parameter list and returns the value, if it is found. Enter the following URL into your browser to see the results from this page:

```
http://localhost:8080/wileyapp/request.jsp?user=Robert
```

After loading this URL, you should see a page similar to Figure 2.12.

response

The implicit response object represents the javax.servlet.http.HttpServletResponse object. The response object is used to pass data back to the requesting client. This implicit object provides all the functionality of the HttpServletRequest, just as if you were executing in a servlet. One of the more common uses for the response object is writing HTML output back to the client browser; however, the JSP API already provides access to a stream back to the client using the implicit out object, as described in the previous implicit out discussion.

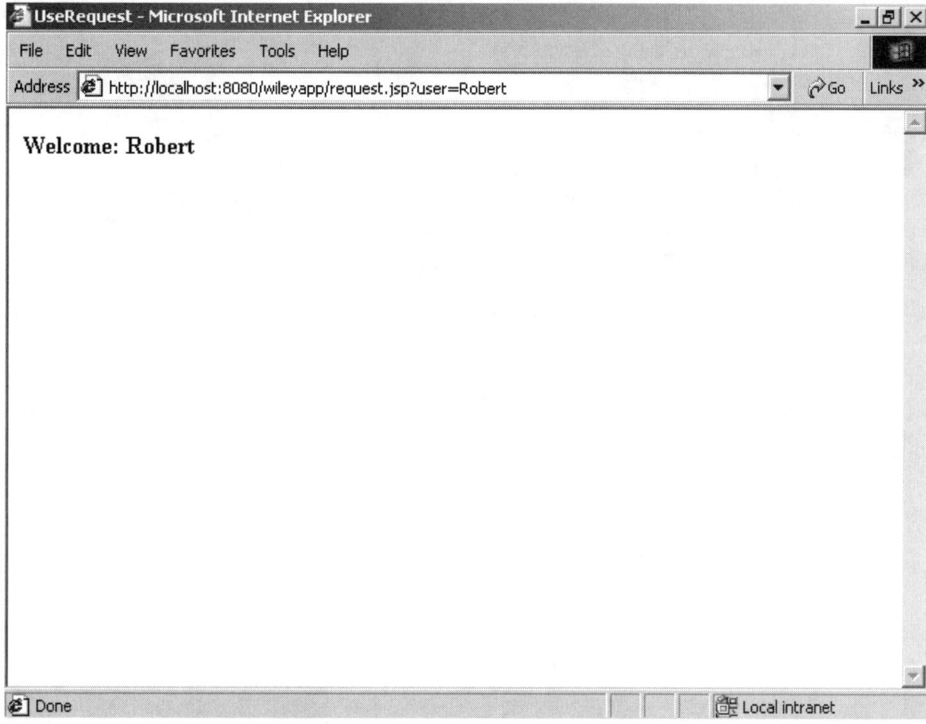

Figure 2.12 The output of request.jsp.

pageContext

The pageContext object provides access to the namespaces associated with a JSP page. It also provides accessors to several other JSP implicit objects. A common use for the pageContext is setting and retrieving objects using the setAttribute() and getAttribute() methods.

session

The implicit session object represents the javax.servlet.http.HttpSession object. It's used to store objects between client requests, thus providing an almost stateful HTTP interactivity.

An example of using the session object is shown in Listing 2.10.

```
<%@ page errorPage="errorpage.jsp" %>

<html>
  <head>
```

Listing 2.10 Using the session object: session.jsp. (continues)

```
    <title>Session Example</title>
  </head>
  <body>
    <%
      // get a reference to the current count from the session
      Integer count = (Integer)session.getAttribute("COUNT");

      if ( count == null ) {

        // If the count was not found create one
        count = new Integer(1);
        // and add it to the HttpSession
        session.setAttribute("COUNT", count);
      }
      else {

        // Otherwise increment the value
        count = new Integer(count.intValue() + 1);
        session.setAttribute("COUNT", count);
      }
      out.println("<b>You have accessed this page: "
        + count + " times.</b>");
    %>
  </body>
</html>
```

Listing 2.10 Using the session object: session.jsp. (continued)

To use this example, copy the JSP to the <*CATALINA_HOME*>/wileyapp/ directory, and open your browser to the following URL:

```
http://localhost:8080/wileyapp/session.jsp
```

If everything went okay, you should see a page similar to Figure 2.13.

Click the Reload button a few times to see the count increment.

application

The application object represents the javax.servlet.ServletContext, discussed earlier in this chapter. The application object is most often used to access objects stored in the ServletContext to be shared between Web components in a global scope. It is a great place to share objects between JSPs and servlets. An example using the application object can be found earlier in this chapter, in the section "The ServletContext."

config

The implicit config object holds a reference to the ServletConfig, which contains configuration information about the JSP/servlet engine containing the Web application where this JSP resides.

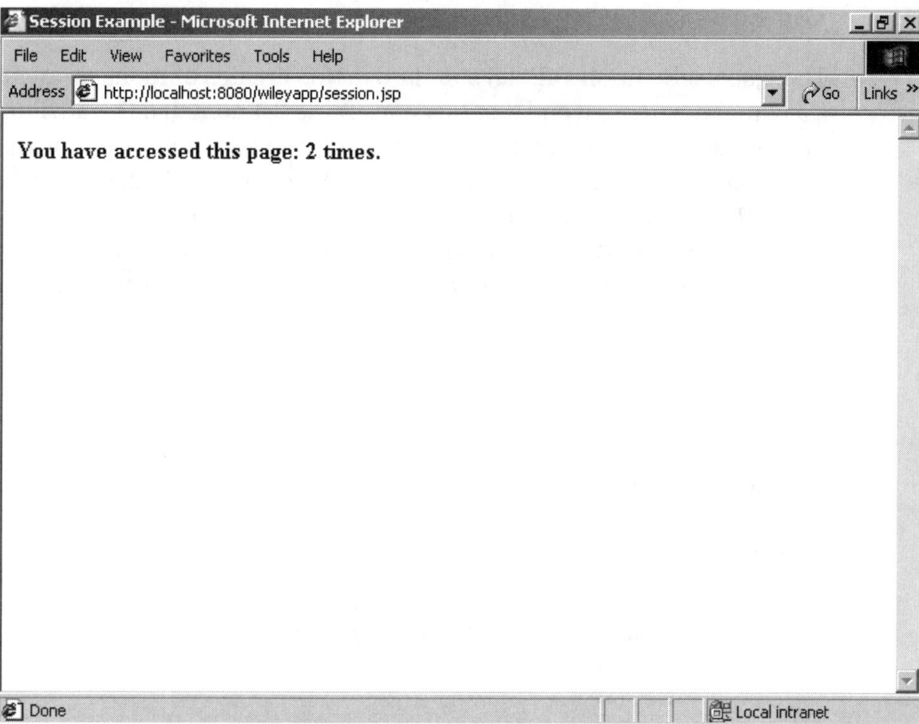

Figure 2.13 The output of session.jsp.

page

The page object contains a reference to the current instance of the JSP being accessed. The page object is used just like this object, to reference the current instance of the generated servlet representing this JSP.

exception

The implicit exception object provides access to an uncaught exception thrown by a JSP. It is available only in JSPs that have a page with the attribute isErrorPage set to true.

Standard Actions

JSP standard actions are predefined custom tags that can be used to encapsulate common actions easily. There are two types of JSP standard actions: the first type is related to JavaBean functionality, and the second type consists of all other standard actions. Each group will be defined and used in the following sections.

Three predefined standard actions relate to using JavaBeans in a JSP: <useBean>, <setProperty>, and <getProperty>. After we define these tags, we will create a simple example that uses them.

<jsp:useBean>

The <jsp:useBean> JavaBean standard action creates or looks up an instance of a JavaBean with a given ID and scope. Table 2.4 contains the attributes of the <jsp:useBean> action, and Table 2.5 defines the scope values for that action. The <jsp:useBean> action is very flexible. When a <useBean> action is encountered, the action tries to find an existing object using the same ID and scope. If it cannot find an existing instance, it will attempt to create the object and store it in the named scope associated with the given ID. The syntax of the <jsp:useBean> action is as follows:

```
<jsp:useBean id="name"
        scope="page|request|session|application"
        typeSpec>
        body
</jsp:useBean>

typeSpec ::=class="className" |
        class="className" type="typeName" |
        type="typeName" class="className" |
        beanName="beanName" type="typeName" |
        type="typeName" beanName="beanName" |
        type="typeName"
```

Table 2.4 Attributes for the <jsp:useBean> Standard Action

ATTRIBUTE	DEFINITION
id	The key associated with the instance of the object in the specified scope. This key is case-sensitive. The id attribute is the same key as used in the page.getAttribute() method.
scope	The life of the referenced object. The scope options are page, request, session, and application. They are defined in Table 2.5.
class	The fully qualified class name that defines the implementation of the object. The class name is case-sensitive.
beanName	The name of the JavaBean.
type	The type of scripting variable defined. If this attribute is unspecified, then the value is the same as the value of the class attribute.

The scope attribute listed in Table 2.4 can have four possible values, which are described in Table 2.5.

Table 2.5 Scope Values for the <jsp:useBean> Standard Action

VALUE	DEFINITION
page	Beans with page scope are accessible only within the page where they were created. References to an object with page scope will be released when the current JSP has completed its evaluation.
request	Beans with request scope are accessible only within pages servicing the same request, in which the object was instantiated, including forwarded requests. All references to the object will be released after the request is complete.
session	Beans with session scope are accessible only within pages processing requests that are in the same session as the one in which the bean was created. All references to beans with session scope will be released after their associated session expires.
application	Beans with application scope are accessible within pages processing requests that are in the same Web application. All references to beans will be released when the JSP/servlet container is shut down.

<jsp:setProperty>

The <jsp:setProperty> standard action sets the value of a bean's property. Its name attribute represents an object that must already be defined and in scope. The syntax for the <jsp:setProperty> action is as follows:

```
<jsp:setProperty name="beanName" propexpr />
```

In the preceding syntax, the name attribute represents the name of the bean whose property you are setting, and propexpr can be represented by any of the following expressions:

```
property="*" |
property="propertyName" |
property="propertyName" param="parameterName" |
property="propertyName" value="propertyValue"
```

Table 2.6 contains the attributes and their descriptions for the <jsp:setProperty> action.

Table 2.6 Attributes for the <jsp:setProperty> Standard Action (continues)

ATTRIBUTE	DEFINITION
name	The name of the bean instance defined by a <jsp:useBean> action or some other action.

Table 2.6 Attributes for the <jsp:setProperty> Standard Action (continued)

ATTRIBUTE	DEFINITION
property	The bean property for which you want to set a value. If you set propertyName to an asterisk (*), then the action will iterate over the current ServletRequest parameters, matching parameter names and value types to property names and setter method types, and setting each matched property to the value of the matching parameter. If a parameter has an empty string for a value, the corresponding property is left unmodified.
param	The name of the request parameter whose value you want to set the named property to. A <jsp:setProperty> action cannot have both param and value attributes referenced in the same action.
value	The value assigned to the named bean's property.

<jsp:getProperty>

The last standard action that relates to integrating JavaBeans into JSPs is <jsp:getProperty>. It takes the value of the referenced bean's instance property, converts it to a java.lang.String, and places it on the output stream. The referenced bean instance must be defined and in scope before this action can be used. The syntax for the <jsp:getProperty> action is as follows:

```
<jsp:getProperty name="name" property="propertyName" />
```

Table 2.7 contains the attributes and their descriptions for the <jsp:getProperty> action.

Table 2.7 Attributes for the <jsp:getProperty> Standard Action

ATTRIBUTE	DEFINITION
name	The name of the bean instance from which the property is obtained, defined by a <jsp:useBean> action or some other action.
property	The bean property for which you want to get a value.

A JavaBean Standard Action Example

To learn how to use the JavaBean standard actions, let's create an example. This example uses a simple JavaBean that acts as a counter. The Counter bean has a single int property, count, that holds the current number of times the bean's property has been accessed. It also contains the appropriate methods for getting and setting this property. Listing 2.11 contains the source code for the Counter bean.

```
package chapter2;

public class Counter {

  int count = 0;

  public Counter() {

  }

  public int getCount() {

    count++;

    return count;
  }

  public void setCount(int count) {

    this.count = count;
  }
}
```

Listing 2.11 Example of a Counter bean: Counter.java.

Let's look at integrating this sample JavaBean into a JSP, using the JavaBean standard actions. Listing 2.12 contains the JSP that leverages the Counter bean.

```
<!-- Set the scripting language to java -->
<%@ page language="java" %>

<HTML>
<HEAD>
<TITLE>Bean Example</TITLE>
</HEAD>

<BODY>

<!-- Instantiate the Counter bean with an id of "counter" -->
<jsp:useBean id="counter" scope="session"
  class="chapter2.Counter" />

<%

  // write the current value of the property count
```

Listing 2.12 A JSP that uses the Counter bean: counter.jsp. (continues)

```
  out.println("Count from scriptlet code : "
    + counter.getCount() + "<BR>");

%>

<!-- Get the the bean's count property, -->
<!-- using the jsp:getProperty action. -->
Count from jsp:getProperty :
  <jsp:getProperty name="counter" property="count" /><BR>

</BODY>
</HTML>
```

Listing 2.12 A JSP that uses the Counter bean: counter.jsp. (continued)

Counter.jsp has four JSP components. The first component tells the JSP container that the scripting language is Java:

```
<%@ page language="java" %>
```

The next step uses the standard action <jsp:useBean> to create an instance of the class Counter with a scope of session and ID of counter. Now you can reference this bean using the name counter throughout the rest of the JSP. The code snippet that creates the bean is as follows:

```
<jsp:useBean id="counter" scope="session"
  class="chapter2.Counter" />
```

The final two actions demonstrate how to get the current value of a bean's property. The first of these two actions uses a scriptlet to access the bean's property, using an explicit method call. It simply accesses the bean by its ID, counter, and calls the getCount() method. The scriptlet snippet is listed here:

```
<%

  // write the current value of the property count
  out.println("Count from scriptlet code : "
    + counter.getCount() + "<BR>");

%>
```

The second example uses the <jsp:getProperty> standard action, which requires the ID of the bean and the property to be accessed. The action takes the attribute, calls the appropriate accessor, and embeds the results directly into the resulting HTML document, as follows:

```
<!-- Get the bean's count property, -->
<!-- using the jsp:getProperty action. -->
Count from jsp:getProperty :
  <jsp:getProperty name="counter" property="count" /><BR>
```

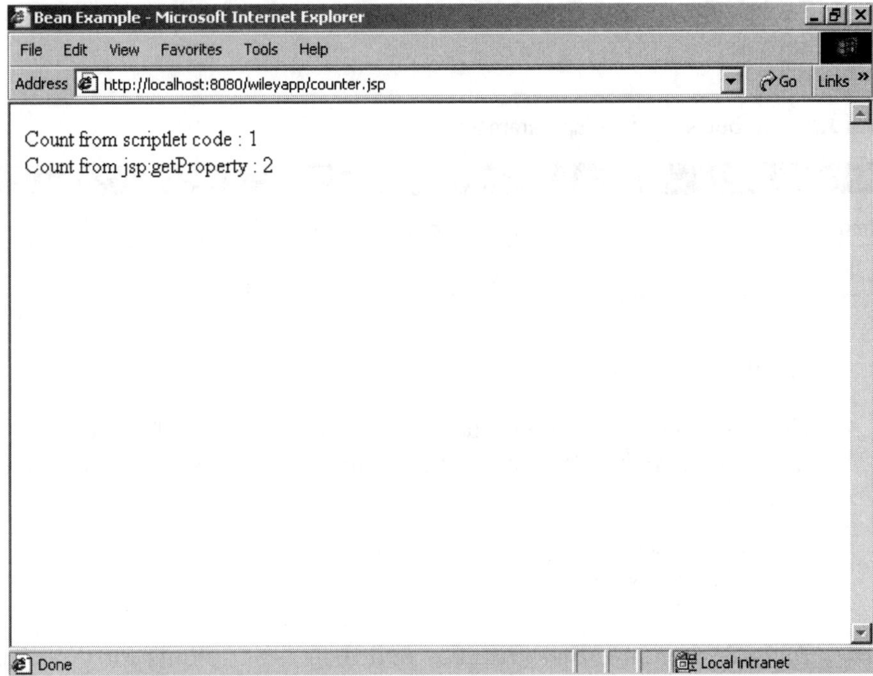

Figure 2.14 The results of counter.jsp.

When you execute the Counter.jsp, notice that the second reference to the count property results in a value that is one greater than the first reference. This is the case because both methods of accessing the count property result in a call to the getCount() method, which increments the value of count.

To see this JSP in action, compile the Counter class, move it to the <*CATALINA_HOME*>/wileyapp/WEB-INF/classes/chapter2/ directory, and copy the Counter.jsp file to the <*CATALINA_HOME*>/wileyapp/ directory. Then, open your browser to the following URL:

```
http://localhost:8080/wileyapp/counter.jsp
```

Once the JSP is loaded, you should see an image similar to Figure 2.14.

The remaining standard actions are used for generic tasks, from basic parameter action to an object plug-in action. These actions are described in the following sections.

<jsp:param>

The <jsp:param> action provides parameters and values to the JSP standard actions <jsp:include>, <jsp:forward>, and <jsp:plugin>. The syntax of the <jsp:param> action is as follows:

```
<jsp:param name="name" value="value"/>
```

Table 2.8 contains the attributes and their descriptions for the <jsp:param> action.

Table 2.8 Attributes for the <jsp:param> Action

ATTRIBUTE	DEFINITION
name	The name of the parameter being referenced
value	The value of the named parameter

<jsp:include>

The <jsp:include> standard action provides a method for including additional static and dynamic Web components in a JSP. The syntax for this action is as follows:

```
<jsp:include page="urlSpec" flush="true">
    <jsp:param ... />
</jsp:include>
```

Table 2.9 contains the attributes and their descriptions for the <jsp:include> action.

Table 2.9 Attributes for the <jsp:include> Action

ATTRIBUTE	DEFINITION
page	The relative URL of the resource to be included
flush	A mandatory Boolean value stating whether the buffer should be flushed

NOTE

It is important to note the difference between the include directive and the include standard action. The directive is evaluated only once, at translation time, whereas the standard action is evaluated with every request.

The syntax description shows a request-time inclusion of a URL that is passed an optional list of param subelements used to argument the request. An example using the include standard action can be found in Listing 2.13.

```
<html>
  <head>
```

Listing 2.13 Example of the include action: include.jsp. (continues)

```
    <title>Include Example</title>
  </head>
  <body>
    <table width="100%" cellspacing="0">
      <tr>
        <td align="left">
          <jsp:include page="header.jsp" flush="true">
            <jsp:param name="user"
              value='<%= request.getParameter("user") %>' />
          </jsp:include>
        </td>
      </tr>
    </table>
  </body>
</html>
```

Listing 2.13 Example of the include action: include.jsp. (continued)

This file contains a single include action that includes the results of evaluating the JSP header.jsp, shown in Listing 2.14.

```
<%
  out.println("<b>Welcome: </b>" +
    request.getParameter("user"));
%>
```

Listing 2.14 The JSP evaluated in include.jsp: header.jsp.

This JSP simply looks for a parameter named user, and outputs a string containing a welcome message. To deploy this example, copy these two JSPs to the <*CATALINA_HOME*>/webapps/wileyapp/ directory. Open your browser to the following URL:

```
http://localhost:8080/wileyapp/include.jsp?user=Bob
```

The results should look similar to Figure 2.15.

<jsp:forward>

The <jsp:forward> standard action enables the JSP engine to execute a runtime dispatch of the current request to another resource existing in the current Web application, including static resources, servlets, or JSPs. The appearance of <jsp:forward> effectively terminates the execution of the current JSP.

NOTE

A <jsp:forward> action can contain <jsp:param> subattributes. These subattributes act as parameters that will be forwarded to the targeted resource.

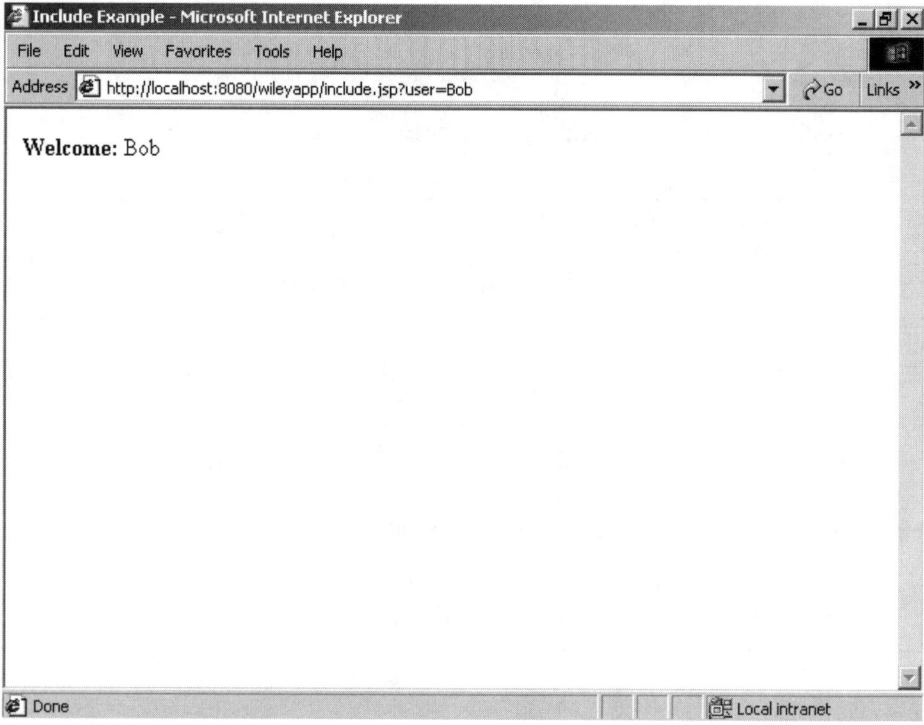

Figure 2.15 The results of include.jsp.

The syntax of the <jsp:forward> action is as follows:

```
<jsp:forward page="relativeURL">
    <jsp:param .../>
</jsp:forward>
```

Table 2.10 contains the attribute and its description for the <jsp:forward> action.

Table 2.10 Attribute for the <jsp:forward> Action

ATTRIBUTE	DEFINITION
page	The relative URL of the target of the forward

The example in Listing 2.15 contains a JSP that uses the <jsp:forward> action. This example checks a request parameter and forwards the request to one of two JSPs based on the value of the parameter.

```
<html>
  <head>
```

Listing 2.15 Example of the forward action: forward.jsp. (continues)

```
    <title>JSP Forward Example</title>
  </head>
  <body>
    <%

      if ( (request.getParameter("role")).equals("manager") ) {

        %>
          <jsp:forward page="management.jsp" />
        <%
      }
      else {
        %>
          <jsp:forward page="welcome.jsp">
          <jsp:param name="user"
            value='<%=request.getParameter("user") %>' />
          </jsp:forward>
        <%
      }
    %>
  </body>
</html>
```

Listing 2.15 Example of the forward action: forward.jsp. (continued)

The forward.jsp simply checks the request for the parameter role, and forwards the request, along with a set of request parameters, to the appropriate JSP based on this value. Listings 2.16 and 2.17 contain the source of the targeted resources.

```
<html>
<!-- Set the scripting language to java -->
<%@ page language="java" %>

<HTML>
<HEAD>
<TITLE>Welcome Home</TITLE>
</HEAD>

<BODY>
<table>
  <tr>
    <td>
      Welcome User: <%= request.getParameter("user") %>
    </td>
  </tr>
</table>
```

Listing 2.16 welcome.jsp.

```
<html>
<!-- Set the scripting language to java -->
<%@ page language="java" %>

<HTML>
<HEAD>
<TITLE>Management Console</TITLE>
</HEAD>

<BODY>
<table>
  <tr>
    <td>
      Welcome Manager: <%= request.getParameter("user") %>
    </td>
  </tr>
</table>
```

Listing 2.17 management.jsp.

To test this example, copy all three JSPs to the <*CATALINA_HOME*>/webapps/ wileyapp/ directory and open your browser to the following URL:

```
http://localhost:8080/wileyapp/forward.jsp?role=user&user=Bob
```

You will see an image similar to Figure 2.16.

You can also change the value of the role parameter to manager, to change the forwarded target.

<jsp:plugin>

The last standard action we will discuss is <jsp:plugin>. This action enables a JSP author to generate the required HTML, using the appropriate client-browser independent constructs, to result in the download and subsequent execution of the specified applet or JavaBeans component.

The <jsp:plugin> tag, once evaluated, will be replaced by either an <object> or <embed> tag, as appropriate for the requesting user agent. The attributes of the <jsp:plugin> action provide configuration data for the presentation of the embedded element. The syntax of the <jsp:plugin> action is as follows:

```
<jsp:plugin type="pluginType"
    code="classFile"
    codebase="relativeURLpath">

    <jsp:params>

    </jsp:params>
</jsp:plugin>
```

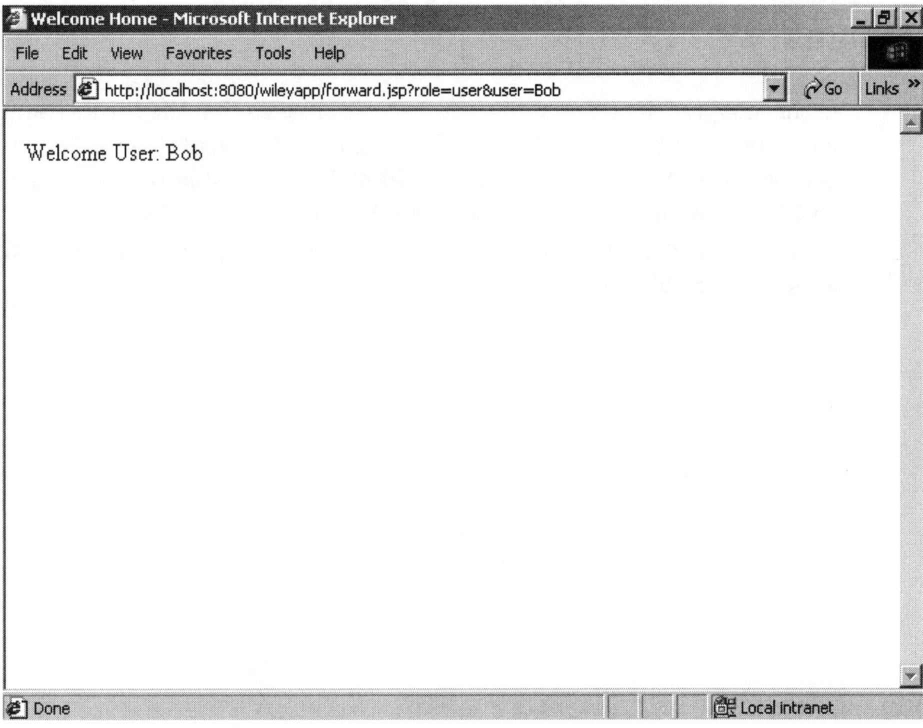

Figure 2.16 The output of forward.jsp.

Table 2.11 contains the attributes and their descriptions for the <jsp:plugin> action.

Table 2.11 Attributes for the <jsp:plugin> Action

ATTRIBUTE	DEFINITION
type	The type of plug-in to include (an applet, for example)
code	The name of the class that will be executed by the plug-in
codebase	The base or relative path where the code attribute can be found

The <jsp:plugin> action also supports the use of the <jsp:params> tag to supply the plug-in with parameters, if necessary.

Summary

In this chapter, we discussed the two technologies that the Struts framework is based on—servlets and JSPs—and we examined both of their architectures and components. At this point, you should feel comfortable with the basic servlet and JSP technologies and how each of these technologies can be used to assemble a Web application. In the next chapter, we are going to take our first hard look at the Struts framework.

CHAPTER 3

Getting Started with Struts

In this chapter, we begin our Jakarta Struts coverage. First, we explain the steps that you must perform when installing and configuring a Struts application. Then, we create a sample application that displays the components of a working Struts application. We conclude this chapter by walking through our sample application.

The goal of this chapter is to provide you with a quick introduction to the components of a Struts application.

Obtaining and Installing the Jakarta Struts Project

Before we can get started with our Struts development, we need to obtain the latest release of the Struts archive and all of its supporting archives. The following list contains all of the items you need to acquire:

- The latest-release Jakarta Struts binary for your operating system. For these examples, we are using Struts 1.1, which can be found at http://jakarta.apache.org.
- The latest Xerces Java parser. We are using Xerces 1.3, which you can find at http://xml.apache.org.

NOTE

For our example, we will use Tomcat 4, which comes packaged with a Xerces parser. If you choose to use another JSP/servlet container, you may need to acquire and install the latest Xerces parser.

Once you have the latest Struts release, you need to complete the following steps to prepare for the remainder of the text. You will have to complete these steps for each Struts Web application that you intend to deploy.

1. Uncompress the Struts archive to your local disk.
2. Create a new Web application, using the directory structure described in Chapter 1, "Introducing the Jakarta Struts Project and Its Supporting Components." Make sure you substitute the name of your Web application for the value *wileyapp*. For our example, the name of our Web application is wileystruts.
3. Copy the following JAR files, extracted from the Jakarta Struts archive, to the <*CATALINA_HOME*>/webapps/wileystruts/WEB-INF/lib directory:
   - struts.jar
   - commons-beanutils.jar
   - commons-collections.jar
   - commons-dbcp.jar
   - commons-digester.jar
   - commons-logging.jar
   - commons-pool.jar
   - commons-services.jar
   - commons-validator.jar
4. Uncompress the Xerces archive to your local disk, if necessary.
5. Copy the xerces.jar file from the Xerces root directory to the <*CATALINA_HOME*>/webapps/wileystruts/WEB-INF/lib/ directory.
6. Create an empty web.xml file, and copy it to the <*CATALINA_HOME*>/webapps/wileystruts/WEB-INF/ directory. A sample web.xml file is shown in the following code snippet:

```
<?xml version="1.0" encoding="ISO-8859-1"?>

<!DOCTYPE web-app
  PUBLIC "-//Sun Microsystems, Inc.//DTD Web Application
  2.3//EN"
  "http://java.sun.com/j2ee/dtds/web-app_2_3.dtd">

<web-app>

</web-app>
```

7. Create a basic strut-config.xml file, and copy it to the *<CATALINA_HOME>*/webapps/wileystruts/WEB-INF/ directory. The struts-config.xml file is the deployment descriptor for Struts applications. It is the file that glues all of the MVC (Model-View-Controller) components together. Its normal location is in the *<CATALINA_HOME>*/webapps/*webappname*/WEB-INF/ directory. We will be using this file extensively throughout the remainder of this text. An empty struts-config.xml file is listed here:

```
<?xml version="1.0" encoding="ISO-8859-1" ?>

<!DOCTYPE struts-config
  PUBLIC
  "-//Apache Software Foundation//DTD Struts Configuration 1.1//EN"
  "http://jakarta.apache.org/struts/dtds/struts-config_1_1.dtd">

<struts-config>

   <message-resources
     parameter="wiley.ApplicationResources"/>

</struts-config>
```

NOTE:

As of Struts 1.1 b1, you are required to have a <message-resources /> element defined in your struts-config.xml file. For now, you simply need to create the struts-config.xml file as shown previously. We will discuss this element's purpose in Chapter 6, "Internationalizing Your Struts Applications."

At this point, you have all of the necessary components to build the simplest of Struts applications. As you begin the design and development of your Struts application, you will need to install and configure further Struts components as necessary. In the next section, we take you through the steps that must be accomplished when developing a Struts application.

Creating Your First Struts Application

Now that you have Struts downloaded and installed, we can begin the development of our own sample Struts application. Our application consists of a simple set of JSP screens that queries a user for a stock symbol, performs a simple stock lookup, and returns the current price of the submitted stock. We will use this example to describe the steps that must be performed when creating any Struts application.

Because Struts is modeled after the MVC design pattern, you can follow a standard development process for all of your Struts Web applications. This process begins with the identification of the application Views, the Controller objects that will service those Views, and the Model components being operated on. This process can be described using the following steps:

1. Define and create all of the Views, in relation to their purpose, that will represent the user interface of our application. Add all ActionForms used by the created Views to the struts-config.xml file.
2. Create the components of the application's Controller.
3. Define the relationships that exist between the Views and the Controllers (struts-config.xml).
4. Make the appropriate modifications to the web.xml file; describe the Struts components to the Web application.
5. Run the application.

These steps provide a high-level description of the Struts development process. In the sections that follow, we will describe each of these steps in much greater detail.

Creating the Views

When creating Views in a Struts application, you are most often creating JSPs that are a combination of JSP/HTML syntax and some conglomeration of prepackaged Struts tag libraries. The JSP/HTML syntax is similar to any other Web page and does not merit discussion, but the specialized Struts custom tag libraries do. Currently, there are three major Struts tag libraries: Bean, HTML, and Logic. We will focus on all of these libraries and more View details in Chapter 5, "The Views," but for now we will use some of the HTML tags in the Views we define in this section. For those tags that we do use, we will include a brief explanation.

To begin the development of our application, we need to first describe the Views that will represent the user interface of our application. Two Views are associated with our sample application: index.jsp and quote.jsp.

NOTE

In our sample application, we do use a single image. This image file, hp_logo_wiley.gif, can be found in the images directory of our sample application's source tree.

The Index View

The Index View, which is represented by the file index.jsp, is our starting View. It is the first page our application users will see, and its purpose is to query the user for a stock symbol and submit the inputted symbol to the appropriate action. The source for index.jsp is found in Listing 3.1.

```
<%@ page language="java" %>
<%@ taglib
  uri="/WEB-INF/struts-html.tld"
  prefix="html" %>

<html>
  <head>
    <title>Wiley Struts Application</title>
  </head>

  <body>
    <table width="500"
    border="0" cellspacing="0" cellpadding="0">
      <tr>
        <td> </td>
      </tr>
      <tr bgcolor="#36566E">
        <td height="68" width="48%">
          <div align="left">
            <img src="images/hp_logo_wiley.gif"
              width="220"
             height="74">
          </div>
        </td>
      </tr>
      <tr>
        <td> </td>
      </tr>
    </table>

    <html:form action="Lookup"
      name="lookupForm"
      type="wiley.LookupForm" >
      <table width="45%" border="0">
        <tr>
          <td>Symbol:</td>
          <td><html:text property="symbol" /></td>
```

Listing 3.1 index.jsp. (continues)

```
        </tr>
        <tr>
          <td colspan="2" align="center"><html:submit /></td>
        </tr>
      </table>
    </html:form>

  </body>
</html>
```

Listing 3.1 index.jsp. (continued)

As you look over the source for the Index View, you will notice that it looks much like any other HTML page containing a form used to gather data, with the exception of the actual form tags. Instead of using the standard HTML Form tag, like most HTML pages, the index.jsp uses a Struts-specific Form tag: <html:form />. This tag, with its child tags, encapsulates Struts form processing. The form tag attributes used in this example are described in Table 3.1.

Table 3.1 Attributes of the Form Tag Used in Our Example

ATTRIBUTE	DESCRIPTION
action	Represents the URL to which this form will be submitted. This attribute is also used to find the appropriate ActionMapping in the Struts configuration file, which we will describe later in this section. The value used in our example is *Lookup*, which will map to an ActionMapping with a path attribute equal to Lookup.
name	Identifies the key that the ActionForm will be referenced by. We use the value *LookupForm*. An ActionForm is an object that is used by Struts to represent the form data as a JavaBean. It main purpose is to pass form data between View and Controller components. We will discuss LookupForm later in this section.
type	Names the fully qualified class name of the form bean to use in this request. For this example, we use the value *wiley.LookupForm*, which is an ActionForm object containing data members matching the inputs of this form.

This instance of the <html:form /> tag is also the parent to two other HTML tags. The first of the tags is the <html:text /> tag. This tag is synonymous with the HTML text input tag; the only difference is the property attribute, which names a unique data member found in the ActionForm bean class named by the form's type attribute. The named data member will be set to the text value of the corresponding input tag.

The second HTML tag that we use is the <html:submit /> tag. This tag simply emulates an HTML submit button. The net effect of these two tags is

- Upon submission, the ActionForm object named by the <html:form /> tag will be created, populated with the value of the <html:text /> tags, and stored in the session.
- Once the ActionForm object is populated with the appropriate values, the action referenced by the <html:form /> will be invoked and passed a reference to the populated ActionForm.

To use the previous two HTML tags, you must first add a taglib entry in the wileystruts application's web.xml file that references the URI /WEB-INF/struts-html.tld. This TLD describes all of the tags in the HTML tag library. The following snippet shows the <taglib> element that must be added to the web.xml file:

```
<taglib>
  <taglib-uri>/WEB-INF/struts-html.tld</taglib-uri>
  <taglib-location>/WEB-INF/struts-html.tld</taglib-location>
</taglib>
```

Second, you must copy the struts-html.tld from the lib directory of the extracted Struts archive to the *<CATALINA_HOME>*/webapps/wileystruts/WEB_INF/ directory.

NOTE

The previous two steps are used to deploy all of the Struts tag libraries. The only difference between each library's deployment is the name of the TLD. We will discuss additional Struts tag libraries in Chapter 5, "The Views."

The ActionForm

The ActionForm used in this example contains a single data member that maps directly to the symbol input parameter of the form defined in the Index View. As I stated in the previous section, when an <html:form /> is submitted, the Struts framework populates the matching data members of the ActionForm with the values entered into the <html:input /> tags. The Struts framework does this by using JavaBean reflection; therefore, the accessors of the ActionForm must follow the JavaBean standard naming convention. An example of this naming convention is shown here:

```
private String symbol;

public void setSymbol(String symbol);
public String getSymbol();
```

In this example, we have a single data member symbol. To satisfy the JavaBean standard, the accessors used to set the data member must be prefixed with *set* and *get*, followed by the data member name with its first letter capitalized. Listing 3.2 contains the source for our ActionForm.

```
package wiley;

import javax.servlet.http.HttpServletRequest;
import org.apache.struts.action.ActionForm;
import org.apache.struts.action.ActionMapping;

public class LookupForm extends ActionForm {

  private String symbol = null;

  public String getSymbol() {

    return (symbol);
  }

  public void setSymbol(String symbol) {

    this.symbol = symbol;
  }

  public void reset(ActionMapping mapping,
    HttpServletRequest request) {

    this.symbol = null;
  }
}
```

Listing 3.2 The LookupForm implementation LookupForm.java.

There is really nothing special about this class. It is a simple bean that extends org.apache.struts.action.ActionForm, as must all ActionForm objects, with get and set accessors that match each of its data members. It does have one method that is specific to an ActionForm bean: the reset() method. The reset() method is called by the Struts framework with each request that uses the LookupForm. The purpose of this method is to reset all of the LookupForm's data members and allow the object to be pooled for reuse.

NOTE

The reset() method is passed a reference to an ActionMapping class. At this point, you can ignore this class; we will fully describe it in Chapters 4 and 5.

To deploy the LookupForm to our Struts application, you need to compile this class, move it to the <*CATALINA_HOME*>/webapps/wileystruts/WEB-INF/classes/wiley directory, and add the following line to the <form-beans> section of the <*CATALINA_HOME*>/webapps/wileystruts/WEB-INF/struts-config.xml file:

```
<form-bean name="lookupForm" type="wiley.LookupForm"/>
```

This entry makes the Struts application aware of the LookupForm and how it should be referenced.

The Quote View

The last of our Views is the quote.jsp. This View is presented to the user upon successful stock symbol lookup. It is a very simple JSP with no Struts specific functionality. Listing 3.3 contains its source.

```
<html>
  <head>
    <title>Wiley Struts Application</title>
  </head>
  <body>

    <table width="500"
      border="0" cellspacing="0" cellpadding="0">
      <tr>
        <td> </td>
      </tr>
      <tr bgcolor="#36566E">
        <td height="68" width="48%">
          <div align="left">
            <img src="images/hp_logo_wiley.gif"
              width="220" height="74">
          </div>
        </td>
      </tr>
      <tr>
        <td> </td>
      </tr>
      <tr>
        <td> </td>
      </tr>
      <tr>
        <td> </td>
```

Listing 3.3 quote.jsp. (continues)

```
        </tr>
        <tr>
          <td>
            Current Price : <%= request.getAttribute("PRICE") %>
          </td>
        </tr>
        <tr>
          <td> </td>
        </tr>
      </table>
    </body>
  </html>
```

Listing 3.3 quote.jsp. (continued)

As you look over this JSP, you will notice that it contains a single JSP functional line of code. This line of code retrieves the current price from the HttpServletRequest of the submitted stock symbol. This value is placed in the HttpServletRequest by the Action object that services this request, as shown in the next section.

Creating the Controller Components

In a Struts application, two components make up the Controller. These two components are the org.apache.struts.action.ActionServlet and the org.apache. struts.action.Action classes. In most Struts applications, there is one org. apache.struts.action.ActionServlet implementation and many org.apache. struts.action.Action implementations.

The org.apache.struts.action.ActionServlet is the Controller component that handles client requests and determines which org.apache.struts.action.Action will process the received request. When assembling simple applications, such as the one we are building, the default ActionServlet will satisfy your application needs, and therefore, you do not need to create a specialized org.apache.struts.action.ActionServlet implementation. When the need arises, however, it is a very simple process. For our example, we will stick with the ActionServlet as it is delivered in the Struts packages. We will cover the process of extending the org.apache.struts.action.ActionServlet in Chapter 4, "The Controller."

The second component of a Struts Controller is the org.apache.struts. action.Action class. As opposed to the ActionServlet, the Action class must be extended for each specialized function in your application. This class is where your application's specific logic begins.

For our example, we have only one process to perform: looking up the value of the submitted stock symbol. Therefore, we are going to create a single org.apache.struts.action.Action bean named LookupAction. The source for our Action is shown in Listing 3.4. As you examine this listing, be sure to pay close attention to the execute() method.

```
package wiley;

import java.io.IOException;
import javax.servlet.ServletException;
import javax.servlet.http.HttpServletRequest;
import javax.servlet.http.HttpServletResponse;
import org.apache.struts.action.Action;
import org.apache.struts.action.ActionForm;
import org.apache.struts.action.ActionForward;
import org.apache.struts.action.ActionMapping;

public class LookupAction extends Action {

  protected Double getQuote(String symbol) {

    if ( symbol.equalsIgnoreCase("SUNW") ) {

      return new Double(25.00);
    }
    return null;
  }

  public ActionForward execute(ActionMapping mapping,
    ActionForm form,
    HttpServletRequest request,
    HttpServletResponse response)
    throws IOException, ServletException {

    Double price = null;

    // Default target to success
    String target = new String("success");

    if ( form != null ) {

      // Use the LookupForm to get the request parameters
      LookupForm lookupForm = (LookupForm)form;

      String symbol = lookupForm.getSymbol();
```

Listing 3.4 The LookupAction bean. (continues)

```
        price = getQuote(symbol);
      }

      // Set the target to failure
      if ( price == null ) {

        target = new String("failure");
      }
      else {

        request.setAttribute("PRICE", price);
      }
      // Forward to the appropriate View
      return (mapping.findForward(target));
    }
  }
```

Listing 3.4 The LookupAction bean. (continued)

After examining this class, you will notice that it extends the org.apache.struts.action.Action class and contains two methods: getQuote() and execute(). The getQuote() method is a simple method that will return a fixed price (if *SUNW* is the submitted symbol).

The second method is the execute() method, where the main functionality of the LookupAction is found. This is the method that must be defined by all Action class implementations. Before we can examine how the logic contained in the execute() method works, we need to examine the four parameters passed to it. These parameters are described in Table 3.2.

Table 3.2 The Parameters of the Action.execute() Method

COMPONENT	DESCRIPTION
ActionMapping	The ActionMapping class contains all of the deployment information for a particular Action bean. This class will be used to determine where the results of the LookupAction will be sent once its processing is complete.
ActionForm	The ActionForm represents the form inputs containing the request parameters from the View referencing this Action bean. The reference being passed to our LookupAction points to an instance of our LookupForm.
HttpServletRequest	The HttpServletRequest attribute is a reference to the current HTTP request object.
HttpServletResponse	The HttpServletResponse is a reference to the current HTTP response object.

Now that we have described the parameters passed to the execute() method, we can move on to describing the actual method body. The first notable action taken by this method is to create a String object named *target* with a value of *success*. This object will be used to determine the View that will present successful results of this action.

The next step performed by this method is to get the request parameters contained in the LookupForm. When the form was submitted, the ActionServlet used Java's reflection mechanisms to set the values stored in this object. You should note that the reference passed to the execute() method is an ActionForm that must be cast to the ActionForm implementation used by this action. The following code snippet contains the source used to access the request parameters:

```
// Use the LookupForm to get the request parameters
LookupForm lookupForm = (LookupForm)form;

String symbol = lookupForm.getSymbol();
```

Once we have references to the symbol parameters, we pass these values to the getQuote() method. This method is a simple user-defined method that will return the Double value *25.00*. If the symbol *String* contains any values other than *SUNW*, then null is returned, and we change the value of our target to *failure*. This will have the effect of changing the targeted View. If the value was not null, then we add the returned value to the request with a key of PRICE.

At this point, the value of target equals either *success* or *failure*. This value is then passed to the ActionMapping.findForward() method, which returns an ActionForward object referencing the physical View that will actually present the results of this action. The final step of the execute() method is to return the ActionForward object to the invoking ActionServlet, which will then forward the request to the referenced View for presentation. This step is completed using the following line of code:

```
return (mapping.findForward(target));
```

To deploy the LookupAction to our Struts application, you need to compile the LookupAction class, move the class file to the <*CATALINA_HOME*>/webapps/wileystruts/WEB-INF/classes/wiley directory, and add the following entry to the <action-mappings> section of the <*CATALINA_HOME*>/webapps/wileystruts/WEB-INF/struts-config.xml file:

```
<action path="/Lookup"
  type="wiley.LookupAction"
  name="lookupForm"
  input="/index.jsp">
  <forward name="success" path="/quote.jsp"/>
  <forward name="failure" path="/index.jsp"/>
</action>
```

This entry contains the data that will be stored in the ActionMapping object that is passed to the execute() method of the LookupAction. It contains all of the attributes required to use this instance of the LookupAction, including a collection of keyed <forward> subelements representing the possible Views that can present the results of the LookupAction.

Deploying Your Struts Application

Now we have all of the necessary Struts components deployed and modified. Next, we need to tell the Web application itself about our application components. To do this, we must make some simple changes to the web.xml file.

The first change we must make is to tell the Web application about our ActionServlet. This is accomplished by adding the following servlet definition to the <*CATALINA_HOME*>/webapps/wileystruts/WEB-INF/web.xml file:

```
<servlet>
  <servlet-name>action</servlet-name>
  <servlet-class>
    org.apache.struts.action.ActionServlet
  </servlet-class>
  <init-param>
    <param-name>config</param-name>
    <param-value>/WEB-INF/struts-config.xml</param-value>
  </init-param>
  <load-on-startup>1</load-on-startup>
</servlet>
```

This entry tells the Web application that we have a servlet named action that is implemented by the class org.apache.struts.action.ActionServlet, which, as we stated earlier, is the default ActionServlet provided with Struts. The entry defines a single servlet initialization parameter, config, that tells the ActionServlet where to find the struts-config.xml file. It also includes a load-on-startup element that tells the JSP/servlet container that we want this servlet to be preloaded when the Web application starts. You must pre-load the ActionServlet, or your Struts Views will not load all of their necessary resources.

Once we have told the container about the ActionServlet, we need to tell it when the action should be executed. To do this, we have to add a <servlet-mapping> element to the <*CATALINA_HOME*>/webapps/wileystruts/WEB-INF/web.xml file:

```
<servlet-mapping>
  <servlet-name>action</servlet-name>
  <url-pattern>*.do</url-pattern>
</servlet-mapping>
```

NOTE

You will notice in the previously listed index.jsp that our action does not include a .do at the end of the URL. We do not have to append the .do because it is automatically appended if we use the <html:form /> tag. If you do not use the <html:form /> tag, then you will need to append .do to the action's URL.

This mapping tells the Web application that whenever a request is received with .do appended to the URL, the servlet named action should service the request.

Walking through the wileystruts Web Application

At this point, you should have completed all of the steps described in the previous section and have a deployed wileystruts Web application. In this section, we will go through this sample application and discuss each of the steps performed by Struts along the way. The purpose of this section is to provide you with a walkthrough that ties together all of the previously assembled components.

To begin using this application, you need to restart Tomcat and open your Web browser to the following URL:

```
http://localhost:8080/wileystruts/
```

If everything went according to plan, you should see a page similar to Figure 3.1.

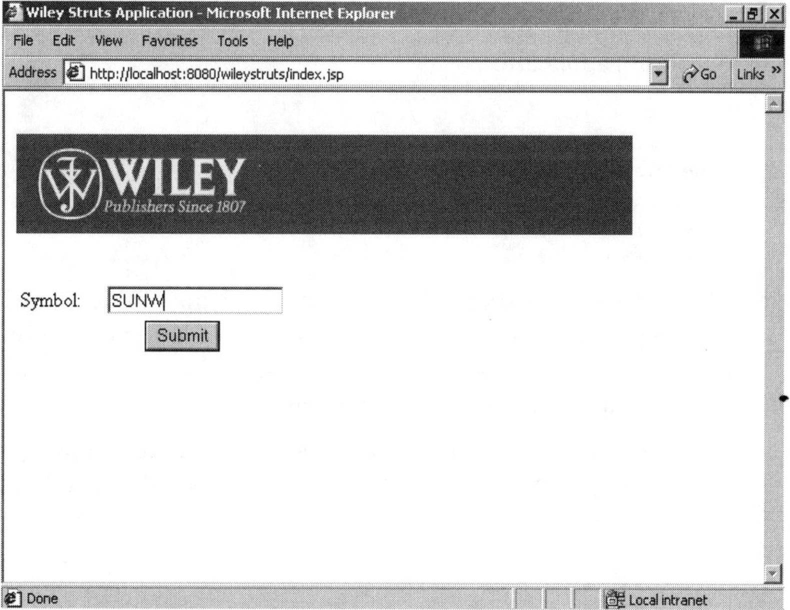

Figure 3.1 The wileystruts Index View.

When this page loads, the following actions occur:

1. The <html:form> creates the necessary HTML used to represent a form and then checks for an instance of the wiley.LookupForm in session scope. If there was an instance of the wiley.LookupForm, then the value stored in the ActionForm's data member will be mapped to the input element value on the form and the HTML form will be written to the response. This is a very handy technique that can be used to handle errors in form data. We will see examples of handling form errors in Chapter 7, "Managing Errors."
2. The Index View is then presented to the user.

To move on to the next step, enter the value *SUNW* into the Symbol text box, and click the Submit button. This will invoke the following functionality:

1. The Submit button will cause the browser to invoke the URL named in the <html:form /> tag's action attribute, which in this case is Lookup. When the JSP/servlet container receives this request, it looks in the web.xml file for a <servlet-mapping> with a <url-pattern> that ends with .do. It will find the following entry, which tells the container to send the request to a servlet that has been deployed with a <servlet-name> of action:

```
<!-- Standard Action Servlet Mapping -->
<servlet-mapping>
  <servlet-name>action</servlet-name>
  <url-pattern>*.do</url-pattern>
</servlet-mapping>
```

2. The container will find the following <servlet> entry with a <servlet-name> of action that points to the ActionServlet, which acts as the Controller for our Struts application:

```
<servlet>
  <servlet-name>action</servlet-name>
  <servlet-class>
    org.apache.struts.action.ActionServlet
  </servlet-class>
</servlet>
```

3. The ActionServlet then takes over the servicing of this request by retrieving the previously created LookupForm, populating its symbol data member with the value passed on the request, and adding the LookupForm to the session with a key of lookupForm.
4. At this point, the ActionServlet looks for an <ActionMapping> entry in the struts-config.xml file with a <path> element equal to Lookup. It finds the following entry:

```
<action path="/Lookup"
  type="wiley.LookupAction"
  name="lookupForm"
  input="/index.jsp">
  <forward name="success" path="/quote.jsp"/>
  <forward name="failure" path="/index.jsp"/>
</action>
```

5. It then creates an instance of the LookupAction class named by the type attribute. It also creates an ActionMapping class that contains all of the values in the <ActionMapping> element.

NOTE

The Struts framework does pool instances of Action classes; therefore, if the wiley.LookupAction had already been requested, then it will be retrieved from the instance pool as opposed to being created with every request.

6. It then invokes the LookupAction.execute() with the appropriate parameters. The LookupAction.execute() method performs its logic, and calls the ActionMapping.findForward() method with a String value of either *success* or *failure*.
7. The ActionMapping.findForward() method looks for a <forward> subelement with a name attribute matching the target value. It then returns an ActionForward object containing the results of the lookup, which is the value of the path attribute /quote.jsp (upon success) or /index.jsp (upon failure).
8. The LookupAction then returns the ActionForward object to the ActionServlet, which in turn forwards the request object to the targeted View for presentation. The results of a successful transaction are shown in Figure 3.2.

NOTE

If you submit any value other than SUNW, you will be sent back index.jsp, which is the failure path of the LookupAction. If this does happen, you will see that the input value on the index page is prepopulated with your originally submitted value. This is one of the handy error-handling techniques provided by the Struts application.

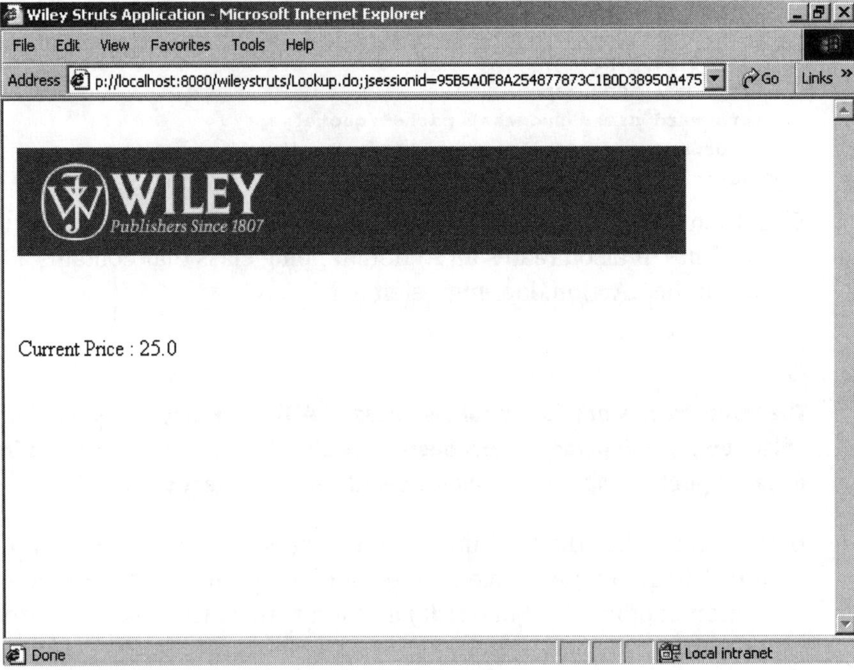

Figure 3.2 The wileystruts Quote View.

Summary

In this chapter, we began our Jakarta Struts coverage. We started by defining the Struts framework, including the steps that must be performed when installing and configuring a Struts application. We created a sample application to display the components that exist in a working Struts application. We concluded the chapter by walking through our sample application and discussing each step performed by Struts as it processes a request.

In the next chapter, we will continue our Struts conversations by digging further into the Controller components, including a discussion of org.apache.struts.action.ActionServlet extensions and a further examination of the org.apache.struts.action.Action class.

CHAPTER 4

The Controller

In this chapter, we dig further into the Controller components of the Struts framework. We begin by looking at three distinct Struts Controller components, including the ActionServlet class, the Action class, Plugins, and the RequestProcesser.

The goal of this chapter is to provide you with a solid understanding of the Struts Controller components, and how they can be used and extended to create a robust and easily extended Web application.

The ActionServlet Class

The org.apache.struts.action.ActionServlet is the backbone of all Struts applications. It is the main Controller component that handles client requests and determines which org.apache.struts.action.Action will process each received request. It acts as an Action factory by creating specific Action classes based on the user's request.

While the ActionServlet sounds as if it might perform some extraordinary magic, it is a simple servlet. Just like any other HTTP servlet, it extends the class javax.servlet.http.HttpServlet and implements each of the HttpServlet's life-cycle methods, including the init(), doGet(), doPost(), and destroy() methods.

The special behavior begins with the ActionServlet's process() method. The process() method is the method that handles all requests. It has the following method signature:

```
protected void process(HttpServletRequest request,
  HttpServletResponse response);
```

When the ActionServlet receives a request, it completes the following steps:

1. The doPost() or doGet() methods receive a request and invoke the process() method.
2. The process() method gets the current RequestProcessor, which is discussed in the final section of this chapter, and invokes its process() method.

NOTE:

If you intend to extend the ActionServlet, the most logical place for customization is in the RequestProcessor object. It contains the logic that the Struts controller performs with each request from the container. We will discuss the RequestProcessor in the final section of this chapter.

3. The RequestProcessor.process() method is where the current request is actually serviced. The RequestProcessor.process() method retrieves, from the struts-config.xml file, the <action> element that matches the path submitted on the request. It does this by matching the path passed in the <html:form /> tag's action element to the <action> element with the same path value. An example of this match is shown below:

```
<html:form action="/Lookup"
  name="lookupForm"
  type="wiley.LookupForm" >

<action path="/Lookup"
  type="wiley.LookupAction"
  name="lookupForm" >
  <forward name="success" path="/quote.jsp"/>
  <forward name="failure" path="/index.jsp"/>
</action>
```

4. When the RequestProcessor.process() method has a matching <action>, it looks for a <form-bean> entry that has a name attribute that matches the <action> element's name attribute. The following code snippet contains a sample match:

```
<form-beans>
  <form-bean name="lookupForm"
    type="wiley.LookupForm"/>
</form-beans>

<action path="/Lookup"
  type="wiley.LookupAction"
  name="lookupForm" >
```

```
    <forward name="success" path="/quote.jsp"/>
    <forward name="failure" path="/index.jsp"/>
  </action>
```

5. When the RequestProcessor.process() method knows the fully qualified name of the FormBean, it creates or retrieves a pooled instance of the ActionForm named by the <form-bean> element's type attribute, and populates its data members with the values submitted on the request.
6. After the ActionForm's data members are populated, the RequestProcessor.process() method calls the ActionForm.validate() method, which checks the validity of the submitted values.

NOTE

There is more to the validate() method than we are discussing in this chapter. We will see exactly how this method is configured and performs in Chapter 7, "Managing Errors."

7. At this point, the RequestProcessor.process() method knows all that it needs to know, and it is time to actually service the request. It does this by retrieving the fully qualified name of the Action class from the <action> element's type attribute, creating or retrieving the named class, and calling the Action.execute() method. We will look at this method in the section titled "The Action Class," later in this chapter.
8. When the Action class returns from its processing, its execute() method returns an ActionForward object that is used to determine the target of this transaction. The RequestProcessor.process() method resumes control, and the request is then forwarded to the determined target.
9. At this point, the ActionServlet instance has completed its processing for this request and is ready to service future requests.

Extending the ActionServlet

Now that you have seen what the ActionServlet is and how it is configured, let's look at how it can be extended to provide additional functionality. As you might have guessed, there are several different ways in which the ActionServlet can be extended, and we are going to examine just one of them. This examination, however, should provide the foundation you need to extend the ActionServlet for your own uses.

To develop your own ActionServlet, you must complete the following four steps. We will perform each of these steps when creating our custom ActionServlet.

1. Create a class that extends the org.apache.struts.action.ActionServlet class.
2. Implement the methods specific to your business logic.
3. Compile the new ActionServlet and move it into the Web application's classpath.
4. Add a <servlet> element to the application's web.xml file; name the new ActionServlet as the mapping to the .do extension.

In the 1.0x version of Struts, this was very common method of extending the ActionServlet. As of Struts 1.1, it is more appropriate to extend a Request-Processor to modify the default ActionServlet processing. We will discuss extending these components later in this chapter.

Configuring the ActionServlet

Now that you have a solid understanding of how the ActionServlet performs its duties, let's take a look at how it is deployed and configured. The ActionServlet is like any other servlet and is configured using a web.xml <serlvet> element.

You can take many approaches when setting up an ActionServlet. You can go with a bare-bones approach, as we did in Chapter 3, "Getting Started with Struts," or you can get more serious and include any combination of the available initialization parameters described in Table 4.1.

Table 4.1 The Initialization Parameters of the ActionServlet (continues)

PARAMETER	DESCRIPTION
bufferSize	Names the size of the input buffer used when uploading files. The default value is 4096 bytes. (optional)
config	Names the context-relative path to the struts-config.xml file. The default location is in the /WEB-INF/struts-config.xml directory. (optional)
content	Names the content type and character encoding to be set on each response. The default value is *text/html*. (optional)
debug	Determines the debugging level for the ActionServlet. The default value is 0, which turns debugging off. (optional)
detail	Sets the debug level for the Digester object, which is used during ActionServlet initialization. The default value is 0. (optional)
factory	Names the fully qualified class name of the object used to create the application's MessageResources object. The default value is *org.apache.struts.util.PropertyMessageResourcesFactory*. In most cases, the default class will handle your application needs. (optional)

Table 4.1 The Initialization Parameters of the ActionServlet (continued)

PARAMETER	DESCRIPTION
locale	If set to true and the requesting client has a valid session, then the Locale object is stored in the user's session bound to the key Action.LOCALE_KEY. The default value is true. (optional)
mapping	Names the fully qualified class name of the ActionMapping implementation used to describe each Action deployed to this application. The default value is *org.apache.struts.action.ActionMapping*. We will create our own ActionMapping extension in Chapter 8, "Creating Custom ActionMappings." (optional)
maxFileSize	Names the maximum file size (in bytes) of a file to be uploaded to a Struts application. This value can be expressed using *K*, *M*, or *G*, understood as kilobytes, megabytes, or gigabytes, respectively. The default size is 250M. (optional)
multipartClass	Names the fully qualified class of the MultipartRequestHandler implementation to be used when file uploads are being processed. The default value is *org.apache.struts.upload.DiskMultipartRequestHandler*. (optional)
nocache	If set to true, will add the appropriate HTTP headers to every response, turning off browser caching. This parameter is very useful when the client browser is not reflecting your application changes. The default value is false. (optional)
null	If set to true, will cause the Struts application resources to return null, as opposed to an error message, if it cannot find the requested key in the application resource bundle. The default value for this parameter is true. (optional)
tempDir	Names a directory to use as a temporary data store when file uploads are being processed. The default value is determined by the container hosting the application. (optional)
validate	If set to true, tells the ActionServlet that we are using the configuration file format defined as of Struts 1.0. The default value is true. (optional)
validating	If set to true, tells the ActionServlet that we want to validate the strut-config.xml file against its DTD. While this parameter is optional, it is highly recommended, and therefore the default is set to true.

While none of these initialization parameters are required, the most common ones include the config, application, and mapping parameters. It is also common practice to use a <load-on-startup> element to ensure that the Action-Servlet is started when the container starts the Web application. An example <serlvet> entry, describing an ActionServlet, is shown in the following code snippet:

```
<servlet>
  <servlet-name>action</servlet-name>
  <servlet-class>
    org.apache.struts.action.ActionServlet
  </servlet-class>
  <init-param>
    <param-name>config</param-name>
    <param-value>/WEB-INF/struts-config.xml</param-value>
  </init-param>
  <init-param>
    <param-name>mapping</param-name>
    <param-value>wiley.WileyActionMapping</param-value>
  </init-param>
  <load-on-startup>1</load-on-startup>
</servlet>
```

We will use all of these <init-param> elements in subsequent chapters of this book.

The Action Class

The second component of a Struts Controller is the org.apache.struts.action. Action class. As we stated in Chapter 3, the Action class must and will be extended for each specialized Struts function in your application. The collection of the Action classes that belong to your Struts application is what defines your Web application.

To begin our discussion of the Action class, we must first look at some of the Action methods that are more commonly overridden or leveraged when creating an extended Action class. The following sections describe five of these methods.

The execute() Method

The execute() method is where your application logic begins. It is the method that you need to override when defining your own Actions. The Struts framework defines two execute() methods.

The first execute() implementation is used when you are defining custom Actions that are not HTTP-specific. This implementation of the execute() method would be analogous to the javax.serlvet.GenericServlet class. The signature of this execute() method is

```
public ActionForward execute(ActionMapping mapping,
                             ActionForm form,
                             ServletRequest request,
                             ServletResponse response)
        throws IOException, ServletException
```

You will notice that this method receives, as its third and fourth parameter, a ServletRequest and a ServletResponse object, as opposed to the HTTP-specific equivalents HttpServletRequest and HttpServletResponse.

The second execute() implementation is used when you are defining HTTP-specific custom Actions. This implementation of the execute() method would be analogous to the javax.serlvet.http.HttpServlet class. The signature of this execute() method is

```
public ActionForward execute(ActionMapping mapping,
                             ActionForm form,
                             HttpServletRequest request,
                             HttpServletResponse response)
        throws IOException, ServletException
```

You will notice that this method receives, as its third and fourth parameter, a HttpServletRequest and a HttpServletResponse object, as opposed to the previously listed execute() method. This implementation of the execute() method is the implementation that you will most often extend. Table 4.2 describes all of the parameters of the Action.execute() method.

Table 4.2 The Parameters of the Action.execute() Method

COMPONENT	DESCRIPTION
ActionMapping	Contains all of the deployment information for a particular Action bean. This class will be used to determine where the results of the LoginAction will be sent after its processing is complete.
ActionForm	Represents the Form inputs containing the request parameters from the View referencing this Action bean. The reference being passed to our LoginAction points to an instance of our LoginForm.
HttpServletRequest	Is a reference to the current HTTP request object.
HttpServletResponse	Is a reference to the current HTTP response object.

Extending the Action Class

Now that you have seen the Action class and some of its configuration options, let's see how we can create our own Action class.

To develop your own Action class, you must complete the following steps. These steps describe the minimum actions that must be completed when creating a new Action:

1. Create a class that extends the org.apache.struts.action.Action class.
2. Implement the appropriate execute() method and your specific to your business logic.
3. Compile the new Action and move it into the Web application's classpath.
4. Add an <action> element to the application's struts-config.xml file describing the new Action.

An example execute() implementation is listed in the following snippet. We will be extending the Action class throughout the remainder of this text.

```
public ActionForward execute(ActionMapping mapping,
  ActionForm form,
  HttpServletRequest request,
  HttpServletResponse response)
  throws IOException, ServletException {

  Double price = null;

  // Default target to success
  String target = new String("success");

  if ( form != null ) {

    // Use the LookupForm to get the request parameters
    LookupForm lookupForm = (LookupForm)form;

    String symbol = lookupForm.getSymbol();

    price = getQuote(symbol);
  }

  // Set the target to failure
  if ( price == null ) {

    target = new String("failure");
  }
  else {

    request.setAttribute("PRICE", price);
  }
  // Forward to the appropriate View
  return (mapping.findForward(target));
}
```

Configuring the Action Class

Now that you have seen the major methods of the Action class, let's examine its configuration options. The Action class is a Struts-specific object, and therefore must be configured using the struts-config.xml file.

The element that is used to configure a Struts action is an <action> element. The class that defines the <action> element's attributes is the org.apache.struts.action.ActionMappings class. We will look at how this class can be extended to define additional <action> attributes in Chapter 8, "Creating Custom ActionMappings." Table 4.3 describes the attributes of an <action> element as they are defined by the default ActionMappings class.

NOTE

When using an <action> element to describe an Action class, you are describing only one instance of the named Action class. There is nothing stopping you from using n-number of <action> elements that describe the same Action class. The only restriction is that the path attribute must be unique for each <action> element.

Table 4.3 Attributes of an <action> Element (continues)

ATTRIBUTE	DESCRIPTION
path	Represents the context-relative path of the submitted request. The path must be unique and start with a / character. (required)
type	Names the fully qualified class name of the Action class being described by this ActionMapping. The type attribute is valid only if no include or forward attribute is specified. (optional)
name	Identifies the name of the form bean, if any, that is coupled with the Action being defined. (optional)
scope	Names the scope of the form bean that is bound to the described Action. The default value is session. (optional)
input	Names the context-relative path of the input form to which control should be returned if a validation error is encountered. The input attribute is where control will be returned if ActionErrors are returned from the ActionForm or Action objects. (optional)
className	Names the fully qualified class name of the ActionMapping implementation class to use in when invoking this Action class. If the className attribute is not included, the ActionMapping defined in the ActionServlet's mapping initialization parameter is used. (optional)
forward	Represents the context-relative path of the servlet or JSP resource that will process this request. This attribute is used if you do not want an Action to service the request to this path. The forward attribute is valid only if no include or type attribute is specified. (optional)

Table 4.3 Attributes of an <action> Element (continued)

ATTRIBUTE	DESCRIPTION
include	Represents the context-relative path of the servlet or JSP resource that will process this request. This attribute is used if you do not want an Action to service the request to this path. The include attribute is valid only if no forward or type attribute is specified. (optional)
validate	If set to true, causes the ActionForm.validate() method to be called on the form bean associated to the Action being described. If the validate attribute is set to false, then the ActionForm.validate() method is not called. The default value is true. (optional)

A sample <action> subelement using some of the previous attributes is shown here:

```
<action-mappings>

  <action path="/Lookup"
    type="wiley.LookupAction"
    name="lookupForm"
    input="/index.jsp">
    <forward name="success" path="/quote.jsp"/>
    <forward name="failure" path="/index.jsp"/>
  </action>

</action-mappings>
```

This <action> element tells the ActionServlet the following things about this Action instance:

- The Action class is implemented by the wiley.LookupAction class.
- This Action should be invoked when the URL ends with the path /Lookup.
- This Action class will use the <form-bean> with the name lookupForm.
- The originating resource that submitted the request to this Action is the JSP index.jsp.
- This Action class will forward the results of its processing to either the quote.jsp or the index.jsp.

The previous <action> element uses only a subset of the possible <action> element attributes, but the attributes that it does use are some of the more common.

Struts Plugins

Struts Plugins are modular extensions to the Struts Controller. They have been introduced in Struts 1.1, and are defined by the org.apache.struts.action.Plugin interface. Struts Plugins are useful when allocating resources or preparing connections to databases or even JNDI resources. We will look at an example of loading application properties on startup later in this section.

This interface, like the Java Servlet architecture, defines two methods that must be implemented by all used-defined Plugins: init() and destroy(). These are the life-cycle methods of a Struts Plugin.

init()

The init() method of a Struts Plugin is called whenever the JSP/Servlet container starts the Struts Web application containing the Plugin. It has a method signature as follows:

```
public void init(ApplicationConfig config)
  throws ServletException;
```

This method is convenient when initializing resources that are important to their hosting applications. As you will have noticed, the init() method receives an ApplicationConfig parameter when invoked. This object provides access to the configuration information describing a Struts application. The init() method marks the beginning of a Plugin's life.

destroy()

The destroy() method of a Struts Plugin is called whenever the JSP/Servlet container stops the Struts Web application containing the Plugin. It has a method signature as follows:

```
public void destroy();
```

This method is convenient when reclaiming or closing resources that were allocated in the Plugin.init() method. This method marks the end of a Plugin's life.

Creating a Plugin

Now that we have discussed what a Plugin is, let's look at an example Plugin implementation. As we stated earlier, all Plugins must implement the two Plugin methods init() and destroy(). To develop your own Plugin, you must complete the following steps. These steps describe the minimum actions that must be completed when creating a new Plugin:

1. Create a class that implements the org.apache.struts.action.Plugin interface.
2. Add a default empty constructor to the Plugin implementation. **You must have a default constructor to ensure that your Plugin is properly created by the ActionServlet.**
3. Implement both the init() and destroy() methods and your implementation.
4. Compile the new Plugin and move it into the Web application's classpath.
5. Add an <plug-in> element to the application's struts-config.xml file describing the new Plugin. We will look at this step in the next section.

An example Plugin implementation is listed in the following snippet.

```
package wiley;

import java.util.Properties;
import java.io.File;
import java.io.FileInputStream;
import java.io.FileNotFoundException;
import java.io.IOException;

import javax.servlet.ServletException;
import javax.servlet.ServletContext;

import org.apache.struts.action.PlugIn;
import org.apache.struts.config.ApplicationConfig;
import org.apache.struts.action.ActionServlet;

public class WileyPlugin implements PlugIn {

  public static final String PROPERTIES = "PROPERTIES";

  public WileyPlugin() {

  }

  public void init(ActionServlet servlet,
    ApplicationConfig applicationConfig)
    throws javax.servlet.ServletException {

    System.err.println("---->The Plugin is starting<----");
    Properties properties = new Properties();

    try {

      // Build a file object referening the properties file
      // to be loaded
      File file =
        new File("PATH TO PROPERTIES FILE");
```

```
            // Create an input stream
            FileInputStream fis =
              new FileInputStream(file);

            // load the properties
            properties.load(fis);

            // Get a reference to the ServletContext
            ServletContext context =
              servlet.getServletContext();

            // Add the loaded properties to the ServletContext
            // for retrieval throughout the rest of the Application
            context.setAttribute(PROPERTIES, properties);
          }
          catch (FileNotFoundException fnfe) {

            throw new ServletException(fnfe.getMessage());
          }
          catch (IOException ioe) {

            throw new ServletException(ioe.getMessage());
          }
        }

        public void destroy() {

          // We don't have anything to clean up, so
          // just log the fact that the Plugin is shutting down
          System.err.println("---->The Plugin is stopping<----");
        }
      }
```

As you look over our example Plugin, you will see just how straightforward Plugin development can be. In this example, we create a simple Plugin that extends the init() method, which contains the property loading logic, and the destroy() method, which contains no specialized implementation. The purpose of this Plugin is to make a set of properties available upon application startup. To make the wiley.WileyPlugin available to your Struts application, you need to move on to the following section on Plugin configuration.

Configuring a Plugin

Now that you have seen a Plugin and understand how they can be used, let's take a look at how a Plugin is deployed and configured. To deploy and configure our wiley.WileyPlugin, you must

1. Compile and move the Plugin class file into the classpath.

2. Add a <plug-in> element to your struts-config.xml file. An example <plug-in> entry, describing the previously defined Plugin, is shown in the following code snippet:

```
<plug-in className="wiley.WileyPlugin"/>
```

NOTE:

The <plug-in> element must follow all <message-resources /> elements in the struts-config.xml.

3. Restart the Struts Web application.

When this deployment is complete, this Plugin will begin its life when the hosting application restarts.

The RequestProcessor

As we stated previously, the org.apache.struts.action.RequestProcessor contains the logic that the Struts controller performs with each servlet request from the container. The RequestProcessor is the class that you will want to override when you want to customize the processing of the ActionServlet.

Creating a New RequestProcessor

Now that we have discussed what the RequestProcessor is, let's look at an example Plugin implementation. The RequestProcessor contains n-number of methods that you can override to change the behavior of the ActionServlet.

To create your own RequestProcessor, you must follow the steps described in the following list:

1. Create a class that extends the org.apache.struts.action.RequestProcessor class.
2. Add a default empty constructor to the RequestProcessor implementation.
3. Implement the method that you want to override. Our example overrides the processPreprocess() method.

In our example, we are going to override one of the more useful RequestProcessor methods, the processPreprocess() method, to log information about every request being made to our application.

The processPreprocess() method is executed prior to the execution of every Action.execute() method. It allows you to perform application-specific business logic before every Action. The method prototype for the processPreprocess() method is shown below:

```
protected boolean processPreprocess(HttpServletRequest request,
  HttpServletResponse response)
```

The default implementation of the processPreprocess() method simply returns true, which tells the framework to continue its normal processing. You must return true from your overridden processPreprocess() method if you want to continue processing the request.

NOTE:

If you do choose to return false from the processPreprocess() method, then the RequestProcessor will stop processing the request and return control back to the doGet() or doPost() of the ActionServlet.

To see how all of this really works, take a look at our example RequestProcessor implementation, which is listed in the following snippet.

```
package wiley;

import javax.servlet.http.HttpServletRequest;
import javax.servlet.http.HttpServletResponse;
import javax.servlet.http.HttpServlet;
import javax.servlet.ServletException;
import javax.servlet.http.Cookie;

import java.io.IOException;
import java.util.Enumeration;

import org.apache.struts.action.RequestProcessor;

public class WileyRequestProcessor extends RequestProcessor {

  public WileyRequestProcessor() {
  }

  public boolean processPreprocess(HttpServletRequest request,
    HttpServletResponse response) {

    log("----------processPreprocess Logging--------------");
    log("Request URI = " + request.getRequestURI());
    log("Context Path = " + request.getContextPath());

    Cookie cookies[] = request.getCookies();
    if (cookies != null) {

      for (int i = 0; i < cookies.length; i++) {
```

```
        log("Cookie = " + cookies[i].getName() + " = " +
        cookies[i].getValue());
      }
    }

    Enumeration headerNames = request.getHeaderNames();

    while (headerNames.hasMoreElements()) {

      String headerName =
        (String) headerNames.nextElement();

      Enumeration headerValues =
        request.getHeaders(headerName);

      while (headerValues.hasMoreElements()) {

        String headerValue =
          (String) headerValues.nextElement();

        log("Header = " + headerName + " = " + headerValue);
      }
    }
    log("Locale = " + request.getLocale());
    log("Method = " + request.getMethod());
    log("Path Info = " + request.getPathInfo());
    log("Protocol = " + request.getProtocol());
    log("Remote Address = " + request.getRemoteAddr());
    log("Remote Host = " + request.getRemoteHost());
    log("Remote User = " + request.getRemoteUser());
    log("Requested Session Id = "
      + request.getRequestedSessionId());
    log("Scheme = " + request.getScheme());
    log("Server Name = " + request.getServerName());
    log("Server Port = " + request.getServerPort());
    log("Servlet Path = " + request.getServletPath());
    log("Secure = " + request.isSecure());
    log("-------------------------------------------------");

    return true;
  }
}
```

In our processPreprocess() method, we are retrieving the information stored in the request and logging it to the ServletContext log. Once the logging is complete, the processPreprocess() method returns the Boolean value true, and normal processing continues. If the processPreprocess() method had returned false, then the ActionServlet would have terminated processing, and the Action would never have been performed.

Configuring an Extended RequestProcessor

Now that you have seen a Plugin and understand how it can be used, let's take a look at how a Plugin is deployed and configured. To deploy and configure our wiley.WileyPlugin, you must

1. Compile the new RequestProcessor and move it into the Web application's classpath.
2. Add a <controller> element to the application's struts-config.xml file describing the new RequestProcessor. An example <controller> entry, describing the our new RequestProcessor, is shown in the following code snippet:

```
<controller
  processorClass="wiley.WileyRequestProcessor" />
```

NOTE:

The <controller> element must follow the <action-mappings> element and precede the <message-resources /> elements in the struts-config.xml. A full description of the <controller> element and its attributes is included in Chapter 12, "The struts-config.xml File."

3. Restart the Struts Web application.

When this deployment is complete, the new RequestProcessor will take effect. To see the results of these log statements, open the *<CATALINA_HOME>*/ logs/localhost_log.*todaysdate*.txt file, and you will see the logged request at the bottom of the log file.

Summary

In this chapter, we described the different Controller components, and discussed how and when they should be extended. In the next chapter, we will discuss the presentation layer of the Struts framework. We will describe the major components of the Struts View, including ActionForm beans and the Struts tag libraries, and how each of these components fit into the Struts framework.

CHAPTER 5

The Views

In this chapter, we examine the View component of the Struts framework. Some of the topics that we discuss are using tags from Struts tag libraries, using ActionForms, and deploying Views to a Struts application.

The goal of this chapter is to give you an understanding of the Struts View and the components that can be leveraged to construct the View.

Building a Struts View

As we discussed in Chapter 1, "Introducing the Jakarta Struts Project and Its Supporting Components," the Struts View is represented by a combination of JSPs, custom tag libraries, and optional ActionForm objects. In the sections that follow, we examine each of these components and how they can be leveraged.

At this point, you should have a pretty good understanding of what JSPs are and how they can be used. We can now focus on how JSPs are leveraged in a Struts application.

JSPs in the Struts framework serve two main functions. The first of these functions is to act as the presentation layer of a previously executed Controller Action. This is most often accomplished using a set of custom tags that are focused around iterating and retrieving data forwarded to the target JSP by the Controller Action. This type of View is not Struts-specific, and does not warrant special attention.

The second of these functions, which is very much Struts-specific, is to gather data that is required to perform a particular Controller Action. This is done most often with a combination of tag libraries and ActionForm objects. This type of View contains several Struts-specific tags and classes, and is therefore the focus of this chapter.

Deploying JSPs to a Struts Application

Before we can begin looking at the role of a JSP in the Struts framework, we must take a look at how JSPs are deployed to the framework. JSPs are most often the target of a previous request; whether they are gathering or presenting data usually makes no difference as to how they are deployed. All JSPs should be deployed to a Struts application by using a <forward> element. This element is used to define the targets of Struts Actions, as shown in the following code snippet:

```
<forward name="login" path="/login.jsp"/>
```

In this example, the <forward> element defines a View named login with a path of /login.jsp.

To make this <forward> element available to a Struts application, we must nest it within one of two possible Struts elements. You can make a JSP available globally to the entire application. This type of JSP deployment is useful for error pages and login pages. You perform this type of deployment by adding the JSP to the <global-forwards> section of the struts-config.xml file. An example of this is shown in the following code snippet:

```
<global-forwards>
  <forward name="login" path="/login.jsp"/>
</global-forwards>
```

The previous <forward> element states that /login.jsp will be the target of all Struts Actions that return an ActionForward instance with the name login, as shown here:

```
return (mapping.findForward("login"));
```

NOTE

The only time that a global forward is not used is when an <action> element has a <forward> declaration with the same name. In this instance, the <action> element's <forward> will take precedence.

The second type of <forward> declaration is defined as an Action <forward>. These types of <forward> elements are defined as subelements of an <action> definition, and are accessible only from within that <action>. The following code snippet shows an example of this type of <forward> declaration:

```
<action path="/Login"
  type="com.wiley.LoginAction"
  validate="true"
  input="/login.jsp"
  name="loginForm"
  scope="request" >
  <forward name="success" path="/employeeList.jsp"/>
  <forward name="failure" path="/login.jsp"/>
</action>
```

This <forward> definition states that /login.jsp will be the target of com.wiley.LoginAction when this Action returns an ActionForward instance with the name “failure”, as shown here:

```
return (mapping.findForward("failure"));
```

JSPs that Gather Data

Now that you know how JSPs are deployed in a Struts application, let’s take a look at one of the two most common uses of a JSP in a Struts application: using JSPs to gather data.

There are several methods that can be leveraged when gathering data using a JSP. The most common of these methods includes using the HTML <form> element and any combination of <input> subelements to build a form. While Struts uses this exact methodology, it does so with a set of JSP custom tags that emulate the HTML <form> and <input> elements, but also includes special Struts functionality. The following code snippet contains a JSP that uses the Struts tags to gather data:

```
<html:form action="/Login"
  name="loginForm"
  type="com.wiley.LoginForm" >

  <table width="45%" border="0">
    <tr>
      <td>Username:</td>
      <td><html:text property="username" /></td>
    </tr>
    <tr>
      <td>Password:</td>
      <td><html:password property="password" /></td>
    </tr>
    <tr>
      <td colspan="2" align="center"><html:submit /></td>
    </tr>
  </table>
</html:form>
```

If we break this JSP into logical sections, you will first take notice of the four Struts HTML tags: <html:form />, <html:text />, <html:password />, and

<html:submit />. These tags include special Struts functionality that is used to gather HTML form data. We look at each of these tags in the sections that follow.

NOTE

The Struts library that includes the HTML tags listed in our JSP is named the HTML Tag Library. It includes tags that closely mimic the same functionality common to HTML form elements. In our example, we saw only a small fraction of the entire HTML tag library. The remaining tags are discussed in Chapter 14, "HTML Tag Library."

The <html:form /> Tag

The first of these tags is the <html:form /> tag. This tag serves as the container for all other Struts HTML input tags. It renders an HTML <form> element, containing all of the child elements associated with this HTML form. While the <html:form /> tag does serve as an HTML input container, it is also used to store and retrieve the data members of the named ActionForm bean. This tag, with its children, encapsulates the presentation layer of Struts form processing. The form tag attributes used in this example are described in Table 5.1.

Table 5.1 The Attributes of the Form Tag Used in this Example

ATTRIBUTE	DESCRIPTION
action	Represents the URL to which this form will be submitted. This attribute is also used to find the appropriate ActionMapping in the Struts configuration file, which we describe later in this section. The value used in our example is /Login, which will map to an ActionMapping with a path attribute equal to /Login.
name	Identifies the key that the ActionForm that we will be using in this request to identify the FormBean associated with this Form. We use the value loginForm. ActionForms are described in the following section.
type	Provides the fully qualified class name of the ActionForm bean used in this request. For this example, we use the value com.wiley.LoginForm, which is described following.

ActionForm Beans

Before we can move on to examining the rest of this form, we must discuss the org.apache.struts.action.ActionForm object. ActionForms are JavaBeans that are used to encapsulate and validate the request parameters submitted by an HTTP request. A sample ActionForm, named LoginForm, is listed in the following code snippet:

```
package com.wiley;

import javax.servlet.http.HttpServletRequest;
import org.apache.struts.action.ActionForm;
import org.apache.struts.action.ActionMapping;
import org.apache.struts.action.ActionErrors;
import org.apache.struts.action.ActionError;

public class LoginForm extends ActionForm {

  private String password = null;

  private String username = null;

  public String getPassword() {

    return (this.password);
  }

  public void setPassword(String password) {

    this.password = password;
  }

  public String getUsername() {

    return (this.username);
  }

  public void setUsername(String username) {

    this.username = username;
  }

  public void reset(ActionMapping mapping,
    HttpServletRequest request) {

    this.password = null;
    this.username = null;
  }

  public ActionErrors validate(ActionMapping mapping,
    HttpServletRequest request) {

    ActionErrors errors = new ActionErrors();

    if ( (username == null ) || (username.length() == 0) ) {

      errors.add("username",
        new ActionError("errors.username.required"));
    }
```

```
        if ( (password == null ) || (password.length() == 0) ) {

          errors.add("password",
            new ActionError("errors.password.required"));
        }
        return errors;
      }
    }
```

As you look over this class, you should first notice that it extends the org.apache.struts.action.ActionForm class; all ActionForm beans must extend this class. After this, you will notice that the LoginForm definition itself contains two data members–username and password–as well as six methods.

The first four of these methods are simple setters and getters used to access and modify the two data members. Each of these setter methods is called by the Struts framework when a request is submitted with a parameter matching the data member's name. This is accomplished using JavaBean reflection; therefore, the accessors of the ActionForm must follow the JavaBean standard naming convention. In the next section, we learn how these data members are mapped to request parameters.

The last two methods of this ActionForm are probably the most important. These methods are defined by the ActionForm object, and are used to perform request-time processing.

The reset() method is called by the Struts framework with each request that uses the defined ActionForm. The purpose of this method is to reset all of the LoginForm's data members prior to the new request values being set. You should implement this method to reset your form's data members to their original values; otherwise, the default implementation will do nothing.

As you look over our reset() method, you will note that it sets both of our data members back to null. This method guarantees that our data members are not holding stale data.

The last method defined by our LoginForm is validate(). This method should be overridden when you are interested in testing the validity of the submitted data prior to the invocation of the Action.execute() method.

The proper use of this method is to test the values of the data members, which have been set to the matching request parameters. If there are no problems with the submitted values, then the validate() method should return null or an empty ActionErrors object, and the execution of the request will continue with normal operation.

If the values of the data members are invalid, then it should create a collection of ActionErrors containing an ActionError object for each invalid parameter and then return this ActionErrors instance to the Controller. If the Controller receives a valid ActionErrors collection, it will forward the request to the path identified by the <action> element's input attribute. If your ActionForm does not implement the validate() method, then the default implementation will simply return null, and processing will continue normally.

NOTE

We will discuss the error management process in much more detail in Chapter 7, "Managing Errors."

After looking at the LoginForm's validate() method, you will see that the request using this ActionForm must contain a username and password that is not null or a 0 length string.

The Input Tags

Once you get past the attributes of this instance of the <html:form /> tag, you will see that it also acts as a parent to three other HTML tags. These tags are synonymous with the HTML input elements.

The <html:text /> Tag

The first of the HTML input tags is the <html:text /> tag. This tag is equivalent to the HTML text input tag, with the only difference being the property attribute, which names a unique data member found in the ActionForm bean class named by the form's type attribute. The following code snippet contains our <html:text /> tag.

```
<html:text property="username" />
```

As you can see, the property attribute of this instance is set to the value *username*; therefore, when the form is submitted, the value of this input tag will be stored in the LoginForm's username data member.

The <html:password /> Tag

The second of the HTML tags is the <html:password /> tag. This tag is equivalent to the HTML password input tag. It functions in the same way as <html:text />; the only difference is that its value is not displayed to the client. The following code snippet contains our <html:password /> tag:

```
<html:password property="password" />
```

As you can see, the property attribute of this instance is set to the value *password*, which results in the LoginForm's password data member being set to the value of this input parameter.

The <html:submit />Tag

The last HTML tag that we use is the <html:submit /> tag. This tag simply emulates an HTML submit button by submitting the request to the targeted action:

```
<html:submit />
```

The Steps of a Struts Form Submission

When a View containing this type of <html:form /> is requested, it will be evaluated and the resulting HTML will look similar to this:

```
<form name="loginForm"
  method="POST"
  action="/employees/Login.do">

      <table width="45%" border="0">
        <tr>
          <td>User Name:</td>
          <td>
            <input type="text"
              name="username"
              value=""></td>
        </tr>
        <tr>
          <td>Password:</td>
          <td>
            <input type="password"
              name="password"
              value=""></td>
        </tr>
        <tr>
          <td colspan="2" align="center">
            <input type="submit"
              name="submit"
              value="Submit"></td>
        </tr>
      </table>
    </form>
```

NOTE

As you examine the evaluated form, you will notice that the value of the <input> elements is an empty string. This will not always be the case. If the session already includes an instance of the ActionForm named by the <form> element's name attribute, then the values stored in its data members will be used to prepopulate the input values. We will see an example of this in Chapter 7.

Once the user of this form has entered the appropriate values and clicked the Submit button, the following actions take place:

1. The Controller creates or retrieves (if it already exists) an instance of the com.wiley.LoginForm object, and stores the instance in the appropriate scope. The default scope is session. To change the scope of the ActionForm, you use the <html:form /> attribute scope.
2. The Controller then calls the com.wiley.LoginForm.reset() method to set the form's data members back to their default values.
3. The Controller next populates the com.wiley.LoginForm username and password data members with the values of the <html:text /> and <html:password /> tags, respectively.
4. Once the data members of the com.wiley.LoginForm have been set, the Controller invokes the com.wiley.LoginForm.validate() method.
5. If the validate() method does not encounter problems with the data, then the Action referenced by the <html:form />'s action attribute is invoked and passes a reference to the populated ActionForm. Processing then continues normally.

That's about it. There is almost no limit to the type of Views that can exist in a Struts application, but this type of View is most tightly bound to the Struts framework. This is also the type of View that you will see evolve throughout the remainder of this text.

Summary

In this chapter, we discussed the View component of the Struts framework, and examined how to use tags from Struts tag libraries, use ActionForms, and deploy Views to a Struts application. The next chapter focuses on how to make use of the internationalization (i18n) features in Struts.

CHAPTER 6

Internationalizing Your Struts Applications

In this chapter, we look at the internationalization (i18n) features of the Struts Framework. We begin by defining each Struts i18n component and how it is used and configured. We then examine the steps involved when internationalizing our existing stock lookup application.

The goal of this chapter is to cover all of the required components and processes involved when internationalizing a Struts application. At the end of this chapter, you should feel comfortable with internationalizing your own Struts applications.

NOTE

In this chapter, you will notice that I use the terms *i18n* and *internationalization* interchangeably. While i18n looks like an acronym, we use it simply to represent "Internationalization," because 18 is the number of letters between the alphabetical characters *i* and *n* in the word *internationalization*.

I18N Components of a Struts Application

Two i18n components are packaged with the Struts Framework. The first of these components, which is managed by the application Controller, is a Message class that references a resource bundle containing Locale-dependent strings. The second i18n component is a JSP custom tag, <bean:message />, which is used in the View layer to present the actual strings managed by the Controller. We examine each of these components in the following sections.

The Controller

The standard method used when internationalizing a Struts application begins with the creation of a set of simple Java properties files. Each file contains a key/value pair for each message that you expect your application to present, in the language appropriate for the requesting client.

Defining the Resource Bundles

The first of these files is one that contains the key/value pairs for the default language of your application. The naming format for this file is *ResourceBundleName*.properties. An example of this default file, using English as the default language, would be

```
ApplicationResources.properties
```

A sample entry in this file would be

```
app.symbol=Symbol
```

This combination tells Struts that when the client has a default Locale that uses English as the language, and the key for app.symbol exists in the requested resource, then the value *Symbol* will be substituted for every occurrence of the app.symbol key.

NOTE

In the following section, which describes the i18n View component, we see how these keys are requested.

Once you have defined the default properties file, you must define a properties file for each language that your application will use. This file must follow the same naming convention as the default properties file, except that it must include the two-letter ISO language code of the language that it represents. An example of this naming convention for an Italian-speaking client would be

```
ApplicationResources_it.properties
```

And a sample entry in this file would be

```
app.symbol=Simbolo
```

NOTE

You can find all of the two-letter ISO language codes at www-old.ics.uci.edu/pub/ietf/http/related/iso639.txt.

This combination tells Struts that when the client has a Locale that uses the Italian language, and the key for app.symbol exists in the requested resource, then the value *Simbolo* will be substituted for every occurrence of the app.symbol key.

NOTE

The ApplicationResources.properties files are loaded upon application startup. If you make changes to this file, you must reload the properties file, either by restarting the entire container or by restarting the Web application referencing the properties files.

Deploying the Resource Bundles

Once you have defined all of the properties files for your application, you need to make Struts aware of them. Prior to 1.1, this was accomplished by setting the application servlet <init-parameter> of the org.apache.struts.actions.ActionServlet. As of Struts 1.1, this is achieved by adding a <message-resources> subelement to the struts-config.xml file. The Struts 1.1 method of configuring a resource bundle will be the focus of the following section.

To make the Struts Framework aware of your application resource bundles, you must copy all of your resource bundles into the application classpath, which in this case is *<CATALINA-HOME>*/webapps/*webapplicationname*/ WEB-INF/classes/wiley, and then use the package path plus the base file name as the value of the <message-resources> subelement. The following snippet shows an example of using the <message-resources> subelement to configure a resource bundle, using the properties files described in the previous section:

```
<message-resources
  parameter="wiley.ApplicationResources"/>
```

This <message-resource> subelement tells the Struts Controller that all of our properties' files exist in the *<CATALINA_HOME>*/webapps/*web applicationname*/WEB-INF/classes/wiley directory, and are named ApplicationResources_*xx*.properties.

NOTE

You will notice that the <param-value> contains only the default filename. This is because Struts will get the Locale of the client and append it to the filename, if it uses a language other than the default language. The behavior is the default method used when loading resource bundles.

The View

The second i18n component defined by the Struts Framework is a JSP custom tag, <bean:message />, which is used to present the actual strings that have been loaded by the Controller. This section will describe the <bean:message /> tag and how it is configured for use.

Deploying the bean Tag Library

Before we can use <bean:message />, we must first deploy the bean tag library, which contains the <bean:message /> tag. Deploying a tag library is a very simple process that requires only the addition of a new <taglib> entry in the web.xml file of the Web application using the bean library. Here is an example of this entry:

```
<taglib>
  <taglib-uri>/WEB-INF/struts-bean.tld</taglib-uri>
  <taglib-location>/WEB-INF/struts-bean.tld</taglib-location>
</taglib>
```

This entry simply tells the JSP/servlet container that this Web application uses a tag library, which exists in the classpath and is described by the TLD located in the *<CATALINA_HOME>*/webapps/*webappname*/WEB-INF/struts-bean.tld file. To make this a true statement, you need to copy this TLD from the Struts archive to this directory, and make sure the struts.jar file exists in the *<CATALINA_HOME>*/webapps/*webapplicationname*/WEB-INF/lib directory.

That's all there is to deploying the bean tag library. To make this change effective, you must restart Tomcat or the Web application that contains the newly deployed bean tag library.

Using the <bean:message /> Tag

The <bean:message /> tag is a useful tag that retrieves keyed values from a previously defined resource bundle—specifically, the properties files defined in the <message-resources> subelement—and displays them in a JSP. The <bean:message /> tag defines nine attributes and has no body. Of these nine attributes, we are interested in only three: key, bundle, and locale:

key—The key attribute is the unique value that is used to retrieve a message from the previously defined resource bundle. The key attribute is a request time attribute that is required.

bundle—The bundle attribute is the name of the bean under which messages are stored. This bean is stored in the ServletContext. If the bundle is not included, the default value of *Action.MESSAGES_KEY* is used. This attribute is an optional request time attribute. If you use the ActionServlet to manage your resource bundles, you can ignore this attribute.

locale—The locale attribute names the session bean that references the requesting client's Locale. If the bundle is not included, the default value of *Action.LOCALE_KEY* is used.

Now that we have described the <bean:message /> tag, it is time to take a look at how it is used. The following code snippet contains a simple example of using the <bean:message /> tag:

```
<%@ taglib uri="/WEB-INF/struts-bean.tld" prefix="bean" %>

<html>
  <head>
    <title><bean:message key="app.title"/></title>
  </head>
  <body>

  </body>
</html>
```

As you look over the previous snippet, you will see two lines in bold. We need to focus on these two areas. The first of these lines is a JSP taglib directive that must be included by all JSPs that will use the <bean:message /> tag.

NOTE

The URI defined in the previous taglib directive should match the <taglib-uri> defined in the previously defined web.xml file.

The second line that we need to look at is the actual <bean:message /> tag. The <bean:message /> instance that we use in this snippet contains only the key attribute; it retrieves the value stored in the resource bundle that is referenced by the key app.title, and substitutes it for the occurrence of the <bean:message /> tag. The result of this is a JSP that will have an HTML <title> that matches the Locale of the requesting client.

Internationalizing the wileystruts Application

Now that we have seen all of the components involved in internationalizing a Struts application, we can apply them to our wileystruts application. In this section, we take you through the step-by-step process that is required when internationalizing a Struts Web application. Each of these steps is described as follows:

1. Create the resource bundles that will contain the key/value pairs used in your application. For our application, we will have two properties files that contain our resource bundles. These properties files appear in Listings 6.1 and 6.2.

```
app.symbol=Simbolo
app.price=Prezzo Corrente
```

Listing 6.1 The Italian ApplicationResources_it.properties file.

```
app.symbol=Symbol
app.price=Current Price
```

Listing 6.2 The English ApplicationResources.properties file.

2. Copy all of the properties files to the <*CATALINA_HOME*>/webapps/*webappname*/WEB-INF/classes/wiley directory.
3. Add an application <message-resources /> subelement, naming the wiley. ApplicationResources to the struts-config.xml file, as shown in Listing 6.3.

```
<?xml version="1.0" encoding="ISO-8859-1" ?>

<!DOCTYPE struts-config PUBLIC
  "-//Apache Software Foundation//DTD Struts Configuration 1.1//EN"
  "http://jakarta.apache.org/struts/dtds/struts-config_1_1.dtd">

<struts-config>

  <form-beans>
    <form-bean name="lookupForm"
      type="wiley.LookupForm"/>
  </form-beans>

  <action-mappings>

    <action path="/Lookup"
      type="wiley.LookupAction"
      name="lookupForm" >
      <forward name="success" path="/quote.jsp"/>
      <forward name="failure" path="/index.jsp"/>
    </action>

  </action-mappings>

  <message-resources
    parameter="wiley.ApplicationResources"/>

</struts-config>
```

4. Add a <taglib> entry, describing the bean tag library to the application's web.xml file, as shown in Listing 6.4.

```
<?xml version="1.0" encoding="ISO-8859-1"?>

<!DOCTYPE web-app
  PUBLIC
  "-//Sun Microsystems, Inc.//DTD Web Application 2.3//EN"
 "http://java.sun.com/dtd/web-app_2_3.dtd">

<web-app>

  <servlet>
    <servlet-name>action</servlet-name>
    <servlet-class>
      org.apache.struts.action.ActionServlet</servlet-class>
    <init-param>
      <param-name>config</param-name>
      <param-value>/WEB-INF/struts-config.xml</param-value>
    </init-param>
    <load-on-startup>1</load-on-startup>
  </servlet>

  <!-- Standard Action Servlet Mapping -->
  <servlet-mapping>
    <servlet-name>action</servlet-name>
    <url-pattern>*.do</url-pattern>
  </servlet-mapping>

  <!-- The Usual Welcome File List -->
  <welcome-file-list>
    <welcome-file>index.jsp</welcome-file>
  </welcome-file-list>

  <!-- Struts Tag Library Descriptors -->
  <taglib>
    <taglib-uri>/WEB-INF/struts-html.tld</taglib-uri>
    <taglib-location>/WEB-INF/struts-html.tld</taglib-location>
  </taglib>

  <taglib>
    <taglib-uri>/WEB-INF/struts-bean.tld</taglib-uri>
    <taglib-location>/WEB-INF/struts-bean.tld</taglib-location>
  </taglib>

</web-app>
```

Listing 6.4 The Modified web.xml file.

NOTE

Make sure that you are using the <load-on-startup> element when describing the ActionServlet. This will ensure that all of the key/value pairs are loaded prior to any requests.

5. Modify your JSP files to include a taglib directive referencing the bean tag library, and replace all text strings presented to the user with matching <bean:message /> tags. Listings 6.4 and 6.5 show our modified JSPs. You will notice that all of the formerly presented strings have been placed in the properties files, listed earlier, and are now referenced using a <bean:message /> tag with the appropriate key.

```
<%@ taglib uri="/WEB-INF/struts-html.tld" prefix="html" %>
<%@ taglib uri="/WEB-INF/struts-bean.tld" prefix="bean" %>

<html>
  <head>
    <title>Wiley Struts Application</title>
  </head>

  <body>
    <table width="500"
      border="0" cellspacing="0" cellpadding="0">
      <tr>
        <td> </td>
      </tr>
      <tr bgcolor="#36566E">
        <td height="68" width="48%">
          <div align="left">
            <img src="images/hp_logo_wiley.gif"
              width="220"
            height="74">
          </div>
        </td>
      </tr>
      <tr>
        <td> </td>
      </tr>
    </table>

    <html:form action="Lookup"
      name="lookupForm"
      type="wiley.LookupForm" >
```

Listing 6.4 The Internationalized index.jsp. (continues)

```
      <table width="45%" border="0">
        <tr>
          <td><bean:message key="app.symbol" />:</td>
          <td><html:text property="symbol" /></td>
        </tr>
        <tr>
          <td colspan="2" align="center"><html:submit /></td>
        </tr>
      </table>
    </html:form>

  </body>
</html>
```

Listing 6.4 The Internationalized index.jsp. (continued)

```
<%@ taglib uri="/WEB-INF/struts-bean.tld" prefix="bean" %>

<html>
  <head>
    <title>Wiley Struts Application</title>
  </head>
  <body>

    <table width="500"
      border="0" cellspacing="0" cellpadding="0">
      <tr>
        <td> </td>
      </tr>
      <tr bgcolor="#36566E">
        <td height="68" width="48%">
          <div align="left">
            <img src="images/hp_logo_wiley.gif"
              width="220" height="74">
          </div>
        </td>
      </tr>
      <tr>
        <td> </td>
      </tr>
      <tr>
        <td> </td>
      </tr>
      <tr>
        <td> </td>
```

Listing 6.5 The Internationalized quote.jsp. (continues)

```
      </tr>
      <tr>
        <td>
          <bean:message key="app.price" />:
            <%= request.getAttribute("PRICE") %>
        </td>
      </tr>
      <tr>
        <td> </td>
      </tr>
    </table>
  </body>
</html>
```

Listing 6.5 The Internationalized quote.jsp. (continued)

That's all there is to it. To see these changes take effect, restart Tomcat, and open the following URL:

```
http://localhost:8080/wileystruts/
```

You should see results that look exactly like your previous encounters with the wileystruts application, except that now all user-presented strings are retrieved from the ApplicationResources.properties file that matched the requesting client's Locale.

Summary

In this chapter, we took a look at the internationalization (i18n) features of the Struts Framework. We began by defining each Struts i18n component, and discussed how it is used and configured. We then went through the steps involved when internationalizing an existing Struts application.

In the next chapter, we will discuss how errors are managed by the Struts framework. We will be discussing how errors are both managed and presented to the user.

CHAPTER 7

Managing Errors

In this chapter, we look at some of the methods available when managing errors in a Struts application. We begin by discussing the various error classes provided by the Struts Framework. We also examine how errors are managed in both the Controller and Views of a Struts application by adding error handling to our wileystruts stock quote application.

The goal of this chapter is to show you how errors can be managed in a Struts application. At the end of this chapter, you will know how and where the Struts error-management component can be leveraged.

Struts Error Management

The Struts Framework is packaged with two main classes that are intended for error management. The first of these classes is the ActionError class, which represents an encapsulation of an error message. The second error management class is the ActionErrors class, which acts as a container for a collection of ActionError instances. We look at both of these classes in this section.

ActionError

The first of our error-management classes, the org.apache.struts.action.ActionError class, represents a single error message. This message—most often created in either an Action or an ActionForm instance—is composed of a message key, which is used to look up a resource from the application resource bundle, and up to four replacement values, which can be used to dynamically modify an error message.

NOTE

The methods of the ActionError class are used by the Struts Framework to assemble the human-readable message and are not often used by the Struts developer; therefore, we will focus only on the constructors of this object.

The ActionError class can be instantiated using one of five different constructors. The method signatures for each of these constructors are shown here:

```
public ActionError(java.lang.String key)
public ActionError(java.lang.String key,
                   java.lang.Object value0)
public ActionError(java.lang.String key,
                   java.lang.Object value0,
                   java.lang.Object value1)
public ActionError(java.lang.String key,
                   java.lang.Object value0,
                   java.lang.Object value1,
                   java.lang.Object value2)
public ActionError(java.lang.String key,
                   java.lang.Object value0,
                   java.lang.Object value1,
                   java.lang.Object value2,
                   java.lang.Object value3)
```

The key attribute of the ActionError class is used to look up a resource from the application resource bundle described in Chapter 6, "Internationalizing Your Struts Applications." This allows you to provide error messages that are i18n-enabled. We will see examples of this when we add error management to our wileystruts application.

The value0..3 attributes allow you to pass up to four replacement objects that can be used to dynamically modify messages. This allows you to parameterize an internationalized message.

Here's an example of constructing an ActionError:

```
ActionError error = new ActionError("errors.lookup.unknown",
                                    symbol);
```

This ActionError instance would look up the resource bundle string with the key errors.lookup.unknown, and substitute the value of the symbol object as the retrieved resource's first parameter. If we were to assume our resource bundle contained the entry

```
errors.lookup.unknown=Unknown Symbol : {0}
```

and the symbol object was a String containing the value BOBCO, then the resulting message would look something like this:

```
Unknown Symbol : BOBCO
```

NOTE

The placeholders used by the ActionError class are formatted according the standard JDK's java.text.MessageFormat, using the replacement symbols of {0}, {1}, {2}, and {3}.

ActionErrors

The second of our error-management classes, the org.apache.struts.action. ActionErrors class, represents a collection of ActionError classes. This class contains an internal HashMap of ActionError objects that are keyed to a property or the global application.

The ActionErrors class is composed of a single default constructor and eight methods that are used to query and manipulate the contained ActionError instances. Table 7.1 describes the methods of the ActionErrors class.

Table 7.1 The Methods of the ActionErrors Class

METHOD	DESCRIPTION
add()	Adds an ActionError instance, associated with a property, to the internal ActionErrors HashMap. You should note that the internal HashMap contains an ArrayList of ActionErrors. This allows you to add multiple ActionError objects bound to the same property.
clear()	Removes all of the ActionError instances currently stored in the ActionErrors object.
empty()	Returns true if no ActionError objects are currently stored in the ActionErrors collection; otherwise, returns false.
get()	Returns a Java Iterator referencing all of the current ActionError objects, without regard to the property they are bound to.
get(java.lang.String)	Returns a Java Iterator referencing all of the current ActionError objects bound to the property represented by the String value passed to this method.
properties()	Returns a Java Iterator referencing all of the current properties bound to ActionError objects.
size()	Returns the number of ActionError objects, without regard to the property they are bound to.
size(java.lang.String)	Returns the number of ActionError objects bound to the property represented by the String value passed to this method.

The add() method is the method most often used when managing collections of errors. The following code snippet contains two add() methods, and shows how ActionError objects can be added to the ActionErrors collection:

```
ActionErrors errors = new ActionErrors();

errors.add("propertyname",
            new ActionError("key");

errors.add(ActionErrors.GLOBAL_ERROR,
            new ActionError("key");
```

As you can see, the only difference between these two add()s is the first parameter. This parameter represents the property to which the ActionError being added should be bound. The first add() example uses a String as the property value. This tells Struts that this error is bound to an input property from the HTML form that submitted this request. This method is most often used to report errors that have occurred when validating the form in the ActionForm.validate() method.

The second add() example uses the value *ActionErrors.GLOBAL_ERROR* as the property value. This tells Struts that this error is not bound to any input property. This method is most often used to report errors that have occurred in an Action.perform() method. We will see examples of both of these methods when we modify the wileystruts application.

Adding Error Handling to the wileystruts Application

Now that we have seen the classes involved in Struts error management, let's look at how they are actually used. We will do this by adding the Struts error-management components to our wileystruts Web application.

Before you can leverage the Struts error-management classes, you must add two attributes to the <action> element that describe the wiley.LookupAction. The following code snippet shows the changes to the struts-config.xml file:

```
<action path="/Lookup"
  type="wiley.LookupAction"
  name="lookupForm"
  validate="true"
  input="/index.jsp">
  <forward name="success" path="/quote.jsp"/>
  <forward name="failure" path="/index.jsp"/>
</action>
```

The new attributes are the validate and input attributes. The first attribute, validate, when set to true tells the Struts framework that validation should be performed. The second attribute tells the Struts frame where the error originated and where the action should be redirected, if any errors have occurred. You must add these attributes to all <action> elements that will use the ActionForm.validate() mechanism described in the following section.

The ActionForm.validate() Method

The first area where we are going to apply error-management techniques is in the ActionForm object. This is probably the best place to begin, because it is the first chance you will have to test the incoming request for errors. The errors that we are checking for are validation errors that occur when the user submitting an HTML form enters incorrect data. The Struts Framework allows us to do this by simply overriding the ActionForm.validate() method. The signature of this method is as follows:

```
public ActionErrors validate(ActionMapping mapping,
  HttpServletRequest request)
```

The ActionForm.validate() method is called by the ActionServlet after the matching HTML input properties have been set. It provides you with the opportunity to test the values of the input properties before the targeted Action.perform() method is invoked. If the validate() method finds no errors in the submitted data, then it returns either an empty ActionErrors object or null, and processing continues normally.

If the validate() method does encounter errors, then it should add an ActionError instance describing each encountered error to an ActionErrors collection, and return the ActionErrors instance. When the ActionServlet receives the returned ActionErrors, it will forward the collection to the JSP that is referenced by the input attribute described previously, which in our case is the index.jsp. We will see what the index.jsp View will do with the ActionErrors collection later in this section. Listing 7.1 contains the changes we have made to our LookupForm to perform input validation.

```
package wiley;

import javax.servlet.http.HttpServletRequest;
import org.apache.struts.action.ActionForm;
import org.apache.struts.action.ActionMapping;
import org.apache.struts.action.ActionError;
import org.apache.struts.action.ActionErrors;
```

Listing 7.1 The Modified LookupForm.java. (continues)

```
public class LookupForm extends ActionForm {

  private String symbol = null;

  public String getSymbol() {

    return (symbol);
  }

  public void setSymbol(String symbol) {

    this.symbol = symbol;
  }

  public void reset(ActionMapping mapping,
    HttpServletRequest request) {

    this.symbol = null;
  }

  public ActionErrors validate(ActionMapping mapping,
    HttpServletRequest request) {

    ActionErrors errors = new ActionErrors();

    if ( (symbol == null ) || (symbol.length() == 0) ) {

      errors.add("symbol",
        new ActionError("errors.lookup.symbol.required"));
    }
    return errors;
  }
      }
```

Listing 7.1 The Modified LookupForm.java. (continued)

As you look over Listing 7.1, you will notice two areas of change. The first is the addition of two import statements. These statements include the ActionError and ActionErrors classes that we will use to handle errors.

The second change is the addition of the validate() method. In this method, we test the symbol data member that was set by the HTML form tag. We test it for both a null and an empty String. If it returns true for either of these tests, then the input data is not valid, and it creates an ActionErrors instance and adds an ActionError object describing the error. It then returns the ActionErrors instance, which will be forwarded to the index.jsp for display.

You should take note of the values passed to the errors.add() method. The first value, *symbol*, binds this error to the symbol input property submitted by the HTML form. This tells the Struts Framework that the input value referenced by the symbol property failed validation.

The second parameter, *errors.lookup.symbol.required*, is a key to the resource bundle of this application. To make this a valid key, you need to add the following entries to both the ApplicationResources.properties and ApplicationResources_it.properties files.

NOTE

You should note that the following errors are surrounded by the HTML list item elements <li>. We do this to make the messages more readable when displayed in an HTML client. We will see the purpose of this in the following section.

```
errors.lookup.symbol.required=<li>A Symbol is Required</li>
errors.lookup.symbol.required=<li>Un simbolo richiesto</li>
```

NOTE

Remember that the resource bundles for our application are found in the ApplicationResources.properties and ApplicationResources_it.properties files.

<html:errors />

To see our new validate() method in action, we need to modify the index.jsp to display any errors resulting from our validation. The easiest way to do this is with <html:errors />, which we described in Chapter 5, "The Views." The <html:errors /> tag is used to display the ActionError objects stored in an ActionErrors collection. It is extremely easy to use, and in most circumstances, you do not need to use any of its available attributes; however, you do need to define its header and footer.

The header and footer consist of HTML text that will be placed before and after the list of ActionErrors. The text that describes the header and footer is stored in the application's resource bundles, allowing the text to be language-independent. Like all other objects in a resource bundle, the header and footer values are identified using text keys. The two keys that describe the header and footer are errors.header and errors.footer, respectively. To use the header and footer values, add the following code snippet to the ApplicationResources.properties file:

```
errors.header=<h3>
  <font color="red">Error List</font></h3>
  <ul>
errors.footer=</ul><hr>
```

and this code snippet to the ApplicationResources_it.properties file:

```
errors.header=<h3>
  <font color="red">Elenco degli errori</font></h3>
  <ul>
errors.footer=</ul><hr>
```

NOTE

Both the header and the footer are surrounded by HTML unnumbered list elements. This is for formatting purposes, as we mentioned earlier, and is not a required format.

Now that we have the header and footer of our error messages defined and in place, we simply need to add the <html:errors /> tag to our JSP. Listing 7.2 shows the index.jsp with the addition of the <html:errors /> tag.

```
<%@ taglib uri="/WEB-INF/struts-html.tld" prefix="html" %>
<%@ taglib uri="/WEB-INF/struts-bean.tld" prefix="bean" %>

<html>
  <head>
    <title>Wiley Struts Application</title>
  </head>

  <body>

    <table width="500"
           border="0"
           cellspacing="0"
           cellpadding="0">
      <tr>
        <td> </td>
      </tr>
      <tr bgcolor="#36566E">
        <td height="68" width="48%">
          <div align="left">
            <img src="images/hp_logo_wiley.gif"
              width="220"
            height="74">
          </div>
        </td>
      </tr>
      <tr>
        <td> </td>
      </tr>
```

Listing 7.2 The modified index.jsp. (continues)

```
    </table>

    <html:errors />

    <html:form action="/Lookup"
      name="lookupForm"
      type="wiley.LookupForm" >
      <table width="45%" border="0">
        <tr>
          <td><bean:message key="app.symbol" />:</td>
          <td><html:text property="symbol" /></td>
        </tr>
        <tr>
          <td colspan="2" align="center"><html:submit /></td>
        </tr>
      </table>
    </html:form>

  </body>
</html>
```

Listing 7.2 The modified index.jsp. (continued)

As you can see, there is really nothing special about this change—you simply need to pick a location in your JSP that will not be missed by the user.

To see these changes take effect, you have to compile the wiley.LookupForm, copy the resulting class file to the *<CATALINA_HOME>*/webapps/wileystruts/WEB_INF/classes directory, restart Tomcat, and open your browser to the wileystruts application. The first time the index.jsp is loaded, you will not see any differences. Recall that we have added code that ensures that the user enters a stock symbol, so to test this change, do not enter any value into the symbol input and click the Submit button. If everything went according to plan, you should see an error message similar to Figure 7.1. If you do not see the error message, check both the LookupForm.validate() method and the resource bundles for this application.

Error Management in the Action.perform() Method

The final area of Struts error management that we will look at addresses how you report errors that occur in the Action.perform() methods of your application. There is really no defined place that errors can occur in a perform() method (as there is in a validate() method), but the important thing to consider is how an error is reported back to the user.

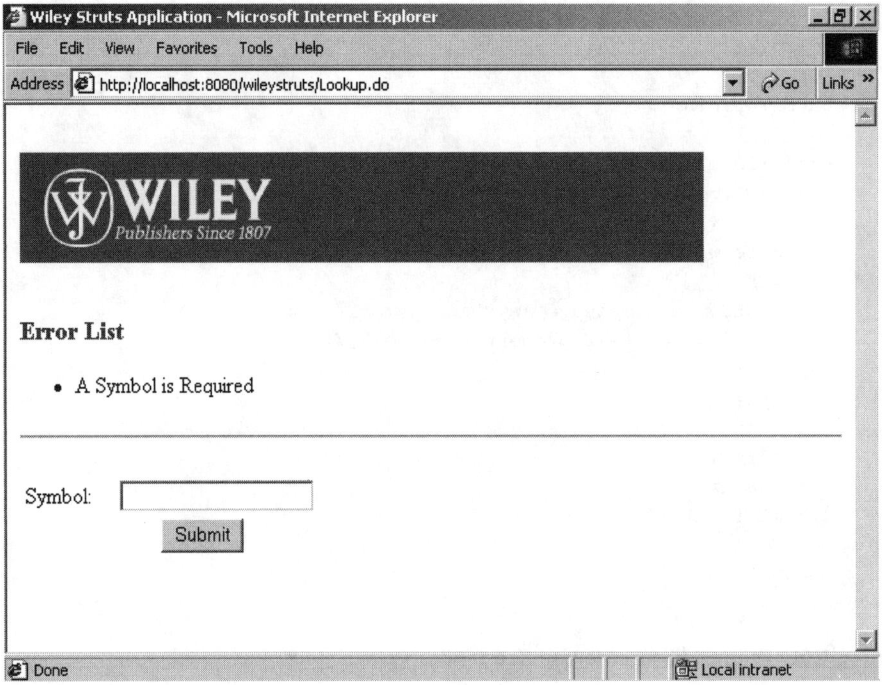

Figure 7.1 An error returned from the LookupForm.validate() method.

When reporting errors in the perform() method, the same two classes, ActionError and ActionErrors, are used. The only difference is how the collection of errors is sent back to the client. If you examine the code in Listing 7.3, you will see the changes that have been added to the wiley.LookupAction to report errors.

```
package wiley;

import java.io.IOException;
import javax.servlet.ServletException;
import javax.servlet.http.HttpServletRequest;
import javax.servlet.http.HttpServletResponse;
import org.apache.struts.action.Action;
import org.apache.struts.action.ActionForm;
import org.apache.struts.action.ActionForward;
import org.apache.struts.action.ActionMapping;
import org.apache.struts.action.ActionError;
import org.apache.struts.action.ActionErrors;
```

Listing 7.3 The modified LookupAction.java. (continues)

```
public class LookupAction extends Action {

  protected Double getQuote(String symbol) {

    if ( symbol.equalsIgnoreCase("SUNW") ) {

      return new Double(25.00);
    }
    return null;
  }

  public ActionForward perform(ActionMapping mapping,
    ActionForm form,
    HttpServletRequest request,
    HttpServletResponse response)
    throws IOException, ServletException {

    Double price = null;

    // Default target to success
    String target = new String("success");
    String symbol = null;

    if ( form != null ) {

      // Use the LoginForm to get the request parameters
      LookupForm lookupForm = (LookupForm)form;

      symbol = lookupForm.getSymbol();

      price = getQuote(symbol);
    }

    // Set the target to failure
    if ( price == null ) {

      target = new String("failure");

      ActionErrors errors = new ActionErrors();
      errors.add(ActionErrors.GLOBAL_ERROR,
        new ActionError("errors.lookup.unknown",symbol));

      // Report any errors we have discovered
      if (!errors.empty()) {
```

Listing 7.3 The modified LookupAction.java. (continues)

```
        saveErrors(request, errors);
      }
    }
    else {

      request.setAttribute("PRICE", price);
    }
    // Forward to the appropriate View
    return (mapping.findForward(target));
  }
}
```

Listing 7.3 The modified LookupAction.java. (continued)

You will see two changes in this file. The first change is just a couple of import statements that include the ActionError and ActionErrors classes.

The second change is the actual error-reporting section. In this section, we test the value of the price variable. If it is null—which it will be if any value other than SUNW was entered—then we need to report an error. This is accomplished by first setting the target to *failure*; then by creating an ActionErrors collection and adding an ActionError object to the collection.

The last thing to note about these changes is how the errors are reported back to the client. This is done using the Action.saveErrors() method, as shown here:

```
if (!errors.empty()) {

  saveErrors(request, errors);
}
```

The saveErrors() method adds the ActionErrors collection to the HttpServ letRequest object. The result of this action is a request containing the errors collection being forwarded to the index.jsp, which is the *failure* target that will display the errors using the <html:errors /> tag.

You should note the parameters passed to the errors.add() method. The first parameter is not an HTML input property (as it was in the validate() method we examined earlier). The value that is passed to the add() method is a predefined value, *ActionErrors.GLOBAL_ERROR*, that indicates that this error is not bound to the validation of an input property, but is instead an application error.

The second parameter acts no different than it did in the validate() method. It is simply a different key representing a different error. To add this error message to the wileystruts application, you need to modify both the ApplicationResources.properties and the ApplicationResources_it.properties files, as shown in Listings 7.4 and 7.5.

```
app.symbol=Symbol
app.price=Current Price

errors.lookup.symbol.required=<li>A Symbol is Required</li>

errors.lookup.unknown=<li>Unknown Symbol {0}</li>

errors.header=<h3><font color="red">Error List</font></h3><ul>
errors.footer=</ul><hr>
```

Listing 7.4 The modified ApplicationResources.properties file.

```
app.symbol=Simbolo
app.price=Prezzo Corrente

errors.lookup.symbol.required=<li>Un simbolo richiesto</li>

errors.lookup.unknown=<li>Simbolo Sconosciuto {0}</li>

errors.header=<h3>
  <font color="red">Elenco degli errori</font></h3>
  <ul>
errors.footer=</ul><hr>
```

Listing 7.5 The modified ApplicationResources_it.properties file.

To see these changes take effect, you need to compile the wiley.LookupAction, copy the resulting class file to the <*CATALINA_HOME*>/webapps/wileystruts/WEB_INF/classes directory, restart Tomcat, and open your browser to the wileystruts application. Now this time, instead of entering an empty stock symbol, enter any value other than SUNW, and click the Submit button. You should see an error message similar to Figure 7.2. If you do not see this message, check both the LookupAction.perform() method and the application resource bundles.

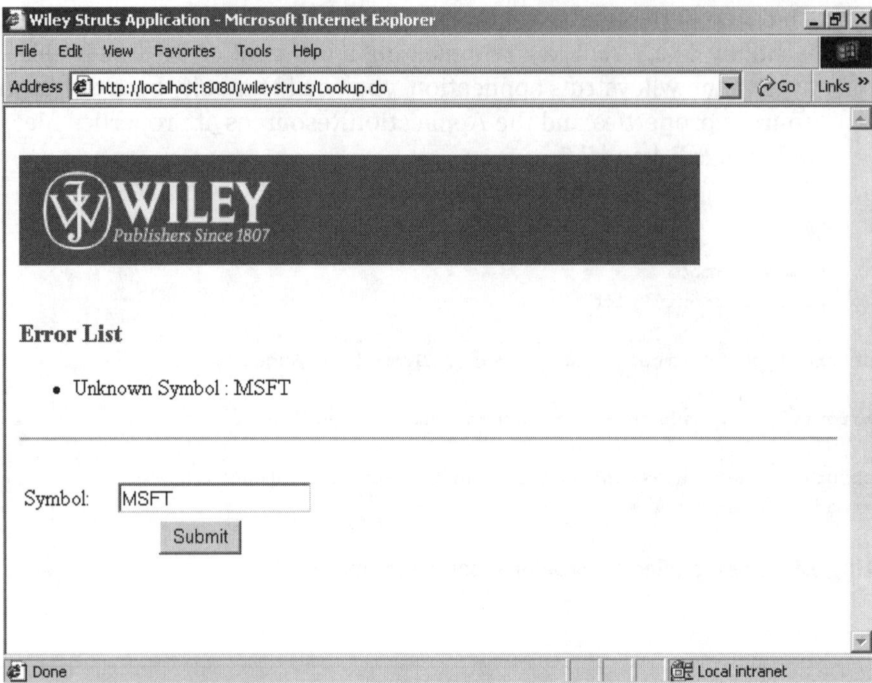

Figure 7.2 An error returned from the LookupAction.perform() method.

Summary

In the next chapter, we take a closer look at the ActionMappings class and how ActionMappings are deployed. We also discuss how to can create custom ActionMappings for your own purposes.

CHAPTER 8

Creating Custom ActionMappings

In this chapter, we discuss the org.apache.struts.action.ActionMapping class and how it can be extended to provide specialized mapping information to the ActionServlet. We conclude this chapter with an example ActionMapping extension that will be leveraged in our wileystruts application.

The goal of this chapter is to show how custom ActionMappings are created and deployed. It is also the goal of this chapter to show an example of how useful an ActionMapping extension can be.

What Is an ActionMapping?

An ActionMapping object describes an Action instance to the ActionServlet. It represents the information that uniquely defines an instance of a particular action class. It also provides useful information to both the Action.execute() and the ActionForm.validate() methods, enabling a developer to alter its behavior based upon the values describing this particular Action. The following two code snippets show the method signatures of both the Action.execute() and the ActionForm.validate() methods.

```
public ActionForward execute(ActionMapping mapping,
  ActionForm form,
  HttpServletRequest request,
  HttpServletResponse response)

public ActionErrors validate(ActionMapping mapping,
  HttpServletRequest request)
```

The default attributes described by an ActionMapping are defined in Table 8.1.

Table 8.1 The Attributes of an ActionMapping Object

ATTRIBUTE	DESCRIPTION
attribute	Represents the names under which the Action's ActionForm bean is bound, if it is other than the bean's specified name attribute. The attribute is optional if the name attribute is included in the Action description.
className	Represents the fully qualified class name of the ActionMapping implementation class to use when invoking this Action class. If the className attribute is not included, then the ActionMapping defined in the ActionServlet's mapping initialization parameter is used.
forward	Represents the context-relative path of the servlet or JSP resource that will process this request. This attribute is used if you do not want an Action to service the request to this path. The forward attribute is only valid if there is no include or type attribute specified.
type	Represents the fully qualified class name of the Action class being described by this ActionMapping. The type attribute is only valid if there is no include or forward attribute specified.
include	Represents the context-relative path of the servlet or JSP resource that will process this request. This attribute is used if you do not want an Action to service the request to this path. The include attribute is only valid if there is no forward or type attribute specified.
input	Represents the context-relative path of the input form to which control should be returned if a validation error is encountered. The input attribute is where control will be returned if ActionErrors are returned from the ActionForm or Action objects.
name	Identifies the name of the form bean, if any, that is coupled with the Action being defined.
path	Represents the context-relative path of the submitted request. The path must start with a / character.
scope	Names the scope of the form bean that is bound to the described Action.
validate	If set to true, causes the ActionForm.validate() method to be called on the form bean associated to the Action being described. If the validate attribute is set to false, then the ActionForm.validate() method is not called.

You have already used the ActionMapping in each one of our prior examples. It is defined by each <action> element in the struts-config.xml file. A sample <action> element is shown in the following code snippet:

```
<action-mappings>

  <action path="/Lookup"
    type="wiley.LookupAction"
    name="lookupForm"
    validate="true"
    input="/index.jsp">
    <forward name="success" path="/quote.jsp"/>
    <forward name="failure" path="/index.jsp"/>
  </action>

</action-mappings>
```

As you may have noticed, we have been using this element throughout this text. The <action> element is how all Action objects are deployed. You should also notice that the <action> element is surrounded by an <action-mappings> element. All <action> elements must be nested within the <action-mappings> element.

Creating a Custom ActionMapping

In the previous section, we saw that the default ActionMapping defines quite a number of attributes. The combination of each of these attributes is used to uniquely describe an Action instance, and in most cases these default attributes will suffice. However, there are times when you need to further describe an Action.

The Struts Framework does provide a solution for this very problem by allowing you to define properties specific to your application needs. You can define these supplementary properties by simply extending the ActionMapping class and adding n-number of <action> subelements and <set-property> elements for each additional property.

NOTE

The Struts Framework provides two extended ActionMapping classes for developer convenience. These two ActionMapping extensions—org.apache.struts.action.SessionActionMapping and org.apache.struts.action.RequestActionMapping—default the form bean scope to session and request, respectively, relieving the developer from specifically setting the ActionMapping scope attribute.

Creating an ActionMapping Extension for the wileystruts Application

To see how a new ActionMapping is created, we will create our own ActionMapping extension that we can use to describe the Actions of our wileystruts application. The ActionMapping extension that we are going to create will allow us to turn logging on or off in our wiley.LookupAction by using a single <set-property> element.

To create an ActionMapping extension, you need to perform these steps:

1. Create a class that extends the org.apache.struts.action.ActionMapping class.
2. Define the additional properties that will be used to describe your Action objects.
3. Call the super() method, which calls the ActionMapping's default constructor, at the beginning of your ActionMapping's constructor.
4. Define matching setters and getters that can be used to modify and retrieve the values of the defined properties.

The source for our new WileyActionMapping is shown in Listing 8.1.

```
package wiley;

import org.apache.struts.action.ActionMapping;

// Step 1. Extend the ActionMapping class
public class WileyActionMapping extends ActionMapping {

  // Step 2. Add the new properties
  protected boolean logResults = false;

  public WileyActionMapping() {

    // Step 3. Call the ActionMapping's default Constructor
    super();
  }

  // Step 4. Add matching setter/getter methods
  public void setLogResults(boolean logResults) {

    this.logResults  = logResults;
  }
```

Listing 8.1 WileyActionMapping.java. (continues)

```
    public boolean getLogResults() {

      return logResults;
    }
  }
```

Listing 8.1 WileyActionMapping.java. (continued)

As you look over this class, you will notice that it is a very simple class that satisfies the previous steps. It defines a single Boolean attribute, logResults, which we will use in our wiley.LookupAction to determine whether or not it should log its results.

Deploying the wiley.WileyActionMapping Extension

Deploying an ActionMapping extension is also a very simple process. The first thing that you need to do is compile the ActionMapping class and place it in the application classpath. For our example, you need to compile the wiley.WileyActionMapping class and move it to the <*CATALINA_HOME*>/webapps/wileystruts/WEB-INF/classes/wiley/ directory.

You then need to tell the Controller about the new ActionMapping. You do this by adding an initialization parameter to the ActionServlet definition. The <param-name> element should be set to the value *mapping* and the <param-value> should be set to the fully qualified class name of the new ActionMapping extension. The following <init-param> subelements define our wiley.WileyActionMapping extension:

```
<servlet>
  <servlet-name>action</servlet-name>
  <servlet-class>
    org.apache.struts.action.ActionServlet
  </servlet-class>
  <init-param>
    <param-name>config</param-name>
    <param-value>/WEB-INF/struts-config.xml</param-value>
  </init-param>
  <init-param>
    <param-name>mapping</param-name>
    <param-value>wiley.WileyActionMapping</param-value>
  </init-param>
  <load-on-startup>1</load-on-startup>
</servlet>
```

That's all there is to it. The new ActionMapping is ready for use.

Using the wiley.WileyActionMapping Extension in the wileystruts Application

To leverage our new ActionMapping, we need to make the appropriate modifications to our LookupAction. The changes that we want to make are both in the source file and the <action> element describing the LookupAction. The first change is to the actual LookupAction source code, and it is shown in Listing 8.2.

```
package wiley;

import java.io.IOException;
import javax.servlet.ServletException;
import javax.servlet.http.HttpServletRequest;
import javax.servlet.http.HttpServletResponse;
import org.apache.struts.action.Action;
import org.apache.struts.action.ActionForm;
import org.apache.struts.action.ActionForward;
import org.apache.struts.action.ActionMapping;
import org.apache.struts.action.SessionActionMapping;
import org.apache.struts.action.ActionError;
import org.apache.struts.action.ActionErrors;

public class LookupAction extends Action {

  protected Double getQuote(String symbol) {

    if ( symbol.equalsIgnoreCase("SUNW") ) {

      return new Double(25.00);
    }
    return null;
  }

  public ActionForward execute(ActionMapping mapping,
    ActionForm form,
    HttpServletRequest request,
    HttpServletResponse response)
    throws IOException, ServletException {

    WileyActionMapping wileyMapping =
     (WileyActionMapping)mapping;

    Double price = null;
    String symbol = null;
```

Listing 8.2 The modified wiley.LookupAction.java. (continues)

```
        // Default target to success
        String target = new String("success");

        if ( form != null ) {

          // Use the LoginForm to get the request parameters
          LookupForm lookupForm = (LookupForm)form;

          symbol = lookupForm.getSymbol();

          price = getQuote(symbol);
        }

        // Set the target to failure
        if ( price == null ) {

          target = new String("failure");

          ActionErrors errors = new ActionErrors();
          errors.add(ActionErrors.GLOBAL_ERROR,
            new ActionError("errors.lookup.unknown",
                            symbol));

          if (!errors.empty()) {

            saveErrors(request, errors);
          }
        }
        else {

          if ( wileyMapping.getLogResults() ) {

            System.err.println("SYMBOL:"
              + symbol + " PRICE:" + price);
          }

          request.setAttribute("PRICE", price);
        }
        // Forward to the appropriate View
        return (mapping.findForward(target));
      }
    }
```

Listing 8.2 The modified wiley.LookupAction.java. (continued)

We need to examine two sections of code from Listing 8.2. The first section takes the ActionMapping instance passed to the execute() method, and casts it to a WileyActionMapping. We can do this because we know that this class is really an instance of the WileyActionMapping, and we must do it to get access to the getLogResults() method. The casting that it performs is shown in the following snippet:

```
WileyActionMapping wileyMapping =
  (WileyActionMapping)mapping;
```

The second section of code actually uses the value retrieved from the getLogResults() method to determine whether it should log the results of its actions. If the value is true, then the action will log its results, which in this case is simply a write to the System.err stream; otherwise, it will skip over the System.err.println() statement. The following snippet shows this test:

```
if ( wileyMapping.getLogResults() ) {

  System.err.println("SYMBOL:"
    + symbol + " PRICE:" + price);
}
```

To see these changes working together, we need to make one last modification. This modification is made to the actual <action> element in the struts-config.xml file, and describes the wiley.LookupAction instance. The change itself includes the addition of the <set-property> element, with its property attribute set to the matching wiley.WileyActionMapping data member and its value attributeset to the value that you want the property set to. The following code snippet shows this modification:

NOTE

If you define an ActionMapping extension that includes more than one property, then you will need to add a <set-property> element for each additional property.

```
<action-mappings>

  <action path="/Lookup"
    type="wiley.LookupAction"
    name="lookupForm"
    validate="true"
    input="/index.jsp">
    <set-property property="logResults" value="true"/>
    <forward name="success" path="/quote.jsp"/>
    <forward name="failure" path="/index.jsp"/>
  </action>

</action-mappings>
```

The result of this entry is a WileyActionMapping instance with a logResults data member set to true.

NOTE

If you do not add the previous property, then the wiley.WileyApplicationMapping defaults to false.

Now you simply need to compile the wiley.WileyActionMapping, copy it to the <*CATALINA_HOME*>/webapps/wileystruts/WEB-INF/classes/wiley directory, restart Tomcat, and go through the normal process of looking up the SUNW stock symbol. If everything went according to plan, you should see the following output in the Tomcat console window:

```
SYMBOL:SUNW PRICE:25.0
```

While this ActionMapping extension seems a bit trivial, in its simplicity it does show how powerful an ActionMapping extension can be. In most applications, you set a debug level for the entire application, which causes all Actions to log at the same level. This can be quite difficult to read in larger applications, where several Actions are being used. This simple class solves this problem by allowing you to turn logging on or off at the individual Action level. This is quite an accomplishment for such a simple class, and it shows just how powerful the ActionMapping mechanism is.

Summary

In this chapter, we discussed the org.apache.struts.action.ActionMapping class and how it can be extended to provide specialized mapping information to the ActionServlet. We then went on to create a sample ActionMapping extension that allows us to turn on and off debug logging on an Action-by-Action level.

At this point, you should feel comfortable with the process of creating and deploying custom ActionMappings. You should also have some insight into how useful an ActionMapping extension can be.

In the next chapter, we discuss the database components of the Struts Framework and examine the org.apache.struts.util.GenericDataSourceclass.

CHAPTER 9

The Struts JDBC Connection Pool

In this chapter, we discuss the process of using a DataSource in a Struts application. At the end of this chapter, you should know how to configure and leverage a DataSource in your Struts applications.

It is important to note that the Struts uses the javax.sql.DataSource interface, so you will need to place the Java Database Connectivity 2.0 Standard Extension package in your Web applications' WEB-INF/lib directory. You can find this package at the http://java.sun.com/products/jdbc/ Web site. It is also packaged with the Struts archive, and you can find it in the Struts lib directory (look for jdbc2_0-stdext.jar).

What Is a DataSource?

A JDBC DataSource is an object described by the JDBC 2.0 extensions package that is used to generically represent a database management system (DBMS). The DataSource described in the JDBC 2.0 extensions package is defined by the interface javax.sql.DataSource; it is described as a factory containing JDBC Connection objects.

Because a DataSource is described as an interface, you must define an implementation class of your own or use a pre-existing implementation to leverage DataSource functions. The JDBC 2.0 extensions package defines three types of DataSource implementations; Table 9.1 describes each type.

Table 9.1 The Three Types of DataSource Implementations

COMPONENT	DESCRIPTION
Basic	Generates standard JDBC Connection objects that are not pooled or used in a distributed environment.
Pooled	Generates a collection of JDBC Connection objects that are managed by a connection pool. This implementation allows a single JDBC Connection to be used multiple times.
Distributed	Generates JDBC Connection objects that can be used by distributed transactions. This allows a single transaction access to two or more DBMS servers.

As of Struts 1.1, the DataSource implementation used by the Struts project models the Pooled implementation.

Using a DataSource in Your Struts Application

As we stated earlier, the Struts Framework leverages a DataSource object to manage its database connections. This DataSource includes all of the necessary functionality to manage a pool of JDBC connections that can be used either in a Java application or in a Struts Web application. For our purposes, we will only configure this DataSource for use in a Struts application.

Creating a Sample Database

Before we can leverage a DataSource, we must have a database to connect to. The database we will use in our Struts application is a MySQL database named stocks that contains a single table, also named stocks. This table contains a list of stock symbols and prices; its layout appears in Table 9.2. Table 9.3 shows the data that populates the stocks table.

Table 9.2 The stocks Table Structure

COLUMN	DESCRIPTION
symbol	Contains a unique key identifying each stock. It is a varchar(15).
price	Contains the current price of the stock symbol being looked up. It is a double.

Table 9.3 The Contents of the stocks Table

SYMBOL	PRICE
SUNW	78.00
YHOO	24.45
MSFT	3.24

For our example, we are going to use the MySQL database. To prepare for this example, you must have an instance of the MySQL database server installed and running on your host machine. You can find the MySQL server at www.mysql.com. You should also download the latest JDBC driver for MySQL, which you can also find at this Web site.

Once you have MySQL installed, you need to complete the following steps to create and configure our MySQL database:

1. Start the MySQL client found in the <*MYSQL_HOME*>/bin/ directory by typing the following command:

```
mysql
```

2. Create the stocks database by executing the following command:

```
create database stocks;
```

3. Make sure you are modifying the correct database by using this command:

```
use stocks;
```

4. Create the stocks table using the following command:

```
create table stocks
(
  symbol varchar(15) not null primary key,
  price double not null
);
```

5. Insert the user data into the stocks table by executing these commands:

```
insert into stocks values("SUNW", 78.00);
insert into stocks values("YHOO", 24.45);
insert into stocks values("MSFT", 3.24);
```

You now have a MySQL database of stocks. To test your installation, make sure you are still running the MySQL client and enter these two commands:

```
use stocks;
select * from stocks;
```

If everything was installed correctly, you should see results similar to the following:

```
+--------+-------+
| symbol | price |
+--------+-------+
| SUNW   |    78 |
| YHOO   | 24.45 |
| MSFT   |  3.24 |
+--------+-------+
3 rows in set (0.00 sec)
```

Using a DataSource in a Struts Application

Now that we have a basic understanding of a DataSource, let's integrate the Struts DataSource into an actual Struts application. For our example, we will revisit our wileystruts application from Chapter 3 ("Getting Started with Struts"), but this time we will use the previously defined database to look up the current stock price, as opposed to the hard-coded response that we are currently using.

There is really no limit as to how you can integrate a DataSource into a Struts application, but there is an existing method that leverages functionality of the org.apache.struts.action.ActionServlet. For our example, we are going to take advantage of this built-in functionality.

To leverage the built-in functionality of the ActionServlet, you simply need to add a new entry to the struts-config.xml file. This entry describes DataSources that are managed by the ActionServlet. To initialize the DataSource, we must add the code snippet shown in Listing 9.1 to our struts-config.xml file.

NOTE

The <data-sources> element, which acts as the parent to all <data-source> elements, must be added prior to the <form-beans> and <action-mappings> elements.

```
<data-sources>
  <data-source>
    <set-property property="driverClass"
      value="org.gjt.mm.mysql.Driver" />
    <set-property property="url"
      value="jdbc:mysql://localhost/stocks" />
    <set-property property="maxCount"
      value="5"/>
```

Listing 9.1 Code added to struts-config.xml to initialize the DataSource. (continues)

```
    <set-property property="minCount"
      value="1"/>
    <set-property property="user"
      value="YOURUSERNAME"/>
    <set-property property="password"
      value="YOURPASSWORD"/>
  </data-source>
</data-sources>
```

Listing 9.1 Code added to struts-config.xml to initialize the DataSource. (continued)

The <data-sources> element acts as a container for *n*-number of <data-source> subelements, which each represent individual DataSource instances. Table 9.4 describes the properties of a <data-source> entry.

Table 9.4 The Properties of a <data-source> Entry

PROPERTY	DESCRIPTION
key	A unique key identifying a DataSource instance stored in the ServletContext. If this property is not used, then the key will be defaulted to Action.DATA_SOURCE_KEY. If you intend to use more than one DataSource in your application, you must include a key for each one.
driverClass	The fully qualified JDBC driver class that will be used to connect to the URL named in the url property.
url	The URL of the database that we are connecting to.
maxCount	The maximum number of Connections that will be open at any given time.
minCount	The minimum number of Connections that will be open at any given time.
user	The username that will be used to connect to the database.
password	The password that will be used to connect to the database.
description	A text description of the DataSource instance.

Now that we have made the appropriate changes to the struts-config.xml file, we need to modify the wiley.LookupAction from Chapter 3. First, we must add the following import statements. These statements represent JDBC packages required to perform most DataSource operations:

```
import javax.servlet.ServletContext;
import javax.sql.DataSource;
```

```
import java.sql.Connection;
import java.sql.Statement;
import java.sql.ResultSet;
import java.sql.SQLException;
```

The second change we must make is to the getQuote() method. This method must be modified to use a DataSource object to retrieve a user from the database as opposed to the hard-coded return that currently exists. These changes are shown in Listing 9.2.

```
protected Double getQuote(String symbol) {

    Double price = null;
    Connection conn = null;
    Statement stmt = null;
    ResultSet rs = null;

    ServletContext context = servlet.getServletContext();
    DataSource dataSource = (DataSource)
      context.getAttribute(Action.DATA_SOURCE_KEY);

    try {

      conn = dataSource.getConnection();
      stmt = conn.createStatement();
      rs = stmt.executeQuery("select * from stocks where "
        + "symbol='" + symbol + "'");

      if ( rs.next() ) {

        double tmp = 0;
        tmp = rs.getDouble("price");

        price = new Double(tmp);

        System.err.println("price : "
          + price);
      }
      else {

        System.err.println("---->Symbol not found<----");
      }
    }
    catch (SQLException e) {

      System.err.println(e.getMessage());
```

Listing 9.2 Modifying the getQuote() method to use a DataSource object. (continues)

```
    }
    finally {

      if (rs != null) {

        try {

          rs.close();
        }
        catch (SQLException sqle) {

          System.err.println(sqle.getMessage());
        }
        rs = null;
      }
      if (stmt != null) {

        try {

          stmt.close();
        }
        catch (SQLException sqle) {

          System.err.println(sqle.getMessage());
        }
        stmt = null;
      }
      if (conn != null) {

        try {

          conn.close();
        }
        catch (SQLException sqle) {

          System.err.println(sqle.getMessage());
        }
        conn = null;
      }
    }
    return price;
  }
```

Listing 9.2 Modifying the getQuote() method to use a DataSource object. (continued)

As you review the new getQuote() method, you will notice that the first thing we do is retrieve our described DataSource from the ServletContext. The code snippet that retrieves the DataSource is shown here:

```
ServletContext context = servlet.getServletContext();
DataSource dataSource = (DataSource)
  context.getAttribute(Action.DATA_SOURCE_KEY);
```

As you can see, this is where the key property used in the <data-source> element comes into play. Because we did not explicitly define a key element in the <data-source> described previously, we can use the default Action.DATA_ SOURCE_KEY to retrieve the DataSource from the ServletContext.

Once we have a reference to the DataSource, we can get a Connection object from it and continue with normal JDBC processing, as shown below:

```
conn = dataSource.getConnection();
  stmt = conn.createStatement();
  rs = stmt.executeQuery("select * from stocks where "
    + "symbol='" + symbol + "'");
```

As you can see, there is really nothing special about this code except for the retrieval of the Connection from the dataSource.getConnection() method. This method requests a Connection from the DataSource's pool of connections and returns the retrieved Connection to the calling action. While the returned Connection object looks and acts just like any other JDBC Connection object, it is actually an instance of the wrapper object around a java.sql.Connection object. The purpose of this wrapped Connection is to allow the DataSource to manage the Connections stored in its pool.

After the getQuote() method has completed its inspection of the ResultSet, it goes through the normal process of resource cleanup; and closes the ResultSet, Statement, and Connection. The only thing notable about this section involves the use of the Connection object. In the normal definition of the Connection class, this method would close the connection to the database and thus render it useless for later processes, but because this Connection object is an instance of a wrapper object, the Connection is returned to the pool for later use, instead of actually being closed.

That's all there is to using the DataSource in a Struts application. You can now test your changes by completing these steps:

1. Copy the MySQL JDBC driver into the <*CATALINA_HOME*>/webapps/wileystruts/lib directory.
2. If the JDBC Extensions Jar is not already there, copy the jdbc2_0-stdext.jar file to the <*CATALINA_HOME*>/webapps/wileystruts/lib directory.
3. Restart Tomcat.
4. Open your browser to the following URL, and enter a stock symbol contained in the database:

```
http://localhost:8080/wileystruts/
```

If everything went according to plan, then you should see the quote.jsp with the price of the symbol that you entered.

Summary

In this chapter, you learned how to configure a DataSource for use in a Struts applications. At this point, you should be able to easily set up almost any Struts application with Database support. Next up, we will discuss how you can use an embedded version of the Tomcat JSP/servlet container to debug your Struts applications.

CHAPTER 10

Debugging Struts Applications

There are many methods you can use to debug a Struts application. In this chapter, we create a Java application that manages an embedded version of the Tomcat JSP/servlet container; then, we deploy our wileystruts stock-quoting application to this embedded version of Tomcat, and step through the source in order to demonstrate a relatively simple method of Struts application debugging. This method allows you to debug your applications with almost any integrated development environment (IDE).

We will be using the JBuilder 6 IDE to step through the source of our wileystruts application. You can choose almost any IDE that includes an integrated debugger; I am simply using my IDE of choice.

Embedding Tomcat into a Java Application

In this section, we will create a Java application that manages an embedded version of the Tomcat JSP/servlet container. Tomcat can be broken down into a set of containers, each with its own purpose. These containers are by default configured using the server.xml file. When embedding a version, you will not be using this file; therefore, you will have to assemble instances of these containers programmatically. The following XML code snippet contains the hierarchy of the Tomcat containers:

```
<Server>
  <Service>
```

```
    <Connector />
    <Engine>
      <Host>
        <Context />
      </Host>
    </Engine>
  </Service>
</Server>
```

NOTE

Each of these elements contains attributes that determine their appropriate behaviors; however, for our purposes, only the element hierarchies and relationships are important.

This is the structure that we need to create with our embedded application. The <Server> and <Service> elements of this structure will be implicitly created; therefore, we do not have to create these objects ourselves. The steps for creating the remainder of the container structure are as follows:

1. Create an instance of an org.apache.catalina.Engine; this object represents the <Engine> element above, and acts as a container to the <Host> element.
2. Create an org.apache.catalina.Host object, which represents a virtual host, and add this instance to the Engine object.
3. Now you need to create *n*-number of org.apache.catalina.Context objects that will represent each Web application in this Host. Add each of the created Contexts to the previously created Host. We will create a single Context that will represent our wileystruts application.
4. The final step is to create an org.apache.catalina.Connector object and associate it with the previously created Engine. The Connector object is the object that actually receives a request from the calling client.

These are the steps that we must perform in order to create our own embedded version of the Tomcat container.

To create this application, let's leverage some existing Tomcat classes that have been developed to ease this type of integration. The main class we will use is the org.apache.catalina.startup.Embedded class, which you can find in the <*CATALINA_HOME*>/src/catalina/src/share/org/apache/catalina/startup directory. Listing 10.1 contains our sample application that builds these containers using the org.apache.catalina.startup.Embedded class:

```
package chapter10;

import java.net.URL;

import org.apache.catalina.Connector;
import org.apache.catalina.Context;
import org.apache.catalina.Deployer;
import org.apache.catalina.Engine;
import org.apache.catalina.Host;
import org.apache.catalina.logger.SystemOutLogger;
import org.apache.catalina.startup.Embedded;
import org.apache.catalina.Container;

public class EmbeddedTomcat {

  private String path = null;

  private Embedded embedded = null;
  private Host host = null;

  /**
    * Default Constructor
    *
    */
  public EmbeddedTomcat() {

  }

  /**
    * Basic Accessor setting the value of the context path
    *
    * @param path - the path
    */
  public void setPath(String path) {

    this.path = path;
  }

  /**
    * Basic Accessor returning the value of the context path
    *
    * @return - the context path
    */
  public String getPath() {

    return path;
  }
```

Listing 10.1 EmbeddedTomcat.java. (continues)

```
/**
  * This method Starts the Tomcat server.
  */
public void startTomcat() throws Exception {

  Engine engine = null;

  // Set the home directory
  System.setProperty("catalina.home", getPath());

  // Create an embedded server
  embedded = new Embedded();
  embedded.setDebug(0);
  embedded.setLogger(new SystemOutLogger());

  // Create an engine
  engine = embedded.createEngine();
  engine.setDefaultHost("localhost");

  // Create a default virtual host
  host = embedded.createHost("localhost", getPath()
    + "/webapps");

  engine.addChild(host);

  // Create the ROOT context
  Context context = embedded.createContext("",
    getPath() + "/webapps/ROOT");
  host.addChild(context);

  // Install the assembled container hierarchy
  embedded.addEngine(engine);

  // Assemble and install a default HTTP connector
  Connector connector =
    embedded.createConnector(null, 8080, false);

  embedded.addConnector(connector);

  // Start the embedded server
  embedded.start();
}

/**
  * This method Stops the Tomcat server.
  */
```

Listing 10.1 EmbeddedTomcat.java. (continues)

```
public void stopTomcat() throws Exception {

  // Stop the embedded server
  embedded.stop();
}

/**
  * Registers a WAR in the web server.
  *
  * @param contextPath - the context path under which the
  *              application will be registered
  * @param warFile - the URL of the WAR to be
  * registered.
  */
public void registerWAR(String contextPath, URL warFile)
  throws Exception {

  if ( contextPath == null ) {

    throw new Exception("Invalid Path : " + contextPath);
  }
  if( contextPath.equals("/") ) {

    contextPath = "";
  }

  if ( warFile == null ) {

    throw new Exception("Invalid WAR : " + warFile);
  }

  Deployer deployer = (Deployer)host;
  Context context = deployer.findDeployedApp(contextPath);

  if (context != null) {

    throw new
      Exception("Context " + contextPath
      + " Already Exists!");
  }
  deployer.install(contextPath, warFile);
}

/**
  * Unregisters a WAR from the web server.
  *
  * @param contextPath - the context path to be removed
```

Listing 10.1 EmbeddedTomcat.java. (continues)

```
    */
  public void unregisterWAR(String contextPath)
    throws   Exception {

    Context context = host.map(contextPath);
    if ( context != null ) {

      embedded.removeContext(context);
    }
    else {

      throw new
        Exception("Context does not exist for named path : "
        + contextPath);
    }
  }

  public static void main(String args[]) {

    try {

      EmbeddedTomcat tomcat = new EmbeddedTomcat();
      tomcat.setPath("d:/jakarta-tomcat-4.0.1");

      tomcat.startTomcat();

      URL url =
        new URL("file:D:/jakarta-tomcat-4.0.1"
        + "/webapps/wileystruts");

      tomcat.registerWAR("/wileystruts", url);

      Thread.sleep(1000000);

      tomcat.stopTomcat();

      System.exit(0);
    }
    catch( Exception e ) {

      e.printStackTrace();
    }
  }
}
```

Listing 10.1 EmbeddedTomcat.java. (continued)

You should begin your examination of the EmbeddedTomcat application source with the main() method. This method first creates an instance of the EmbeddedTomcat class. It then sets the path of the Tomcat installation that will be hosting our Tomcat instance. This path is equivalent to the *<CATALINA_HOME>* environment variable. The next action performed by the main() method is to invoke the startTomcat() method. This method implements the container construction steps we described earlier. The steps performed by this method are as follows:

1. The method begins by setting the system property to the value of the path attribute:

```
  // Set the home directory
System.setProperty("catalina.home", getPath());
```

NOTE

Make sure you use the value of *<CATALINA_HOME>* as the directory value passed to the setPath() method.

2. The next step is to create an instance of the Embedded object, and set the debug level and current logger:

```
  // Create an embedded server
embedded = new Embedded();
embedded.setDebug(5);
embedded.setLogger(new SystemOutLogger());
```

NOTE

The debug level should be 0 when you're deploying a production Web application. Setting the debug level to 0 reduces the amount of logging performed by Tomcat, which will improve performance significantly.

3. After the application has an instance of the Embedded object, it creates an instance of an org.apache.catalina.Engine and sets the name of the default host. The Engine object represents the entire Catalina servlet container:

```
// Create an engine
 engine = embedded.createEngine();
 engine.setDefaultHost("localhost");
```

4. After an Engine has been instantiated, we create an org.apache.catalina.Host object named localhost, with a path pointing to the *<CATALINA_HOME>*/webapps/ directory, and add it the Engine object. The Host object defines the virtual hosts that are contained in each instance of a Catalina Engine.

```
        // Create a default virtual host
host = embedded.createHost("localhost", getPath() +
"/webapps");

       engine.addChild(host);
```

5. Next, the startTomcat() method creates an org.apache.catalina.Context object that represents the ROOT Web application packaged with Tomcat, and then adds it to the previously created Host. The ROOT Web application is the only application that will be installed by default:

```
// Create the ROOT context
Context context = embedded.createContext("",
  getPath() + "/webapps/ROOT");
host.addChild(context);
```

6. The next step adds the Engine containing the created Host and Context to the Embedded object:

```
// Install the assembled container hierarchy
  embedded.addEngine(engine);
```

7. After the engine is added to the Embedded object, the startTomcat() method creates an org.apache.catalina.Connector object, and associates it with the previously created Engine. The <Connector> element defines the class that does the actual handling requests and responses to and from a calling client application. In the following snippet, an HTTP connector that listens to port 8080 is created and added to the Embedded object:

```
// Assemble and install a default HTTP connector
Connector connector = embedded.createConnector(null,
  8080, false);

embedded.addConnector(connector);
```

8. The final step performed by the startTomcat() method starts the Tomcat container:

```
embedded.start();
```

When startTomcat() returns, the main() method calls the registerWAR() method, which installs the previously deployed wileystruts application to the Embedded object:

```
URL url =
  new URL("file:D:/jakarta-tomcat-4.0.1"
  + "/webapps/wileystruts");

tomcat.registerWAR("/wileystruts", url);
```

The main application is then put to sleep to allow the embedded server time to service requests. When the application awakes, the embedded server is stopped and the application exits.

To test this application, you must complete the following steps:

1. Compile the EmbeddedTomcat.java class.
2. Make sure all other instances of Tomcat are shut down.
3. Add the following Jar files, all of which can be found in the Tomcat installation, to your application classpath.

   <*CATALINA_HOME*>/bin/bootstrap.jar

   <*CATALINA_HOME*>/server/lib/catalina.jar

   <*CATALINA_HOME*>/server/lib/servlet-cgi.jar

   <*CATALINA_HOME*>/server/lib/servlets-common.jar

   <*CATALINA_HOME*>/server/lib/servlets-default.jar

   <*CATALINA_HOME*>/server/lib/servlets-invoker.jar

   <*CATALINA_HOME*>/server/lib/servlets-manager.jar

   <*CATALINA_HOME*>/server/lib/servlets-snoop.jar

   <*CATALINA_HOME*>/server/lib/servlets-ssi.jar

   <*CATALINA_HOME*>/server/lib/servlets-webdav.jar

   <*CATALINA_HOME*>/server/lib/jakarta-regexp-1.2.jar

   <*CATALINA_HOME*>/lib/naming-factory.jar

   <*CATALINA_HOME*>/common/lib/crimson.jar

   <*CATALINA_HOME*>/common/lib/jasper-compiler.jar

   <*CATALINA_HOME*>/common/lib/jasper-runtime.jar

   <*CATALINA_HOME*>/common/lib/jaxp.jar

   <*CATALINA_HOME*>/common/lib/jndi.jar

   <*CATALINA_HOME*>/common/lib/naming-common.jar

   <*CATALINA_HOME*>/common/lib/naming-resources.jar

   <*CATALINA_HOME*>/common/lib/servlet.jar

   <*CATALINA_HOME*>/common/lib/tools.jar

4. Make sure that your classpath includes the directory containing the compiled EmbeddedTomcat class.
5. Execute the following command:

```
java chapter10.EmbeddedTomcat
```

If everything went according to plan, you should see some log statements in the console window:

```
HttpProcessor[8080][0] Starting background thread
HttpProcessor[8080][0]  Background thread has been started
HttpProcessor[8080][1] Starting background thread
HttpProcessor[8080][1]  Background thread has been started
HttpProcessor[8080][2] Starting background thread
HttpProcessor[8080][2]  Background thread has been started
HttpProcessor[8080][3] Starting background thread
HttpProcessor[8080][3]  Background thread has been started
HttpProcessor[8080][4] Starting background thread
HttpProcessor[8080][4]  Background thread has been started
```

Once you see this text, you will be able to access the ROOT and /wileystruts Web applications using the following URLs, respectively:

```
http://localhost:8080/
http://localhost:8080/wileystruts/
```

Debugging a Struts Application

Now that we have an embedded version of Tomcat, we can begin the process of debugging our wileystruts application. As I stated at the beginning of this chapter, we are going to use the JBuilder 6 IDE and the EmbeddedTomcat application to step through the source of Chapter 3's wileystruts application.

NOTE

The goal of this section is to examine the steps that must be completed when debugging a Struts application using any IDE. While we are using JBuilder 6 as our sample IDE, the process should be very similar on most other IDEs.

When you first launch the JBuilder IDE, you should see a screen similar to Figure 10.1.

Setting Up the Debug Environment

Once you have the IDE open, you must complete the following steps to set up a JBuilder project. JBuilder projects are used to manage application information, including classpath, source paths, and other miscellaneous project information.

1. Launch the New Project Wizard by selecting File, New Project.

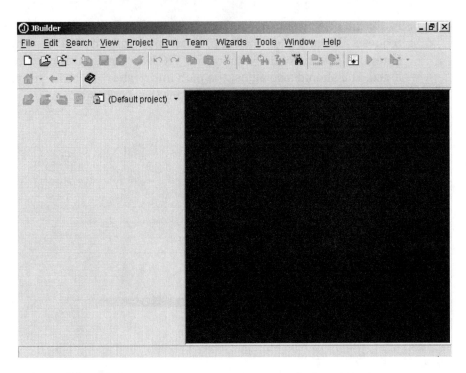

Figure 10.1 The JBuilder 6 IDE.

2. Fill in the text fields with the appropriate values for your application paths. I am using the values *chapter10* and *F:/Struts/Chapter10/* for the Name and Directory entries, as shown in Figure 10.2. After you have entered the appropriate values, click the Next button.

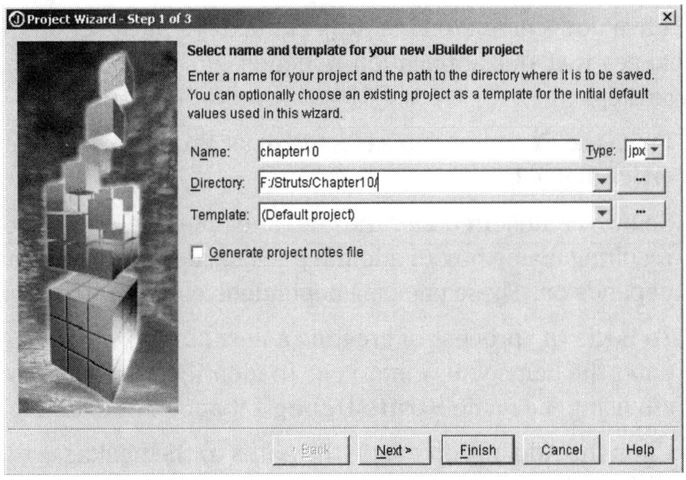

Figure 10.2 The New Project Wizard.

3. At this point, you should see Step 2 of the New Project Wizard. This step requests JDK and additional application path information. You should enter the location of the your *<JAVA_HOME>* path, if it is not already listed. You should also adjust the path information according to your environment. Figure 10.3 displays the values that I am using.

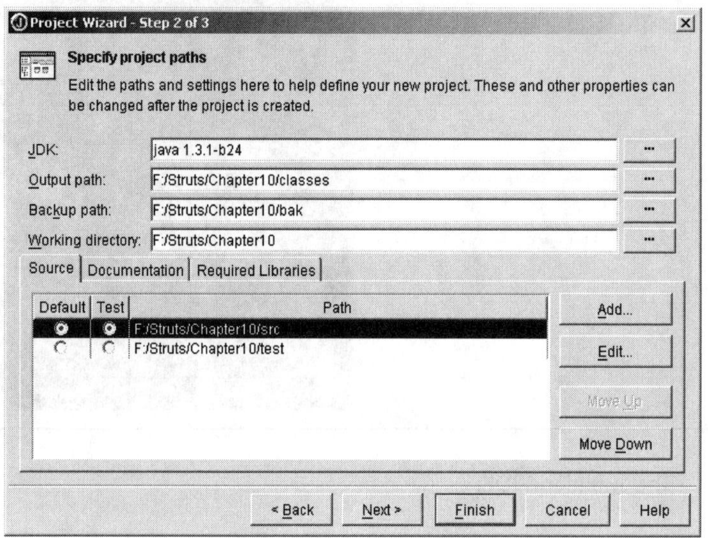

Figure 10.3 Step 2 of the New Project Wizard.

4. You can now click the Finish button to complete the creation of the chapter10 project.

We have now completed the project; next we must set up the classpaths of the packages that our application depends on. To do this, we need to complete these steps:

1. From the Project menu, select Project Properties to open the Project Properties dialog box.
2. Select the Required Libraries tab and click the Add button. We will use the resulting dialog box to add the package dependencies that our new project depends on. These package dependencies are called *libraries*.
3. To begin the process of creating a new library, click the New button, and enter the name you want to use to identify the library you are creating. I am using the name **Struts Debug Libs** for this example.
4. Click the Add button to add the paths to the packages that the wileystruts Web application depends on. The paths values that you want to use are listed here:

<*CATALINA_HOME*>/webapps/wileystruts/WEB-INF/classes/

<*CATALINA_HOME*>/bin/bootstrap.jar

<*CATALINA_HOME*>/server/lib/catalina.jar

<*CATALINA_HOME*>/server/lib/servlet-cgi.jar

<*CATALINA_HOME*>/server/lib/servlets-common.jar

<*CATALINA_HOME*>/server/lib/servlets-default.jar

<*CATALINA_HOME*>/server/lib/servlets-invoker.jar

<*CATALINA_HOME*>/server/lib/servlets-manager.jar

<*CATALINA_HOME*>/server/lib/servlets-snoop.jar

<*CATALINA_HOME*>/server/lib/servlets-ssi.jar

<*CATALINA_HOME*>/server/lib/servlets-webdav.jar

<*CATALINA_HOME*>/server/lib/jakarta-regexp-1.2.jar

<*CATALINA_HOME*>/lib/naming-factory.jar

<*CATALINA_HOME*>/common/lib/crimson.jar

<*CATALINA_HOME*>/common/lib/jasper-compiler.jar

<*CATALINA_HOME*>/common/lib/jasper-runtime.jar

<*CATALINA_HOME*>/common/lib/jaxp.jar

<*CATALINA_HOME*>/common/lib/jndi.jar

<*CATALINA_HOME*>/common/lib/naming-common.jar

<*CATALINA_HOME*>/common/lib/naming-resources.jar

<*CATALINA_HOME*>/common/lib/servlet.jar

<*CATALINA_HOME*>/common/lib/tools.jar

<*CATALINA_HOME*>/webapps/wileystruts/WEB-INF/lib/struts.jar

<*CATALINA_HOME*>/webapps/wileystruts/WEB-INF/lib/struts.jar

<*CATALINA_HOME*>/webapps/wileystruts/WEB-INF/lib/commons-beanutils.jar

<*CATALINA_HOME*>/webapps/wileystruts/WEB-INF/lib/commons-collections.jar

<*CATALINA_HOME*>/webapps/wileystruts/WEB-INF/lib/commons-dbcp.jar

<*CATALINA_HOME*>/webapps/wileystruts/WEB-INF/lib/commons-digester.jar

<*CATALINA_HOME*>/webapps/wileystruts/WEB-INF/lib/commons-logging.jar

<*CATALINA_HOME*>/webapps/wileystruts/WEB-INF/lib/commons-pool.jar

<*CATALINA_HOME*>/webapps/wileystruts/WEB-INF/lib/commons-services.jar

<*CATALINA_HOME*>/webapps/wileystruts/WEB-INF/lib/commons-validator.jar

NOTE

While you are browsing around the file system selecting the appropriate path, you should note that you can select multiple paths using the Ctrl key.

5. Once all of the paths have been added, click the OK button to commit them to the project.

At this point, we have completed the project and defined all of the library dependencies. Before we can begin debugging our wileystruts application, we must add the source paths of the previously included packages. This will allow us to step into the source code as the application is servicing requests. To add the source paths, follow these steps:

NOTE

We are using the source code from Chapter 3, "Getting Started with Struts," for this example.

1. From the Project menu, select Project Properties.
2. Select the Required Libraries tab, select the Struts Debug Libs Library, and click the Edit button. You should see the path of the packages that we have previously added.
3. Select the Source tab, and click the Add button.
4. Select the directories that contain both the wileystruts Web application and the Struts source files. The paths for my environment are shown here:

```
f:/Struts/Chapter3/src
f:/Struts/jakarta-struts /src/share
```

NOTE

The first path listed here is the path that you would want to replace when debugging your own Struts applications.

Now, click the OK button until you are back at the main JBuilder window.

Debugging the wileystruts Application

We now have our IDE's environment configured for debugging Struts Web applications, and we can begin stepping into the source code of a running Struts application. To do this, we must first set a breakpoint.

Breakpoints are like stop signs to the IDE's debugger that tell it where we want to start examining running source code. To set a breakpoint, we must first open the file we want to examine. For our application, the easiest object to examine is the wiley.LookupAction class, so open the File menu, select the Open File submenu, locate the wiley.LookupAction.java file, and open it.

You should see the source for the LookupAction in the main editor window. We can now set the breakpoint by scrolling down to the line you want to look at, placing the cursor on that line, and pressing the F5 key. Move to the line that contains the following line of code, and press the F5 key:

```
String symbol = lookupForm.getSymbol();
```

You should now see a red line marking the code that we have selected. The results of this action are shown in Figure 10.4.

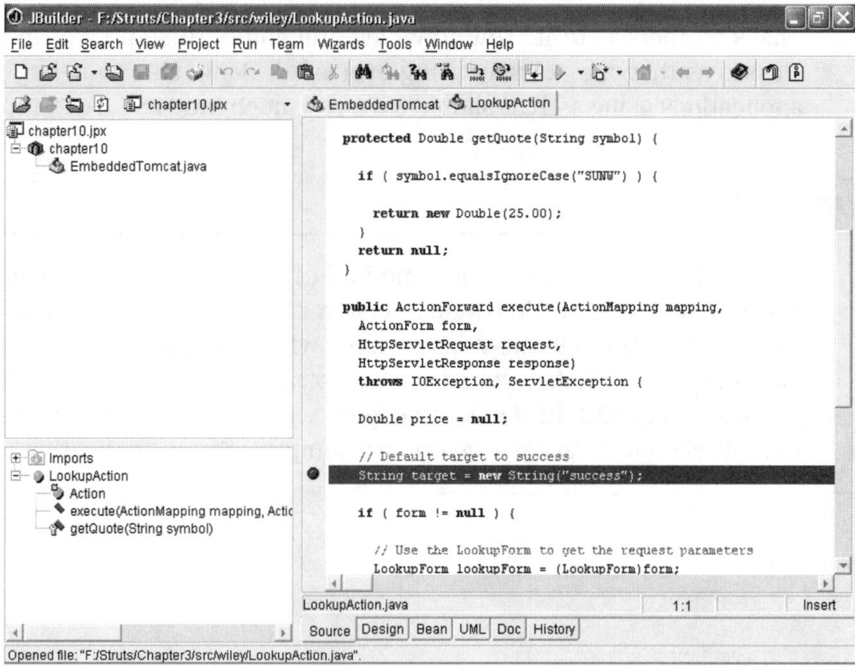

Figure 10.4 A selected breakpoint.

To begin debugging the application, right-click on the EmbeddedTomcat tab in the source window, and select Debug from the context menu. You will see several messages in the Message window. When you see the following message, Tomcat is ready to service requests:

```
StandardWrapper[/wileystruts:invoker]: Loading container servlet invoker
invoker: init
jsp: init
```

Now you can open your browser to the starting page of the wileystruts application, which you can find at http://localhost:8080/wileystruts/index.jsp. Enter a stock symbol, and submit the value to the LookupAction. The result of this action will cause the JBuilder debugger to process the request until it reaches the breakpoint that you specified. When you switch back to the JBuilder environment, you should the line that you selected highlighted in blue. You can now step through the application using the JBuilder Debug toolbar, shown in Figure 10.5.

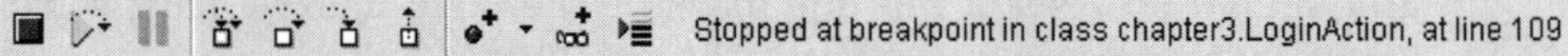

Figure 10.5 The JBuilder Debug toolbar.

That's all there is to it. You now have the ability to step through your Struts classes as they are actually being evaluated. Being able to debug your Struts applications using an IDE should save you much time and frustration.

Summary

In this chapter, we looked at a method of debugging Struts applications. We began by building an Embedded version of the Tomcat JSP/servlet container. We then went through the steps required when using the JBuilder IDE to debug Struts applications. As I stated earlier, you can debug a Struts application with just about any IDE. In the next chapter, we bring together everything that we have discussed so far by developing a complete Struts application.

CHAPTER 11

Developing a Complete Struts Application

In this chapter, we develop a complete Struts application. We begin by defining each component of the application and then continue with the actual development and implementation of the application. The goal of this chapter is to tie all of our previous discussions together through the use of an example that leverages the components most often used from the Struts Framework.

The Employees Application Definition

Our sample application, named *employees*, acts as an employee directory service that will allow a user (with the appropriate access) to list, add, edit, and delete employee records stored in the company database. First, we define the application's components, including the Models, the Views, and the Controller.

Preparing the Employees Application

Before we can begin developing our sample, we must perform the basic steps of preparing the application. What follows are the minimum number of steps that you must complete when defining any Struts application:

1. Create a new Web application; use the directory structure described in Chapter 1, "Introducing the Jakarta Struts Project and Its Supporting Components." Be sure to substitute the name of your Web application for the value *employees*.

2. Copy the struts.jar file, extracted from the Jakarta Struts archive, to the <*CATALINA_HOME*>/webapps/employees/WEB-INF/lib directory.
3. Copy the xerces.jar file (version 1.3.1 or above) to the <*CATALINA_HOME*>/webapps/employees/WEB-INF/lib directory.
4. Copy the jdbc2_0-stdext.jar file to the <*CATALINA_HOME*>/webapps/employees/WEB-INF/lib directory. (You can skip this step if your application does not leverage the GenericDataSource.)
5. Create an empty struts-config.xml file, and copy it to the <*CATALINA_HOME*>/webapps/employees/WEB-INF/ directory. Listing 11.1 contains an example of an empty struts-config.xml file.

```
<?xml version="1.0" encoding="ISO-8859-1" ?>

<!DOCTYPE struts-config PUBLIC
  "-//Apache Software Foundation//DTD Struts Configuration 1.1//EN"
  "http://jakarta.apache.org/struts/dtds/struts-config_1_1.dtd">

<struts-config

</struts-config>
```

Listing 11.1 An empty struts-config.xml file.

6. Create a web.xml file with a Servlet definition for the ActionServlet, and copy this file to the <*CATALINA_HOME*>/webapps/employees/WEB-INF/ directory. Listing 11.2 shows our initial web.xml file; this file will evolve as we add components to our employees application.

NOTE

We discussed the configuration of the ActionServlet in Chapter 4, "The Controller."

```
<?xml version="1.0" encoding="ISO-8859-1"?>

<!DOCTYPE web-app
  PUBLIC "-//Sun Microsystems, Inc.//DTD Web Application 2.3//EN"
  "http://java.sun.com/dtd/web-app_2_3.dtd">

<web-app>
```

Listing 11.2 The web.xml file in its initial stages. (continues)

```
  <servlet>
    <servlet-name>action</servlet-name>
    <servlet-class>
      org.apache.struts.action.ActionServlet
    </servlet-class>
    <init-param>
      <param-name>debug</param-name>
      <param-value>5</param-value>
    </init-param>
    <init-param>
      <param-name>config</param-name>
      <param-value>/WEB-INF/struts-config.xml</param-value>
    </init-param>
    <load-on-startup>1</load-on-startup>
  </servlet>

  <servlet-mapping>
    <servlet-name>action</servlet-name>
    <url-pattern>*.do</url-pattern>
  </servlet-mapping>

</web-app>
```

Listing 11.2 The web.xml file in its initial stages. (continued)

7. Create the application resource bundles, and copy them to the *<CATALINA_HOME>*/webapps/employees/WEB-INF/classes/com/wiley directory. In our examples, we resource bundles for the English language only. Listing 11.3 contains the resource bundle for our application.

```
app.title=Wiley Employee Database
app.username=User Name
app.password=Password
app.name=Name
app.phone=Phone
app.email=Email
app.role=Role
app.department=Department
app.administration=Administration
app.network=Network
app.sales=Sales
app.engineering=Engineering
app.manager=Manager
```

Listing 11.3 The English resource bundle for ApplicationResources.properties. (continues)

```
app.employee=Employee

errors.login.unknown=<li>Unknown User : {0}</li>
errors.login.required=<li>You must login before proceeding</li>
errors.username.required=<li>A Username is Required</li>
errors.password.required=<li>A Password is Required</li>
errors.name.required=<li>A Name is Required</li>
errors.phone.required=<li>A Phone is Required</li>
errors.email.required=<li>An Email Address is Required</li>
errors.roleid.required=<li>A Role is Required</li>
errors.depid.required=<li>A Department is Required</li>
errors.database.error=<li>A Database error occurred : {0}</li>

errors.header=<h3><font color="red">Error List</font></h3><ul>
errors.footer=</ul><hr>
```

Listing 11.3 The English resource bundle for ApplicationResources.properties. (continued)

8. Add this resource bundle to the employees application. This modification requires adding a <message-resources> subelement to the previously defined struts-config.xml file. Listing 11.4 contains the application's new struts-config.xml (featuring this modification).

NOTE

We discussed creating new resource bundles in Chapter 6, "Internationalizing Your Struts Applications."

```
<?xml version="1.0" encoding="ISO-8859-1" ?>

<!DOCTYPE struts-config PUBLIC
  "-//Apache Software Foundation//DTD Struts Configuration 1.1//EN"
  "http://jakarta.apache.org/struts/dtds/struts-config_1_1.dtd">

<struts-config>

  <message-resources
    parameter="com.wiley.ApplicationResources"/>

</struts-config>
```

Listing 11.4 Our struts-config.xml file after we added the application resource bundle.

9. We next need to add the tag libraries that we intend to leverage in our application development. This is an optional step, and is necessary only when your application leverages one or more custom tag libraries. The libraries that we use are the HTML, Logic, and Bean libraries. To add these libraries, you must add a <taglib> entry describing each library to the <*CATALINA_HOME*>/webapps/employees/WEB-INF/web.xml file; then copy the HTML, Logic, and Bean TLDs to the <*CATALINA_HOME*>/webapps/employees/WEB-INF/ directory. Listing 11.5 shows the application's web.xml file with the addition of these libraries.

NOTE

We will further define each of these libraries in Chapters 13-16.

```
<?xml version="1.0" encoding="ISO-8859-1"?>

<!DOCTYPE web-app
  PUBLIC "-//Sun Microsystems, Inc.//DTD Web Application 2.3//EN"
  "http://java.sun.com/dtd/web-app_2_3.dtd">

<web-app>

  <servlet>
    <servlet-name>action</servlet-name>
    <servlet-class>
      org.apache.struts.action.ActionServlet
    </servlet-class>
    <init-param>
      <param-name>debug</param-name>
      <param-value>5</param-value>
    </init-param>
    <init-param>
      <param-name>config</param-name>
      <param-value>/WEB-INF/struts-config.xml</param-value>
    </init-param>
    <load-on-startup>1</load-on-startup>
  </servlet>

  <servlet-mapping>
    <servlet-name>action</servlet-name>
```

Listing 11.5 Our web.xml file after we added the HTML, Logic, and Bean tag libraries. (continues)

```
    <url-pattern>*.do</url-pattern>
  </servlet-mapping>

  <taglib>
    <taglib-uri>/WEB-INF/struts-html.tld</taglib-uri>
    <taglib-location>/WEB-INF/struts-html.tld</taglib-location>
  </taglib>

  <taglib>
    <taglib-uri>/WEB-INF/struts-logic.tld</taglib-uri>
    <taglib-location>
      /WEB-INF/struts-logic.tld
    </taglib-location>
  </taglib>

  <taglib>
    <taglib-uri>/WEB-INF/struts-bean.tld</taglib-uri>
    <taglib-location>/WEB-INF/struts-bean.tld</taglib-location>
  </taglib>

</web-app>
```

Listing 11.5 Our web.xml file after we added the HTML, Logic, and Bean tag libraries. (continued)

10. Add any custom ActionMappings to the application. Again, this step is optional; it's only necessary when your application defines a custom Action-Mapping. In this application, we've added a custom ActionMapping that will be associated with the Action class; the custom mapping will specify whether the user must be logged in to perform the Action that it applies to. The default value is false, which allows a user who is not logged in to execute the Action. Our custom ActionMapping is shown in Listing 11.6.

```
package com.wiley;

import org.apache.struts.action.ActionMapping;

public class EmployeesActionMapping extends ActionMapping {

  protected boolean loginRequired = false;

  public EmployeesActionMapping() {

    super();
  }
```

Listing 11.6 com.wiley.EmployeesActionMapping.java. (continues)

```
  public void setLoginRequired(boolean loginRequired) {

    this.loginRequired = loginRequired;
  }

  public boolean isLoginRequired() {

    return loginRequired;
  }
}
```

Listing 11.6 com.wiley.EmployeesActionMapping.java. (continued)

To add this ActionMapping to the employees application, you need to compile this class, move it to the <*CATALINA_HOME*>/webapps/employees/WEB-INF/classes/com/wiley directory, and then add the EmployeesActionMapping to the ActionServlet's definition. This modification requires adding a new <init-param> to the previously defined <servlet> element. Listing 11.7 contains the application's current web.xml.

NOTE

We discussed creating and deploying custom ActionMappings in Chapter 8, "Creating Custom ActionMappings."

```
<?xml version="1.0" encoding="ISO-8859-1"?>

<!DOCTYPE web-app
  PUBLIC "-//Sun Microsystems, Inc.//DTD Web Application 2.3//EN"
  "http://java.sun.com/dtd/web-app_2_3.dtd">

<web-app>

  <servlet>
    <servlet-name>action</servlet-name>
    <servlet-class>
      org.apache.struts.action.ActionServlet
    </servlet-class>
    <init-param>
      <param-name>debug</param-name>
      <param-value>5</param-value>
    </init-param>
```

Listing 11.7 Our web.xml file after we added the com.wiley.EmployeesActionMapping. (continues)

```
    <init-param>
      <param-name>config</param-name>
      <param-value>/WEB-INF/struts-config.xml</param-value>
    </init-param>
    <init-param>
      <param-name>mapping</param-name>
      <param-value>
        com.wiley.EmployeesActionMapping
      </param-value>
    </init-param>

    <load-on-startup>1</load-on-startup>
  </servlet>

  <servlet-mapping>
    <servlet-name>action</servlet-name>
    <url-pattern>*.do</url-pattern>
  </servlet-mapping>

  <taglib>
    <taglib-uri>/WEB-INF/struts-html.tld</taglib-uri>
    <taglib-location>/WEB-INF/struts-html.tld</taglib-location>
  </taglib>

  <taglib>
    <taglib-uri>/WEB-INF/struts-logic.tld</taglib-uri>
    <taglib-location>
      /WEB-INF/struts-logic.tld
    </taglib-location>
  </taglib>

  <taglib>
    <taglib-uri>/WEB-INF/struts-bean.tld</taglib-uri>
    <taglib-location>/WEB-INF/struts-bean.tld</taglib-location>
  </taglib>

</web-app>
```

Listing 11.7 Our web.xml file after we added the com.wiley.EmployeesActionMapping. (continued)

That's it. We now have our application defined at the Web level. It's now time to define the remainder of the application.

Creating the Employees Model

In this section, we define the persistent data layer of the employees application. This layer, defined as the Model, is represented by a relational database and a single Java object, employee.

The employees application's persistent data will be stored in three database tables: employees, roles, and departments. In the sections that follow, we describe each of these tables and their contents.

The Employees Table

The employees table holds the actual list of employees found in the application. It is the main table of our application. Its structure is defined in Table 11.1.

Table 11.1 The Employees Table Structure

COLUMN	DESCRIPTION
username	A unique key identifying the employee. It is a varchar(10).
password	A password that acts as the security credentials of the employee. It is a varchar(10).
name	The string representing the employee's name. It is a varchar(30).
roleid	An element used to identify the role that the employee belongs to. It is an integer.
phone	The string representation of the employee's phone number. It is a varchar(30).
email	The string representation of the employee's e-mail address. It is a varchar(30).
depid	An element used to identify the department that the employee belongs to. It is an integer.

Table 11.2 contains the data that populates this table.

Table 11.2 The Contents of the Employees Table

USERNAME	PASSWORD	NAME	ROLEID	PHONE	EMAIL	DEPID
abrickey	$word	Art Brickey	1	(303) 555-1214	abrickey@ where.com	2
tharris	ralph	Todd Harris	1	(206) 555-9482	tharris@ where.com	2
sriley	$mindy$	Sean Riley	2	(206) 555-3412	sriley@ where.com	4
jgoodwill	$pass$	James Goodwill	1	(303) 555-1214	jgoodwill@ where.com	3
tgray	password	Tim Gray	2	(303) 555-9876	tgray@ anywhere.com	1

The Roles Table

The roles table holds the list of roles that a user may be assigned. This is the table that we use to determine the rights of the current user. Its structure is described in Table 11.3.

Table 11.3 The Roles Table Structure

COLUMN	DESCRIPTION
roleid	An element used to uniquely identify the roles of the application. It is an integer.
rolename	The string representation of the role. It is a varchar(30).

The data that populates this table can be found in Table 11.4.

Table 11.4 The Contents of the Roles Table

ROLEID	ROLENAME
1	manager
2	employee

The Departments Table

The departments table holds the list of departments that an employee may be assigned to. Its structure is described in Table 11.5.

Table 11.5 The Departments Table Structure

COLUMN	DESCRIPTION
depid	An element used to uniquely identify the departments of the application. It is an integer.
depname	The string representation of the department. It is a varchar(30).

Table 11.6 shows the data that populates this table.

Table 11.6 The Contents of the Departments Table

DEPID	DEPNAME
1	Administration
2	Network
3	Sales
4	Engineering

Creating the Employees Database

Now that you have seen the employees database structure and its contents, it's time to actually create this database.

Make sure you have MySQL installed and running on your host machine. Then complete the following steps:

1. Start the mysql client found in the <*MYSQL_HOME*>/bin/ directory by typing the following command:

```
mysql
```

2. Create the employees database by executing the following command:

```
create database employees;
```

3. Make sure you are modifying the appropriate database by executing the following command:

```
use employees;
```

4. Create and populate the employees table by executing these commands:

```
create table employees
(
  username varchar(15) not null primary key,
  password varchar(15) not null,
  roleid integer not null,
  name varchar(30) not null,
  phone varchar(15) not null,
  email varchar(30) not null,
  depid integer not null
);

insert into employees values("abrickey", "$word", 1,
  "Art Brickey", "(303) 555-1214",
  "abrickey@where.com", 2);

insert into employees values("tharris", "ralph", 1,
  "Todd Harris", "(303) 555-9482",
  "tharris@where.com", 2);

insert into employees values("sriley", "$mindy$", 2,
  "Sean Riley", "(303) 555-3412",
  "sriley@where.com", 4);

insert into employees values("jgoodwill", "$pass$", 1,
  "James Goodwill", "(303) 555-1214",
  "jgoodwill@where.com", 3);

insert into employees values("tgray", "password", 2,
  "Tim Gray", "(303) 555-9876",
  "tgray@where.com", 1);
```

5. Create and populate the roles table by executing these commands:

```
create table roles
(
  roleid integer not null primary key,
  rolename varchar(30) not null
);

insert into roles values(1, "manager");
insert into roles values(2, "employee");
```

6. Create and populate the departments table by executing the following commands:

```
create table departments
(
  depid integer not null primary key,
  depname varchar(30) not null
);

insert into departments values(1, "Administration");
insert into departments values(2, "Network");
insert into departments values(3, "Sales");
insert into departments values(4, "Engineering");
```

The Employee Object

Now that we have defined the database that will house our employee data, we must create the Java object that will model this data. For our example, we use the com.wiley.Employee object, a simple JavaBean used only to hold the values of an individual employee. The code for the Employee object appears in Listing 11.8.

NOTE

We could have modeled each table in the employees database, but to keep things simple, we've chosen only to model the Employee object, which has both a role and a department.

```
package com.wiley;

public class Employee {

  protected String username;
  protected String name;
  protected String department;
```

Listing 11.8 The Employee model. (continues)

```
protected String rolename;
protected String phone;
protected String email;
protected Integer depid;
protected Integer roleid;

public void setUsername(String username) {

  this.username = username;
}

public String getUsername() {

  return username;
}

public void setName(String name) {

  this.name = name;
}

public String getName() {

  return name;
}

public void setDepartment(String department) {

  this.department = department;
}

public String getDepartment() {

  return this.department;
}

public void setRolename(String rolename) {

  this.rolename = rolename;
}

public String getRolename() {

  return rolename;
}

public void setPhone(String phone) {
```

Listing 11.8 The Employee model. (continues)

```
    this.phone = phone;
  }

  public String getPhone() {

    return phone;
  }

  public void setEmail(String email) {

    this.email = email;
  }

  public String getEmail() {

    return email;
  }

  public void setDepid(Integer depid) {

    this.depid = depid;
  }

  public Integer getDepid() {

    return depid;
  }

  public void setRoleid(Integer roleid) {

    this.roleid = roleid;
  }

  public Integer getRoleid() {

    return roleid;
  }
}
```

Listing 11.8 The Employee model. (continued)

After you've had a chance to look over the Employee object, go ahead and compile it, and move the resulting class file to the *<CATALINA_HOME>*/ webapps/employees/WEB-INF/classes/com/wiley directory.

DataSource Configuration

The final step that we must complete to make our data layer available to the remainder of the employees application is to add a DataSource definition to the employees Struts configuration file. To accomplish this, we add a <data-sources> entry to the *<CATALINA_HOME>*/webapps/employees/WEB-INF/struts-config.xml file. The following snippet contains our new DataSource:

```
<data-sources>
  <data-source>
    <set-property property="driverClass"
      value="org.gjt.mm.mysql.Driver" />
    <set-property property="url"
      value="jdbc:mysql://localhost/employees" />
    <set-property property="maxCount"
      value="5"/>
    <set-property property="minCount"
      value="1"/>
    <set-property property="user"
      value="username"/>
    <set-property property="password"
      value="password"/>
  </data-source>
</data-sources>
```

NOTE

Before continuing with this example, make sure you've copied the MySQL JDBC driver to the *<CATALINA_HOME>*/webapps/employees/WEB-INF/lib directory. Chapter 9, "The Struts JDBC Connection Pool," describes this process.

Building the Employees Application

As we discussed earlier, the employees application is intended to be used as an employee directory service that allows a user to list, add, edit, and delete employee records stored in the company database. To accomplish these tasks, we need to define the Views and Actions that will allow the user to perform each of these functions. In the following sections, we describe each of these functions—from the input View through the Action ending with the target View.

NOTE

In this section, I will use the term *transaction* to describe an entire application function, which consists of the Views and Actions associated with one application requirement, such as the add transaction or the edit transaction.

The Login Transaction

The Login transaction is the entry point of our application. All users must perform a login before they can continue with any further actions. The Login transaction presents its components in the following order:

1. Login JSP
2. LoginForm
3. LoginAction
4. EmployeeListAction
5. Employee List JSP

NOTE

As we progress through each transaction, you will notice that the Views and Actions require a user to be logged in prior to execution. This applies to all Views and Actions, excluding the Login View and Action.

The Login JSP

The Login View, represented by the JSP login.jsp, acts as the entry point to the employees application. It requires users to enter their username and password and submit these values to the action named Login. The code for the login.jsp appears in Listing 11.9.

```
<%@ page language="java" %>
<%@ taglib uri="/WEB-INF/struts-html.tld" prefix="html" %>
<%@ taglib uri="/WEB-INF/struts-bean.tld" prefix="bean" %>

<html>
  <head>
    <title><bean:message key="app.title" /></title>
  </head>

  <body>
    <table width="500"
      border="0" cellspacing="0" cellpadding="0">
      <tr>
        <td> </td>
      </tr>
      <tr bgcolor="#36566E">
        <td height="68" width="48%">
```

Listing 11.9 login.jsp. (continues)

```
          <div align="left">
            <img src="images/hp_logo_wiley.gif"
              width="220"
             height="74">
          </div>
        </td>
      </tr>
      <tr>
        <td> </td>
      </tr>
    </table>

    <html:errors />

    <html:form action="/Login"
      name="loginForm"
      type="com.wiley.LoginForm" >
      <table width="45%" border="0">
        <tr>
          <td><bean:message key="app.username" />:</td>
          <td><html:text property="username" /></td>
        </tr>
        <tr>
          <td><bean:message key="app.password" />:</td>
          <td><html:password property="password" /></td>
        </tr>
        <tr>
          <td colspan="2" align="center"><html:submit /></td>
        </tr>
      </table>
    </html:form>

  </body>
</html>
```

Listing 11.9 login.jsp. (continued)

As you look over the source for the Login View, you should pay particular attention to the text in boldface. You'll note several occurrences of the <bean: message /> tag. As you may recall, this tag is used to retrieve a human-readable string that is determined by the Locale of the requesting client. We use this tag throughout our application when presenting text to the user of the application, which makes the employees application language-independent.

NOTE

We discussed language independence in Chapter 6.

The next bit of code we'll focus on is the <html:errors /> tag. We use this tag in all our JSPs to report errors in the processing of the Action targeted by this View.

NOTE

We discussed error handling in Chapter 7, "Managing Errors."

The next piece of code we'd like to point out is the <html:form /> tag. This tag represents the HTML form that will gather the submitted data and populate with these gathered values the ActionForm named by the name attribute. The target of this View is Login, which will be mapped to the LoginAction class described later in this section.

As I stated earlier, login.jsp acts as the entry point to our application; therefore, we need to add it to the application's web.xml file as one of the welcome files. Listing 11.10 contains the web.xml file at this point.

```
<?xml version="1.0" encoding="ISO-8859-1"?>

<!DOCTYPE web-app
  PUBLIC "-//Sun Microsystems, Inc.//DTD Web Application 2.3//EN"
  "http://java.sun.com/dtd/web-app_2_3.dtd">

<web-app>

  <servlet>
    <servlet-name>action</servlet-name>
    <servlet-class>
      org.apache.struts.action.ActionServlet
    </servlet-class>
    <init-param>
      <param-name>debug</param-name>
      <param-value>5</param-value>
    </init-param>
    <init-param>
      <param-name>config</param-name>
      <param-value>/WEB-INF/struts-config.xml</param-value>
    </init-param>
    <init-param>
      <param-name>mapping</param-name>
      <param-value>
        com.wiley.EmployeesActionMapping
      </param-value>
```

Listing 11.0 Our web.xml file after we added login.jsp as a welcome file. (continues)

```
    </init-param>

    <load-on-startup>1</load-on-startup>
  </servlet>

  <servlet-mapping>
    <servlet-name>action</servlet-name>
    <url-pattern>*.do</url-pattern>
  </servlet-mapping>

  <welcome-file-list>
    <welcome-file>login.jsp</welcome-file>
  </welcome-file-list>

  <taglib>
    <taglib-uri>/WEB-INF/struts-html.tld</taglib-uri>
    <taglib-location>/WEB-INF/struts-html.tld</taglib-location>
  </taglib>

  <taglib>
    <taglib-uri>/WEB-INF/struts-logic.tld</taglib-uri>
    <taglib-location>
      /WEB-INF/struts-logic.tld
    </taglib-location>
  </taglib>

  <taglib>
    <taglib-uri>/WEB-INF/struts-bean.tld</taglib-uri>
    <taglib-location>/WEB-INF/struts-bean.tld</taglib-location>
  </taglib>

</web-app>
```

Listing 11.0 Our web.xml file after we added login.jsp as a welcome file. (continued)

The Login ActionForm

Now that you have seen the data that will be submitted by the Login View, we must create an ActionForm that will validate and encapsulate the submitted values. The code for this ActionForm appears in Listing 11.11.

```
package com.wiley;

import javax.servlet.http.HttpServletRequest;
```

Listing 11.11 LoginForm.java. (continues)

```
import org.apache.struts.action.ActionForm;
import org.apache.struts.action.ActionMapping;
import org.apache.struts.action.ActionErrors;
import org.apache.struts.action.ActionError;

public class LoginForm extends ActionForm {

  private String password = null;

  private String username = null;

  // Password Accessors
  public String getPassword() {

    return (this.password);
  }

  public void setPassword(String password) {

    this.password = password;
  }

  // Username Accessors
  public String getUsername() {

    return (this.username);
  }

  public void setUsername(String username) {

    this.username = username;
  }

  // This method is called with every request. It resets the
  // Form attribute prior to setting the values in the new
  // request.
  public void reset(ActionMapping mapping,
    HttpServletRequest request) {

    this.password = null;
    this.username = null;
  }

  public ActionErrors validate(ActionMapping mapping,
    HttpServletRequest request) {

    ActionErrors errors = new ActionErrors();
```

Listing 11.11 LoginForm.java. (continues)

```
    if ( (username == null ) || (username.length() == 0) ) {

      errors.add("username",
        new ActionError("errors.username.required"));
    }
    if ( (password == null ) || (password.length() == 0) ) {

      errors.add("password",
        new ActionError("errors.password.required"));
    }
    return errors;
  }
}
```

Listing 11.11 LoginForm.java. (continued)

As you look over the LoginForm.java, you'll notice that there's really nothing special about it. It provides accessors to data members that map to the values submitted by the Login View—username and password—and it performs some simple validation of those values. If the values pass the validation, then the transaction continues; otherwise, ActionErrors are created and the request is forwarded back to the value defined by this Actions input subelement, which in this case is login.jsp. We will see the input subelement when we deploy this transaction.

The only things especially notable about this object are the keys used when creating an ActionError when validation fails. These keys are used to look up Locale-specific text stored in the application's resource bundle. We examine this bundle later in this chapter.

NOTE

We discussed ActionForm objects in Chapter 5, "The Views."

The LoginAction

Once the submitted values have been validated by the LoginForm, the LoginAction.execute() method is invoked. The LoginAction tries to retrieve a user from the employees database. If it finds the user, the user is added to the HttpSession and then forwarded to the success target—which in this case is another Action, the EmployeeListAction. If the user is not found, then an ActionError is created, and the results are forwarded to the failure target—the login.jsp. The code for the LoginAction is shown in Listing 11.12.

```
package com.wiley;

import java.io.IOException;
import javax.servlet.ServletContext;
import javax.servlet.ServletException;
import javax.servlet.http.HttpServletRequest;
import javax.servlet.http.HttpServletResponse;
import javax.servlet.http.HttpSession;
import org.apache.struts.action.Action;
import org.apache.struts.action.ActionForm;
import org.apache.struts.action.ActionForward;
import org.apache.struts.action.ActionMapping;
import org.apache.struts.action.ActionErrors;
import org.apache.struts.action.ActionError;

import javax.sql.DataSource;
import java.sql.Connection;
import java.sql.Statement;
import java.sql.ResultSet;
import java.sql.SQLException;

public class LoginAction extends Action {

  protected String getUser(String username, String password) {

    String user = null;
    Connection conn = null;
    Statement stmt = null;
    ResultSet rs = null;

    ServletContext context = servlet.getServletContext();

    DataSource dataSource = (DataSource)
      context.getAttribute(Action.DATA_SOURCE_KEY);

    try {

      conn = dataSource.getConnection();
      stmt = conn.createStatement();
      rs =
        stmt.executeQuery("select * from employees where "
          + "username='" + username + "' "
          + "and password='" + password + "'");

      if ( rs.next() ) {

        user = rs.getString("username");
```

Listing 11.12 The LoginAction. (continues)

```
        // Iterate over the results
        System.err.println("Username : "
          + rs.getString("username")
          + " Password : " + rs.getString("password"));
      }
      else {

        System.err.println("---->User not found<----");
      }
    }
    catch (SQLException e) {

      System.err.println(e.getMessage());
    }
    finally {

      if (rs != null) {

        try {

          rs.close();
        }
        catch (SQLException sqle) {

          System.err.println(sqle.getMessage());
        }
        rs = null;
      }
      if (stmt != null) {

        try {

          stmt.close();
        }
        catch (SQLException sqle) {

          System.err.println(sqle.getMessage());
        }
        stmt = null;
      }
      if (conn != null) {

        try {

          conn.close();
        }
        catch (SQLException sqle) {
```

Listing 11.12 The LoginAction. (continues)

```
        System.err.println(sqle.getMessage());
      }
      conn = null;
    }
  }
  return user;
}

public ActionForward execute(ActionMapping mapping,
  ActionForm form,
  HttpServletRequest request,
  HttpServletResponse response)
  throws IOException, ServletException {

  String user = null;

  // Default target to success
  String target = "success";

  // Use the LoginForm to get the request parameters
  String username = ((LoginForm)form).getUsername();
  String password = ((LoginForm)form).getPassword();

  user = getUser(username, password);

  // Set the target to failure
  if ( user == null ) {

    target = "login";
    ActionErrors errors = new ActionErrors();

    errors.add(ActionErrors.GLOBAL_ERROR,
      new ActionError("errors.login.unknown",
                      username));

    // Report any errors we have discovered back to the
    // original form
    if (!errors.empty()) {

      saveErrors(request, errors);
    }
  }
  else {

    HttpSession session = request.getSession();
    session.setAttribute("USER", user);
```

Listing 11.12 The LoginAction. (continues)

```
    }
    // Forward to the appropriate View
    return (mapping.findForward(target));
  }
}
```

Listing 11.12 The LoginAction. (continued)

The EmployeeListAction

Once the LoginAction has added the USER session attribute, then the EmployeeListAction.execute() method is invoked. The EmployeeListAction is used to retrieve all of the employees currently contained in the employees database.

If the employees are successfully retrieved from the employees database, then an Employee object (which was described in the section "Creating the Employees Model," earlier in this chapter) is created and populated with the contents of each returned row. Each one of these Employee objects is added to an ArrayList. The ArrayList is then added to the request, and the request is forwarded to the success target—which in this case is the employeelist.jsp. If the EmployeeListAction encounters errors, then an ActionError is created, and the results are forwarded to the failure target, which is the login.jsp. The source for the EmployeeListAction can be found in Listing 11.13.

```
package com.wiley;

import java.io.IOException;
import javax.servlet.ServletException;
import javax.servlet.ServletContext;
import javax.servlet.http.HttpServletRequest;
import javax.servlet.http.HttpServletResponse;
import javax.servlet.http.HttpSession;
import org.apache.struts.action.Action;
import org.apache.struts.action.ActionForm;
import org.apache.struts.action.ActionForward;
import org.apache.struts.action.ActionMapping;
import org.apache.struts.action.ActionErrors;
import org.apache.struts.action.ActionError;

import javax.sql.DataSource;
import java.sql.Connection;
import java.sql.Statement;
import java.sql.ResultSet;
```

Listing 11.13 EmployeeListAction.java. (continues)

```
import java.sql.SQLException;
import java.util.HashMap;
import java.util.ArrayList;

public class EmployeeListAction extends Action {

  protected ArrayList getEmployees() {

    Employee employee = null;
    ArrayList employees = new ArrayList();
    Connection conn = null;
    Statement stmt = null;
    ResultSet rs = null;

    ServletContext context = servlet.getServletContext();
    DataSource dataSource = (DataSource)
      context.getAttribute(Action.DATA_SOURCE_KEY);

    try {

      conn = dataSource.getConnection();
      stmt = conn.createStatement();
      rs =
        stmt.executeQuery("select * from employees, roles, "
        + "departments where employees.roleid=roles.roleid "
        + "and employees.depid=departments.depid");

      while ( rs.next() ) {

        employee = new Employee();

        employee.setUsername(rs.getString("username"));
        employee.setName(rs.getString("name"));
        employee.setRolename(rs.getString("rolename"));
        employee.setPhone(rs.getString("phone"));
        employee.setEmail(rs.getString("email"));
        employee.setRoleid(new Integer(rs.getInt("roleid")));
        employee.setDepid(new Integer(rs.getInt("depid")));
        employee.setDepartment(rs.getString("depname"));

        employees.add(employee);

        System.err.println("Username : "
          + employee.getUsername()
          + " Department : " + rs.getString("depname"));
      }
    }
    catch (SQLException e) {
```

Listing 11.13 EmployeeListAction.java. (continues)

```
      System.err.println(e.getMessage());
    }
    finally {

      if (rs != null) {

        try {

          rs.close();
        }
        catch (SQLException sqle) {

          System.err.println(sqle.getMessage());
        }
        rs = null;
      }
      if (stmt != null) {

        try {

          stmt.close();
        }
        catch (SQLException sqle) {

          System.err.println(sqle.getMessage());
        }
        stmt = null;
      }
      if (conn != null) {

        try {

          conn.close();
        }
        catch (SQLException sqle) {

          System.err.println(sqle.getMessage());
        }
        conn = null;
      }
    }
    return employees;
  }

  public ActionForward execute(ActionMapping mapping,
    ActionForm form,
    HttpServletRequest request,
    HttpServletResponse response)
    throws IOException, ServletException {
```

Listing 11.13 EmployeeListAction.java. (continues)

```
    // Default target to success
    String target = "success";

    EmployeesActionMapping employeesMapping =
      (EmployeesActionMapping)mapping;

    // Does this action require the user to login
    if ( employeesMapping.isLoginRequired() ) {

      HttpSession session = request.getSession();
      if ( session.getAttribute("USER") == null ) {

        // The user is not logged in
        target = "login";
        ActionErrors errors = new ActionErrors();

        errors.add(ActionErrors.GLOBAL_ERROR,
          new ActionError("errors.login.required"));

        // Report any errors we have discovered back to
        // the original form
        if (!errors.empty()) {

          saveErrors(request, errors);
        }
        return (mapping.findForward(target));
      }
    }

    ArrayList employees = null;

    employees = getEmployees();

    // Set the target to failure
    if ( employees == null ) {

      target = new String("login");
    }
    else {

      request.setAttribute("employees", employees);
    }

      // Forward to the appropriate View
       return (mapping.findForward(target));
      }
}
```

Listing 11.13 EmployeeListAction.java. (continued)

As you look over the EmployeeListAction, you will notice that it is relatively ordinary, except for one section of code. This section, found at the beginning of the EmployeeListAction.execute() method, is shown in the following code snippet:

```
EmployeesActionMapping employeesMapping =
  (EmployeesActionMapping)mapping;

// Does this action require the user to login
if ( employeesMapping.isLoginRequired() ) {

  HttpSession session = request.getSession();
  if ( session.getAttribute("USER") == null ) {

    // The user is not logged in
    target = new String("login");
    ActionErrors errors = new ActionErrors();

    errors.add(ActionErrors.GLOBAL_ERROR,
      new ActionError("errors.login.required"));

    // Report any errors we have discovered back to
    // the original form
    if (!errors.empty()) {

      saveErrors(request, errors);
    }
  }
}
```

You will see this section of code at the beginning of all of our Action classes except the LoginAction. This bit of code checks the custom ActionMapping, EmployeesActionMapping, to determine whether this transaction requires that the user be logged in. If the employeesMapping.isLoginReuired() method returns true, then the user must be logged in to perform this Action. If users are not logged in, they are forwarded to the login.jsp screen.

NOTE

You will see how the EmployeesActionMapping is applied to each transaction as we deploy each Action in the struts-config.xml file.

The Employee List JSP

The Employee List JSP is used to display all of the employees stored in the employees database. The Employees List View is a simple JSP that takes an ArrayList of Employee objects (forwarded by the EmployeeListAction, as described earlier) and iterates over them, printing the contents of each Employee object to the output stream. This View also presents the user with the ability to initiate an edit or deletion of an employee. The source for the employeelist.jsp appears in Listing 11.14.

```
<%@ taglib uri="/WEB-INF/struts-bean.tld" prefix="bean" %>
<%@ taglib uri="/WEB-INF/struts-logic.tld" prefix="logic" %>

<logic:notPresent name="USER">
  <logic:forward name="login" />
</logic:notPresent>

<html>
  <head>
    <title><bean:message key="app.title" /></title>
  </head>
  <body>

    <table width="650"
      border="0" cellspacing="0" cellpadding="0">
      <tr>
        <td colspan="7"> </td>
      </tr>
      <tr bgcolor="#36566E">
        <td  colspan="7" height="68" width="48%">
          <div align="left">
            <img src="images/hp_logo_wiley.gif"
            width="220" height="74">
          </div>
        </td>
      </tr>
      <tr>
        <td colspan="7"> </td>
      </tr>
    </table>

    <html:errors />

    <table width="650"
      border="0" cellspacing="0" cellpadding="0">
      <tr align="left">
        <th><bean:message key="app.username" /></th>
        <th><bean:message key="app.name" /></th>
        <th><bean:message key="app.phone" /></th>
        <th><bean:message key="app.email" /></th>
        <th><bean:message key="app.department" /></th>
        <th><bean:message key="app.role" /></th>
```

Listing 11.14 The employeelist.jsp. (continues)

```
      </tr>
      <!-- iterate over the results of the query -->
      <logic:iterate id="employee" name="employees">
      <tr align="left">
        <td>
         <bean:write name="employee" property="username" />
        </td>
        <td>
         <bean:write name="employee" property="name" />
        </td>
        <td>
         <bean:write name="employee" property="phone" />
        </td>
        <td>
         <bean:write name="employee" property="email" />
        </td>
        <td>
         <bean:write name="employee" property="department" />
        </td>
        <td>
         <bean:write name="employee" property="rolename" />
        </td>
        <td>
         <a href="Edit.do?username=<bean:write
           name="employee" property="username" />">Edit</a>
          <a href="Delete.do?username=<bean:write
           name="employee" property="username" />">Delete</a>
        </td>
      </tr>
      </logic:iterate>
      <tr>
        <td colspan="7">
        <hr>
      </td>
      </tr>
    </table>
    <font size="-1" face="arial">
      <a href="addemployee.jsp">Add New Employee</a>
    </font>

  </body>
</html>
```

Listing 11.14 The employeelist.jsp. (continued)

As you look over the source for the Employee List View, pay close attention to the text in boldface, particularly the occurrences of the <logic:notPresent /> and the <logic:iterate /> tags.

NOTE

You can find more information about both the <logic:notPresent /> and the <logic:iterate /> tags in Chapter 15, "Logic Tag Library."

The first of these tags, <logic:notPresent />, is used to determine if an attribute exists in the named scope. We use this tag to ensure that the user is logged in; it tests for the existence of the USER attribute in the session. If this attribute does not exist in the session, then the body of this tag is evaluated, which results in the request being forwarded to the login screen.

The second of these tags, <logic:iterate />, is used to iterate over the ArrayList forwarded to the employeelist.jsp by the EmployeeListAction.

Deploying the Components of the Login Transaction

Now that we've defined all of the components of the Login transaction, we need to deploy them to our employees application. Listing 11.15 contains the struts-config.xml file at this point, including the changes necessary to deploy the Login and Employee List components.

```
<?xml version="1.0" encoding="ISO-8859-1" ?>

<!DOCTYPE struts-config PUBLIC
  "-//Apache Software Foundation//DTD Struts Configuration 1.1//EN"
  "http://jakarta.apache.org/struts/dtds/struts-config_1_1.dtd">

<struts-config>

  <data-sources>
    <data-source>
      <set-property property="driverClass"
        value="org.gjt.mm.mysql.Driver" />
      <set-property property="url"
        value="jdbc:mysql://localhost/employees" />
      <set-property property="maxCount"
        value="5"/>
      <set-property property="minCount"
        value="1"/>
      <set-property property="user"
        value="username"/>
```

Listing 11.15 Our web.xml file after we added the Login and Employee List components. (continues)

```
      <set-property property="password"
        value="password"/>
    </data-source>
  </data-sources>

  <form-beans>
    <form-bean name="loginForm"
      type="com.wiley.LoginForm" />
  </form-beans>

  <global-forwards>
    <forward name="login" path="/login.jsp"/>
  </global-forwards>

  <action-mappings>

    <action path="/Login"
      type="com.wiley.LoginAction"
      validate="true"
      input="/login.jsp"
      name="loginForm"
      scope="request" >
      <forward name="success" path="/EmployeeList.do"/>
    </action>

    <action path="/EmployeeList"
      type="com.wiley.EmployeeListAction"
      scope="request" >
      <set-property property="loginRequired" value="true"/>
      <forward name="success" path="/employeelist.jsp"/>
    </action>

  </action-mappings>

  <message-resources
    parameter="com.wiley.ApplicationResources"/>
</struts-config>
```

Listing 11.15 Our web.xml file after we added the Login and Employee List components. (continued)

Once you've looked over the new struts-config.xml file, notice that it looks very similar to any other struts-config.xml file, except for two lines of code. The first of these two lines is the forward subelement of the <action> element that defines the instance of the LoginAction. This subelement is shown in the following code snippet:

```
<forward name="success" path="/EmployeeList.do"/>
```

This <forward> subelement is very similar to most <forward> subelements, with the exception of the value of the path attribute. This value has the string *.do* appended to its end. We must do this because the target is not being constructed from the <html:form /> tag, which appends this string automatically.

NOTE

This is a good example of how you can chain Actions together by specifying the <forward> path of one Action using the path of another Action with *.do* appended to it.

The second line we want to point out contains the <set-property> subelement of the EmployeeList action. This subelement appears in the following code snippet:

```
<set-property property="loginRequired" value="true"/>
```

The <set-property> subelement is used to set the loginRequired data member of the EmployeesActionMapping we defined earlier. In this case, we are saying that the user must be logged in to perform the EmployeeListAction.

The Add Employee Transaction

The Add Employee transaction is used to add employees to the employees database. It is initiated when a user selects the Add New Employee link from the employeelist.jsp. When this link is selected, the Add Employee transaction presents its components in the following order:

1. Add Employee JSP
2. EmployeeForm
3. AddEmployeeAction
4. EmployeeListAction
5. Employee List JSP

The Add Employee JSP

The Add Employee View, represented by the JSP addemployee.jsp, is used to retrieve the values of the new employee being added to the employees database. The code for the addemployee.jsp appears in Listing 11.16.

```
<%@ page language="java" %>
<%@ taglib uri="/WEB-INF/struts-html.tld" prefix="html" %>
<%@ taglib uri="/WEB-INF/struts-bean.tld" prefix="bean" %>

<html>
  <head>
    <title><bean:message key="app.title" /></title>
  </head>

  <body>
    <table width="500"
      border="0" cellspacing="0" cellpadding="0">
      <tr>
        <td> </td>
      </tr>
      <tr bgcolor="#36566E">
        <td height="68" width="48%">
          <div align="left">
            <img src="images/hp_logo_wiley.gif"
               width="220"
             height="74">
          </div>
        </td>
      </tr>
      <tr>
        <td> </td>
      </tr>
    </table>

    <html:errors />

    <html:form action="/Add"
      name="employeeForm"
      type="com.wiley.EmployeeForm" >
      <table width="500" border="0">
        <tr>
          <td><bean:message key="app.username" />:</td>
          <td><html:text property="username" /></td>
          <td><bean:message key="app.password" />:</td>
          <td><html:text property="password" /></td>
        </tr>
        <tr>
          <td><bean:message key="app.name" />:</td>
```

Listing 11.16 The Add Employee View. (continues)

```
          <td><html:text property="name" /></td>
          <td><bean:message key="app.phone" />:</td>
          <td><html:text property="phone" /></td>
        </tr>
        <tr>
          <td><bean:message key="app.email" />:</td>
          <td><html:text property="email" /></td>
          <td><bean:message key="app.department" />:</td>
        <td>
          <html:select property="depid" size="1">
            <html:option value="1">
             <bean:message key="app.administration" />
            </html:option>
            <html:option value="2">
              <bean:message key="app.network" />
            </html:option>
            <html:option value="3">
              <bean:message key="app.sales" />
            </html:option>
             <html:option value="4">
              <bean:message key="app.engineering" />
            </html:option>
            </html:select>
          </td>
        </tr>
        <tr>
          <td><bean:message key="app.role" />:</td>
        <td>
          <html:select property="roleid" size="1">
            <html:option value="1">
              <bean:message key="app.manager" />
            </html:option>
              <html:option value="2">
              <bean:message key="app.employee" />
            </html:option>
          </html:select>
        </td>
        <td colspan="2" align="center">
          <html:submit /><html:cancel /><html:reset />
        </td>
      </tr>
    </table>
  </html:form>

  </body>
</html>
```

Listing 11.16 The Add Employee View. (continued)

The EmployeeForm

Now that you have seen the JSP that will submit the new employee values, we must create an ActionForm that will validate and encapsulate these new employee values. Listing 11.17 contains the code for the EmployeeForm.

NOTE

The EmployeeForm is used by both the Add and Edit Employee transactions.

```
package com.wiley;

import javax.servlet.http.HttpServletRequest;
import javax.servlet.http.HttpSession;
import org.apache.struts.action.ActionForm;
import org.apache.struts.action.ActionMapping;
import org.apache.struts.action.ActionErrors;
import org.apache.struts.action.ActionError;

public class EmployeeForm extends ActionForm {

  protected String username;
  protected String password;
  protected String name;
  protected String phone;
  protected String email;
  protected String depid;
  protected String roleid;

  public void setUsername(String username) {

    this.username = username;
  }

  public String getUsername() {

    return username;
  }

  public void setPassword(String password) {

    this.password = password;
  }

  public String getPassword() {
```

Listing 11.17 The EmployeeForm.java. (continues)

```
    return password;
  }

  public void setName(String name) {

    this.name = name;
  }

  public String getName() {

    return name;
  }

  public void setPhone(String phone) {

    this.phone = phone;
  }

  public String getPhone() {

    return phone;
  }

  public void setEmail(String email) {

    this.email = email;
  }

  public String getEmail() {

    return email;
  }

  public void setDepid(String depid) {

    this.depid = depid;
  }

  public String getDepid() {

    return depid;
  }

  public void setRoleid(String roleid) {

    this.roleid = roleid;
```

Listing 11.17 The EmployeeForm.java. (continues)

```
  }

  public String getRoleid() {

    return roleid;
  }

  public void reset(ActionMapping mapping,
    HttpServletRequest request) {

    this.username = "";
    this.password = "";
    this.name = "";
    this.phone = "";
    this.email = "";
    this.depid = "1";
    this.roleid = "1";
  }

  public ActionErrors validate(ActionMapping mapping,
    HttpServletRequest request) {

    ActionErrors errors = new ActionErrors();

    EmployeesActionMapping employeesMapping =
      (EmployeesActionMapping)mapping;

    // Does this action require the user to login
    if ( employeesMapping.isLoginRequired() ) {

      HttpSession session = request.getSession();
      if ( session.getAttribute("USER") == null ) {

        // return null to force action to handle login
        // error
        return null;
      }
    }

    if ( (roleid == null ) || (roleid.length() == 0) ) {

      errors.add("roleid",
        new ActionError("errors.roleid.required"));
    }
    if ( (depid == null ) || (depid.length() == 0) ) {

      errors.add("depid",
```

Listing 11.17 The EmployeeForm.java. (continues)

```
        new ActionError("errors.depid.required"));
    }
    if ( (email == null ) || (email.length() == 0) ) {

      errors.add("email",
        new ActionError("errors.email.required"));
    }
    if ( (phone == null ) || (phone.length() == 0) ) {

      errors.add("phone",
        new ActionError("errors.phone.required"));
    }
    if ( (name == null ) || (name.length() == 0) ) {

      errors.add("name",
        new ActionError("errors.name.required"));
    }
    if ( (password == null ) || (password.length() == 0) ) {

      errors.add("password",
        new ActionError("errors.password.required"));
    }
    if ( (username == null ) || (username.length() == 0) ) {

      errors.add("username",
        new ActionError("errors.username.required"));
    }
    return errors;
  }
}
```

Listing 11.17 The EmployeeForm.java. (continued)

There's really nothing special about the EmployeeForm.java: It provides accessors to data members that map to the values submitted by the Add Employee View, and it performs some simple validation of those values. If the values pass the validation, then the transaction continues; otherwise, ActionErrors are created and the request is forwarded back to the addemployee.jsp, which is named by the input attribute of the AddEmployeeAction definition.

The AddEmployeeAction

The AddEmployeeAction is a very simple Struts Action. After making sure that the user is logged in, this Action takes the values submitted in the EmployeeForm object and inserts them into the employees database as a new employee record.

If the insert is successful, then the request is forwarded to the Employee ListAction, which retrieves all of the employees from the database—including the newly inserted record—and forwards the results to the employeelist.jsp for display. You can see the code for the AddEmployeeAction in Listing 11.18.

```
package com.wiley;

import java.io.IOException;
import javax.servlet.ServletContext;
import javax.servlet.ServletException;
import javax.servlet.http.HttpServletRequest;
import javax.servlet.http.HttpServletResponse;
import javax.servlet.http.HttpSession;
import org.apache.struts.action.Action;
import org.apache.struts.action.ActionForm;
import org.apache.struts.action.ActionForward;
import org.apache.struts.action.ActionMapping;
import org.apache.struts.action.ActionErrors;
import org.apache.struts.action.ActionError;

import javax.sql.DataSource;
import java.sql.Connection;
import java.sql.Statement;
import java.sql.ResultSet;
import java.sql.SQLException;

public class AddEmployeeAction extends Action {

  protected void insertUser(ActionForm form)
    throws Exception {

    String user = null;
    Connection conn = null;
    Statement stmt = null;
    ResultSet rs = null;

    ServletContext context = servlet.getServletContext();
    DataSource dataSource = (DataSource)
      context.getAttribute(Action.DATA_SOURCE_KEY);

    try {

      EmployeeForm eForm = (EmployeeForm)form;
      conn = dataSource.getConnection();
      stmt = conn.createStatement();

      StringBuffer sqlString =
```

Listing 11.18 The AddEmployeeAction.java. (continues)

```
        new StringBuffer("insert into employees ");

      sqlString.append("values (\""
        + eForm.getUsername() + "\", ");
      sqlString.append("\"" +
        eForm.getPassword() + "\", ");
      sqlString.append("\""
        + eForm.getRoleid() + "\", ");
      sqlString.append("\""
        + eForm.getName() + "\", ");
      sqlString.append("\""
        + eForm.getPhone() + "\", ");
      sqlString.append("\""
        + eForm.getEmail() + "\", ");
      sqlString.append("\""
        + eForm.getDepid() + "\")");

      stmt.execute(sqlString.toString());
    }
    finally {

      if (rs != null) {

          rs.close();
      }
      if (stmt != null) {

          stmt.close();
      }
      if (conn != null) {

          conn.close();
      }
    }
  }

  public ActionForward execute(ActionMapping mapping,
    ActionForm form,
    HttpServletRequest request,
    HttpServletResponse response)
    throws IOException, ServletException {

    // Default target to success
    String target = "success";

    EmployeesActionMapping employeesMapping =
      (EmployeesActionMapping)mapping;
```

Listing 11.18 The AddEmployeeAction.java. (continues)

```
    // Does this action require the user to login
    if ( employeesMapping.isLoginRequired() ) {

      HttpSession session = request.getSession();
      if ( session.getAttribute("USER") == null ) {

        // The user is not logged in
        target = "login";
        ActionErrors errors = new ActionErrors();

        errors.add(ActionErrors.GLOBAL_ERROR,
          new ActionError("errors.login.required"));

        // Report any errors we have discovered back
        // to the original form
        if (!errors.empty()) {

          saveErrors(request, errors);
        }
        return (mapping.findForward(target));
      }
    }

    if ( isCancelled(request) ) {

      // Cancel pressed back to employee list
      return (mapping.findForward("success"));
    }

    try {

      insertUser(form);
    }
    catch (Exception e) {

      System.err.println("Setting target to error");
      target = "error";
      ActionErrors errors = new ActionErrors();

      errors.add(ActionErrors.GLOBAL_ERROR,
        new ActionError("errors.database.error",
        e.getMessage()));

      // Report any errors
      if (!errors.empty()) {
```

Listing 11.18 The AddEmployeeAction.java. (continues)

```
        saveErrors(request, errors);
      }
    }
    // Forward to the appropriate View
    return (mapping.findForward(target));
  }
}
```

Listing 11.18 The AddEmployeeAction.java. (continued)

Deploying the Components of the Add Employee Transaction

Once the components of the Add Employee transaction are defined, we can deploy them to our employees application. Listing 11.19 contains our struts-config.xml file at this point, including the changes necessary to deploy the Add Employee components.

```
<?xml version="1.0" encoding="ISO-8859-1" ?>

<!DOCTYPE struts-config PUBLIC
  "-//Apache Software Foundation//DTD Struts Configuration 1.1//EN"
  "http://jakarta.apache.org/struts/dtds/struts-config_1_1.dtd">

<struts-config>

  <data-sources>
    <data-source>
      <set-property property="driverClass"
        value="org.gjt.mm.mysql.Driver" />
      <set-property property="url"
        value="jdbc:mysql://localhost/employees" />
      <set-property property="maxCount"
        value="5"/>
      <set-property property="minCount"
        value="1"/>
      <set-property property="user"
        value="username"/>
      <set-property property="password"
        value="password"/>
    </data-source>
  </data-sources>

  <form-beans>
```

Listing 11.19 Our web.xml file after we added the Login and Employee List components. (continues)

```
    <form-bean name="loginForm"
      type="com.wiley.LoginForm" />
    <form-bean name="employeeForm"
      type="com.wiley.EmployeeForm" />
  </form-beans>

  <global-forwards>
    <forward name="login" path="/login.jsp"/>
  </global-forwards>

  <action-mappings>

    <action path="/Login"
      type="com.wiley.LoginAction"
      validate="true"
      input="/login.jsp"
      name="loginForm"
      scope="request" >
      <forward name="success" path="/EmployeeList.do"/>
    </action>

    <action path="/EmployeeList"
      type="com.wiley.EmployeeListAction"
      scope="request" >
      <set-property property="loginRequired" value="true"/>
      <forward name="success" path="/employeelist.jsp"/>
    </action>

    <action path="/Add"
      type="com.wiley.AddEmployeeAction"
      name="employeeForm"
      scope="request"
      input="/addemployee.jsp"
      validate="true" >
      <set-property property="loginRequired" value="true"/>
      <forward name="success" path="/EmployeeList.do"/>
      <forward name="error" path="/addemployee.jsp"/>
    </action>

  </action-mappings>

  <message-resources
    parameter="com.wiley.ApplicationResources"/>

</struts-config>
```

Listing 11.19 Our web.xml file after we added the Login and Employee List components. (continued)

In Listing 11.19, notice that we added two new subelements. The first is a new <form-bean> subelement named employeeForm, which references the com.wiley.EmployeeForm object. This subelement tells the application that we want to use the EmployeeForm when performing an AddEmployee Action.

The second subelement we added to the struts-config.xml file actually defines the AddEmployeeAction. The only thing to note about this entry is that the success target, like the LoginAction, is the EmployeeList.do, which will cause the updated list of employees to be displayed.

The Edit Employee Transaction

The Edit Employee transaction is used to modify employees that currently exist in the employees database. It is initiated when a user selects an Edit link from the employeelist.jsp. When this link is selected, the Edit Employee transaction presents its components in the following order:

1. GetEmployeeAction
2. Edit Employee JSP
3. EmployeeForm
4. EditEmployeeAction
5. EmployeeListAction
6. Employee List JSP

The GetEmployeeAction

The GetEmployeeAction is the first Action that is invoked in the Edit Employee transaction. It is invoked from the employeelist.jsp using the following code snippet:

```
<a href="Edit.do?username=<bean:write name="employee"
  property="username" />">Edit</a>
```

As you will notice, this link executes a get request to the Edit.do path with the request parameter username set to the username to be edited. The purpose of the GetEmployeeAction is to retrieve the selected employee from the database and populate an EmployeeForm with the retrieved values. This allows the editemployee.jsp—which is the successful target of the GetEmployeeAction—to prepopulate the input elements of the <html:form /> with the values of the created EmployeeForm object. The code for the GetEmployeeAction object is shown in Listing 11.20.

```
package com.wiley;

import java.io.IOException;
import javax.servlet.ServletException;
import javax.servlet.http.HttpServletRequest;
import javax.servlet.http.HttpServletResponse;
import javax.servlet.http.HttpSession;
import org.apache.struts.action.Action;
import org.apache.struts.action.ActionForm;
import org.apache.struts.action.ActionForward;
import org.apache.struts.action.ActionMapping;
import org.apache.struts.action.ActionErrors;
import org.apache.struts.action.ActionError;

import javax.sql.DataSource;
import java.sql.Connection;
import java.sql.Statement;
import java.sql.ResultSet;
import java.sql.SQLException;

public class GetEmployeeAction extends Action {

  protected ActionForm buildEmployeeForm(String username)
    throws Exception {

    String user = null;
    Connection conn = null;
    Statement stmt = null;
    ResultSet rs = null;
    EmployeeForm form = null;

    DataSource dataSource = (DataSource)
      servlet.getServletContext().getAttribute(Action.DATA_SOURCE_KEY);

    try {

      conn = dataSource.getConnection();
      stmt = conn.createStatement();
      rs =
        stmt.executeQuery("select * from employees "
        + "where username='"
        + username + "'");

      if ( rs.next() ) {
```

Listing 11.20 The GetEmployeeAction.java file. (continues)

```
        form = new EmployeeForm();

        form.setUsername(rs.getString("username"));
        form.setPassword(rs.getString("password"));
        form.setDepid(rs.getString("depid"));
        form.setRoleid(rs.getString("roleid"));

        form.setName(rs.getString("name"));
        form.setPhone(rs.getString("phone"));
        form.setEmail(rs.getString("email"));
      }
      else {

        throw new Exception("Employee " + username
          + " not found!");
      }
    }
    finally {

      if (rs != null) {

        rs.close();
      }
      if (stmt != null) {

        stmt.close();
      }
      if (conn != null) {

        conn.close();
      }
    }
    return form;
  }

  public ActionForward execute(ActionMapping mapping,
    ActionForm form,
    HttpServletRequest request,
    HttpServletResponse response)
    throws IOException, ServletException {

    // Default target to success
    String target = "success";

    EmployeesActionMapping employeesMapping =
      (EmployeesActionMapping)mapping;
```

Listing 11.20 The GetEmployeeAction.java file. (continues)

```
    // Does this action require the user to login
    if ( employeesMapping.isLoginRequired() ) {

      HttpSession session = request.getSession();
      if ( session.getAttribute("USER") == null ) {

        // The user is not logged in
        target = "login";
        ActionErrors errors = new ActionErrors();

        errors.add(ActionErrors.GLOBAL_ERROR,
          new ActionError("errors.login.required"));

        // Report any errors we have discovered back to the
        // original form
        if (!errors.empty()) {

          saveErrors(request, errors);
        }
   return (mapping.findForward(target));
      }
    }

    if ( isCancelled(request) ) {

      // Cancel pressed back to employee list
      return (mapping.findForward(target));
    }

    try {

      // Build the EmployeeForm with the Retrieved values
      form =
        buildEmployeeForm(request.getParameter("username"));

      // Add the form to the request or session, bound to the
      // key named in the <action> attribute name
      if ("request".equals(mapping.getScope())) {

        request.setAttribute(mapping.getAttribute(), form);
      }
      else {

        HttpSession session = request.getSession();
        session.setAttribute(mapping.getAttribute(), form);
      }
    }
```

Listing 11.20 The GetEmployeeAction.java file. (continues)

```
    catch (Exception e) {

      target = "error";
      ActionErrors errors = new ActionErrors();

      errors.add(ActionErrors.GLOBAL_ERROR,
        new ActionError("errors.database.error",
        e.getMessage()));

      // Report any errors
      if (!errors.empty()) {

        saveErrors(request, errors);
      }
    }
    // Forward to the appropriate View
    return (mapping.findForward(target));
  }
}
```

Listing 11.20 The GetEmployeeAction.java file. (continued)

The GetEmployeeAction begins its processing—just like any other Action class—with the execute() method. It first makes sure the user is logged in and then verifies that the Action was not cancelled.

At this point, the GetEmployeeAction is ready to perform its specific logic. It begins by invoking the buildEmployeeForm() method, which retrieves the employee with the passed-in username, creates and populates an EmployeeForm object, and returns the newly created form to the execute() method.

The execute() method then determines where the EmployeeForm object should be stored by using the ActionMapping.getScope() method. Once the Action has this information, it then retrieves the name attribute of the <action> element and adds the EmployeeForm bound to the retrieved name to the appropriate scope. This logic is performed using the following code snippet:

```
// Build the EmployeeForm with the Retrieved values
form =
  buildEmployeeForm(request.getParameter("username"));

// Add the form to the request or session, bound to the
// key named in the <action> attribute name
if ("request".equals(mapping.getScope())) {

  request.setAttribute(mapping.getAttribute(), form);
}
else {
```

```
    HttpSession session = request.getSession();
    session.setAttribute(mapping.getAttribute(), form);
  }
```

Once the EmployeeForm is added to the appropriate object (the request or the session), the execute() method forwards the request to the success target, which in this case will be the editemployee.jsp. At this point, either the request or the session should contain an EmployeeForm instance with the values retrieved from the employees database.

The Edit Employee JSP

The Edit Employee View, represented by the JSP editemployee.jsp, is used to modify the values of the selected employee. The editemployee.jsp presents the user with an HTML form that should be prepopulated by the GetEmployeeAction described previously. When users have completed their modifications they click the Submit button, and the modified values, stored in an EmployeeForm instance, are submitted to the EditEmployeeAction. The code for the editemployee.jsp appears in Listing 11.21.

```
<%@ page language="java" %>
<%@ taglib uri="/WEB-INF/struts-html.tld" prefix="html" %>
<%@ taglib uri="/WEB-INF/struts-bean.tld" prefix="bean" %>

<html>
  <head>
    <title><bean:message key="app.title" /></title>
  </head>

  <body>
    <table width="500"
      border="0" cellspacing="0" cellpadding="0">
      <tr>
        <td> </td>
      </tr>
      <tr bgcolor="#36566E">
        <td height="68" width="48%">
          <div align="left">
            <img src="images/hp_logo_wiley.gif"
               width="220"
             height="74">
          </div>
        </td>
      </tr>
```

Listing 11.21 The Edit Employee View. (continues)

```
    <tr>
      <td> </td>
    </tr>
  </table>

  <html:errors />

  <html:form action="/EditEmployee"
    name="employeeForm"
    type="com.wiley.EmployeeForm"
    scope="request" >
    <table width="500" border="0">
      <tr>
        <td><bean:message key="app.username" />:</td>
        <td><html:text property="username" /></td>
        <td><bean:message key="app.password" />:</td>
        <td><html:password property="password" /></td>
      </tr>
      <tr>
        <td><bean:message key="app.name" />:</td>
        <td><html:text property="name" /></td>
        <td><bean:message key="app.phone" />:</td>
        <td><html:text property="phone" /></td>
      </tr>
      <tr>
        <td><bean:message key="app.email" />:</td>
        <td><html:text property="email" /></td>
        <td><bean:message key="app.department" />:</td>
      <td>

        <html:select property="depid" size="1">
            <html:option value="1">
            <bean:message key="app.administration" />
          </html:option>
            <html:option value="2">
            <bean:message key="app.network" />
          </html:option>
            <html:option value="3">
            <bean:message key="app.sales" />
          </html:option>
            <html:option value="4">
            <bean:message key="app.engineering" />
          </html:option>
          </html:select>

        </td>
      </tr>
```

Listing 11.21 The Edit Employee View. (continues)

```
        <tr>
          <td>
            <bean:message key="app.role" />:
          </td>
        <td>
          <html:select property="roleid" size="1">
            <html:option value="1">
              <bean:message key="app.manager" />
            </html:option>
            <html:option value="2">
              <bean:message key="app.employee" />
            </html:option>
          </html:select>

        </td>
        <td colspan="2" align="center">
          <html:submit />
          <html:cancel />
          <html:reset />
        </td>
      </tr>
    </table>
  </html:form>

  </body>
</html>
```

Listing 11.21 The Edit Employee View. (continued)

The EmployeeForm

The EmployeeForm object used in the Edit Employee transaction is the same EmployeeForm used by the Add Employee transaction.

The EditEmployeeAction

The EditEmployeeAction is a very basic Struts Action that takes the submitted employee values from the editemployee.jsp View and performs a SQL update on the record with the matching username. Listing 11.22 shows the code for the EditEmployeeAction object.

```
package com.wiley;

import java.io.IOException;
```

Listing 11.22 The EditEmployeeAction. (continues)

```
import javax.servlet.ServletContext;
import javax.servlet.ServletException;
import javax.servlet.http.HttpServletRequest;
import javax.servlet.http.HttpServletResponse;
import javax.servlet.http.HttpSession;
import org.apache.struts.action.Action;
import org.apache.struts.action.ActionForm;
import org.apache.struts.action.ActionForward;
import org.apache.struts.action.ActionMapping;
import org.apache.struts.action.ActionErrors;
import org.apache.struts.action.ActionError;

import javax.sql.DataSource;
import java.sql.Connection;
import java.sql.Statement;
import java.sql.ResultSet;
import java.sql.SQLException;

public class EditEmployeeAction extends Action {

  protected void updateUser(ActionForm form)
    throws Exception {

    String user = null;
    Connection conn = null;
    Statement stmt = null;
    ResultSet rs = null;

    ServletContext context = servlet.getServletContext();
    DataSource dataSource = (DataSource)
      context.getAttribute(Action.DATA_SOURCE_KEY);

    try {

      EmployeeForm eForm = (EmployeeForm)form;
      conn = dataSource.getConnection();
      stmt = conn.createStatement();

      StringBuffer sqlString =
        new StringBuffer("update employees ");

      sqlString.append("set password='"
        + eForm.getPassword() + "', ");
      sqlString.append("roleid="
        + eForm.getRoleid() + ", ");
      sqlString.append("name='"
        + eForm.getName() + "', ");
```

Listing 11.22 The EditEmployeeAction. (continues)

```
      sqlString.append("phone='"
        + eForm.getPhone() + "', ");
      sqlString.append("email='"
        + eForm.getEmail() + "', ");
      sqlString.append("depid="
        + eForm.getDepid());
      sqlString.append(" where username='"
        + eForm.getUsername() + "'");

      stmt.execute(sqlString.toString());
    }
    finally {

      if (rs != null) {

        rs.close();
      }
      if (stmt != null) {

        stmt.close();
      }
      if (conn != null) {

        conn.close();
      }
    }
  }

  public ActionForward execute(ActionMapping mapping,
    ActionForm form,
    HttpServletRequest request,
    HttpServletResponse response)
    throws IOException, ServletException {

    // Default target to success
    String target = "success";

    EmployeesActionMapping employeesMapping =
      (EmployeesActionMapping)mapping;

    // Does this action require the user to login
    if ( employeesMapping.isLoginRequired() ) {

      HttpSession session = request.getSession();
      if ( session.getAttribute("USER") == null ) {

        // The user is not logged in
```

Listing 11.22 The EditEmployeeAction. (continues)

```
        target = new "login";
        ActionErrors errors = new ActionErrors();

        errors.add(ActionErrors.GLOBAL_ERROR,
          new ActionError("errors.login.required"));

        // Report any errors we have discovered
        //back to the original form
        if (!errors.empty()) {

          saveErrors(request, errors);
        }
        return (mapping.findForward(target));

      }
    }

    if ( isCancelled(request) ) {

      // Cancel pressed back to employee list
      return (mapping.findForward("success"));
    }

    try {

      updateUser(form);
    }
    catch (Exception e) {

      System.err.println("Setting target to error");
      target = "error";
      ActionErrors errors = new ActionErrors();

      errors.add(ActionErrors.GLOBAL_ERROR,
        new ActionError("errors.database.error",
          e.getMessage()));

      // Report any errors
      if (!errors.empty()) {

        saveErrors(request, errors);
      }
    }
    // Forward to the appropriate View
    return (mapping.findForward(target));
  }
}
```

Listing 11.22 The EditEmployeeAction. (continued)

The EditEmployeeAction begins by first verifying that the user is logged in and the Action was not cancelled. Once these conditions are satisfied, the EditEmployeeAction.execute() method is ready to perform its specific logic, which is simply to invoke the updateUser() method with the submitted EmployeeForm.

The updateUser() method then performs a SQL update to the employee record referenced by the username contained in the EmployeeForm instance, and returns control back to the execute() method. Assuming that no Exceptions were thrown by the updateUser() method, the request is forwarded to the success target—the previously described employeelist.jsp.

If the updateUser() method does throw Exceptions, then an ActionError is created and the request is forwarded to the failure target, which in this case is the editemployee.jsp.

Deploying the Components of the Edit Employee Transaction

At this point, we've defined the components of the Edit Employee transaction; we can now deploy them to our employees application. Listing 11.23 contains our struts-config.xml file at this stage, including the changes necessary to deploy the Edit Employee components.

```
<?xml version="1.0" encoding="ISO-8859-1" ?>

<!DOCTYPE struts-config PUBLIC
  "-//Apache Software Foundation//DTD Struts Configuration 1.1//EN"
  "http://jakarta.apache.org/struts/dtds/struts-config_1_1.dtd">

<struts-config>

  <data-sources>
    <data-source>
      <set-property property="driverClass"
        value="org.gjt.mm.mysql.Driver" />
      <set-property property="url"
        value="jdbc:mysql://localhost/employees" />
      <set-property property="maxCount"
        value="5"/>
      <set-property property="minCount"
        value="1"/>
      <set-property property="user"
        value="username"/>
```

Listing 11.23 Our struts-config.xml file after we added the Edit Employee components. (continues)

```
        <set-property property="password"
          value="password"/>
      </data-source>
    </data-sources>

    <form-beans>
      <form-bean name="loginForm"
        type="com.wiley.LoginForm" />
      <form-bean name="employeeForm"
        type="com.wiley.EmployeeForm" />
    </form-beans>

    <global-forwards>
      <forward name="login" path="/login.jsp"/>
    </global-forwards>

    <action-mappings>

      <action path="/Login"
        type="com.wiley.LoginAction"
        validate="true"
        input="/login.jsp"
        name="loginForm"
        scope="request" >
        <forward name="success" path="/EmployeeList.do"/>
      </action>

      <action path="/EmployeeList"
        type="com.wiley.EmployeeListAction"
        scope="request" >
        <set-property property="loginRequired" value="true"/>
        <forward name="success" path="/employeelist.jsp"/>
      </action>

      <action path="/Add"
        type="com.wiley.AddEmployeeAction"
        name="employeeForm"
        scope="request"
        input="/addemployee.jsp"
        validate="true" >
        <set-property property="loginRequired" value="true"/>
        <forward name="success" path="/EmployeeList.do"/>
        <forward name="error" path="/addemployee.jsp"/>
      </action>
```

Listing 11.23 Our struts-config.xml file after we added the Edit Employee components. (continues)

```
    <action path="/Edit"
      type="com.wiley.GetEmployeeAction"
      name="employeeForm"
      scope="request"
      validate="false" >
      <set-property property="loginRequired" value="true"/>
      <forward name="success" path="/editemployee.jsp"/>
      <forward name="error" path="/EmployeeList.do"/>
    </action>

    <action path="/EditEmployee"
      type="com.wiley.EditEmployeeAction"
      name="employeeForm"
      scope="request"
      input="/editemployee.jsp"
      validate="true" >
      <set-property property="loginRequired" value="true"/>
      <forward name="success" path="/EmployeeList.do"/>
      <forward name="error" path="/editemployee.jsp"/>
    </action>

  </action-mappings>

  <message-resources
    parameter="com.wiley.ApplicationResources"/>

</struts-config>
```

Listing 11.23 Our struts-config.xml file after we added the Edit Employee components. (continued)

As you examine the new struts-config.xml file, you will notice that we added two new <action> elements. These two elements are used to describe the GetEmployeeAction and EditEmployeeAction, respectively.

Note that we have set the validate attribute of the GetEmployeeAction to false. This is because the instance of the EmployeeForm will be empty when first submitted to the GetEmployeeAction.

NOTE

In the <action> element defining the GetEmployeeAction, we are setting the name attribute to point to employeeForm. This would not be necessary if we weren't retrieving the name attribute in the GetEmployeeAction.execute() method, but because we're using the name as the key to bind our EmployeeForm instance, we must specify the name attribute.

The Delete Employee Transaction

The Delete Employee transaction is used to remove a selected employee from the employees database. It is initiated when a user selects the Delete link next to the employee to be removed. When this link is selected, the Delete Employee transaction presents its components in the following order:

1. DeleteEmployeeAction
2. EmployeeListAction
3. Employee List JSP

The DeleteEmployeeAction

The final transaction we'll add to our employees application is also the simplest. It is invoked from the employeelist.jsp using the following code snippet:

```
<a href="Delete.do?username=<bean:write name="employee"
  property="username" />">Delete</a>
```

As you will notice, this link executes a get request to the Delete.do path with the request parameter username, which will contain the username of the employee to be deleted. The code for the DeleteEmployeeAction object appears in Listing 11.24.

```
package com.wiley;

import java.io.IOException;
import javax.servlet.ServletContext;
import javax.servlet.ServletException;
import javax.servlet.http.HttpServletRequest;
import javax.servlet.http.HttpServletResponse;
import javax.servlet.http.HttpSession;
import org.apache.struts.action.Action;
import org.apache.struts.action.ActionForm;
import org.apache.struts.action.ActionForward;
import org.apache.struts.action.ActionMapping;
import org.apache.struts.action.ActionErrors;
import org.apache.struts.action.ActionError;

import javax.sql.DataSource;
import java.sql.Connection;
import java.sql.Statement;
import java.sql.ResultSet;
import java.sql.SQLException;

public class DeleteEmployeeAction extends Action {
```

Listing 11.24 The Delete Employee Action. (continues)

```
protected void deleteEmployee(String username)
  throws Exception {

  String user = null;
  Connection conn = null;
  Statement stmt = null;
  ResultSet rs = null;

  ServletContext context = servlet.getServletContext();
  DataSource dataSource = (DataSource)
    context.getAttribute(Action.DATA_SOURCE_KEY);

  try {

    conn = dataSource.getConnection();
    stmt = conn.createStatement();

    StringBuffer sqlString =
      new StringBuffer("delete from employees ");
    sqlString.append("where username='" + username + "'");

    stmt.execute(sqlString.toString());
  }
  finally {

    if (rs != null) {

      rs.close();
    }
    if (stmt != null) {

      stmt.close();
    }
    if (conn != null) {

      conn.close();
    }
  }
}

public ActionForward execute(ActionMapping mapping,
  ActionForm form,
  HttpServletRequest request,
  HttpServletResponse response)
  throws IOException, ServletException {
```

Listing 11.24 The Delete Employee Action. (continues)

```
    // Default target to success
    String target = "success";

    EmployeesActionMapping employeesMapping =
      (EmployeesActionMapping)mapping;

    // Does this action require the user to login
    if ( employeesMapping.isLoginRequired() ) {

      HttpSession session = request.getSession();
      if ( session.getAttribute("USER") == null ) {

        // The user is not logged in
        target = "login";
        ActionErrors errors = new ActionErrors();

        errors.add(ActionErrors.GLOBAL_ERROR,
          new ActionError("errors.login.required"));

        // Report any errors we have discovered
        // back to the original form
        if (!errors.empty()) {

          saveErrors(request, errors);
        }
        return (mapping.findForward(target));
      }
    }

    try {

      deleteEmployee(request.getParameter("username"));
    }
    catch (Exception e) {

      System.err.println("Setting target to error");
      target = "error";
      ActionErrors errors = new ActionErrors();

      errors.add(ActionErrors.GLOBAL_ERROR,
        new ActionError("errors.database.error",
        e.getMessage()));

      // Report any errors
      if (!errors.empty()) {

        saveErrors(request, errors);
```

Listing 11.24 The Delete Employee Action. (continues)

```
            }
        }
        // Forward to the appropriate View
        return (mapping.findForward(target));
    }
}
```

Listing 11.24 The Delete Employee Action. (continued)

The DeleteEmployeeAction begins by first verifying that the user is logged in and that the Action was not cancelled. Once these conditions are satisfied, the DeleteEmployeeAction.execute() method invokes the deleteEmployee() method with the submitted username.

The deleteEmployee() method performs a SQL delete, removing the employee record referenced by the username, and then returns control to the execute() method. Assuming that no Exceptions were thrown by the deleteEmployee() method, the request is forwarded to the success target—the previously described EmployeeListAction.

If the deleteEmployee() method does throw Exceptions, then an ActionError is created and the request is forwarded to the failure target, which in this case is the same as the success target.

Deploying the Delete Employee Transaction

The Delete Employee transaction has only a single component, the DeleteEmployeeAction. To deploy this action, we simply need to include a single <action> element describing it. Listing 11.25 contains the struts-config.xml file with the changes necessary to deploy the DeleteEmployeeAction.

```
<?xml version="1.0" encoding="ISO-8859-1" ?>

<!DOCTYPE struts-config PUBLIC
  "-//Apache Software Foundation//DTD Struts Configuration 1.1//EN"
  "http://jakarta.apache.org/struts/dtds/struts-config_1_1.dtd">

<struts-config>

  <data-sources>
    <data-source>
      <set-property property="driverClass"
```

Listing 11.25 The struts-config.xml file after we added the Delete Employee components. (continues)

```
        value="org.gjt.mm.mysql.Driver" />
      <set-property property="url"
        value="jdbc:mysql://localhost/employees" />
      <set-property property="maxCount"
        value="5"/>
      <set-property property="minCount"
        value="1"/>
      <set-property property="user"
        value="username"/>
      <set-property property="password"
        value="password"/>
    </data-source>
  </data-sources>

  <form-beans>
    <form-bean name="loginForm"
      type="com.wiley.LoginForm" />
    <form-bean name="employeeForm"
      type="com.wiley.EmployeeForm" />
  </form-beans>

  <global-forwards>
    <forward name="login" path="/login.jsp"/>
  </global-forwards>

  <action-mappings>

    <action path="/Login"
      type="com.wiley.LoginAction"
      validate="true"
      input="/login.jsp"
      name="loginForm"
      scope="request" >
      <forward name="success" path="/EmployeeList.do"/>
    </action>

    <action path="/EmployeeList"
      type="com.wiley.EmployeeListAction"
      scope="request" >
      <set-property property="loginRequired" value="true"/>
      <forward name="success" path="/employeelist.jsp"/>
    </action>

    <action path="/Add"
      type="com.wiley.AddEmployeeAction"
      name="employeeForm"
```

Listing 11.25 The struts-config.xml file after we added the Delete Employee components. (continues)

```
      scope="request"
      input="/addemployee.jsp"
      validate="true" >
      <set-property property="loginRequired" value="true"/>
      <forward name="success" path="/EmployeeList.do"/>
      <forward name="error" path="/addemployee.jsp"/>
    </action>

    <action path="/Edit"
      type="com.wiley.GetEmployeeAction"
      name="employeeForm"
      scope="request"
      validate="false" >
      <set-property property="loginRequired" value="true"/>
      <forward name="success" path="/editemployee.jsp"/>
      <forward name="error" path="/EmployeeList.do"/>
    </action>

    <action path="/EditEmployee"
      type="com.wiley.EditEmployeeAction"
      name="employeeForm"
      scope="request"
      input="/editemployee.jsp"
      validate="true" >
      <set-property property="loginRequired" value="true"/>
      <forward name="success" path="/EmployeeList.do"/>
      <forward name="error" path="/editemployee.jsp"/>
    </action>

    <action path="/Delete"
      type="com.wiley.DeleteEmployeeAction"
      scope="request"
      validate="false" >
      <set-property property="loginRequired" value="true"/>
      <forward name="success" path="/EmployeeList.do"/>
      <forward name="error" path="/EmployeeList.do"/>
    </action>
  </action-mappings>

  <message-resources
    parameter="com.wiley.ApplicationResources"/>

</struts-config>
```

Listing 11.25 The struts-config.xml file after we added the Delete Employee components. (continued)

Notice in Listing 11.25 that we added a single <action> element that describes the DeleteEmployeeAction with a very basic definition.

Walkthrough

We have now described and deployed all of the components of our employees application To see this application in action, follow these steps:

1. Move all of your JSPs to the <*CATALINA_HOME*>/webapps/employees directory.
2. Compile all of the Java classes and move them to the <*CATALINA_HOME*>/webapps/employees/classes/com/wiley directory.
3. Copy the MySQL JDBC driver to the <CATALINA_HOME>/webapps/employees/lib directory.
4. Copy the jdbc2_0-stdext.jar file driver to the <*CATALINA_HOME*>/webapps/employees/lib directory.
5. Start MySQL, if it is not already running.
6. Start Tomcat, if it is not already running.
7. Open your browser to the following URL:

```
http://localhost:8080/employees/
```

If everything started correctly, you should see the employees Login View, as shown in Figure 11.1.

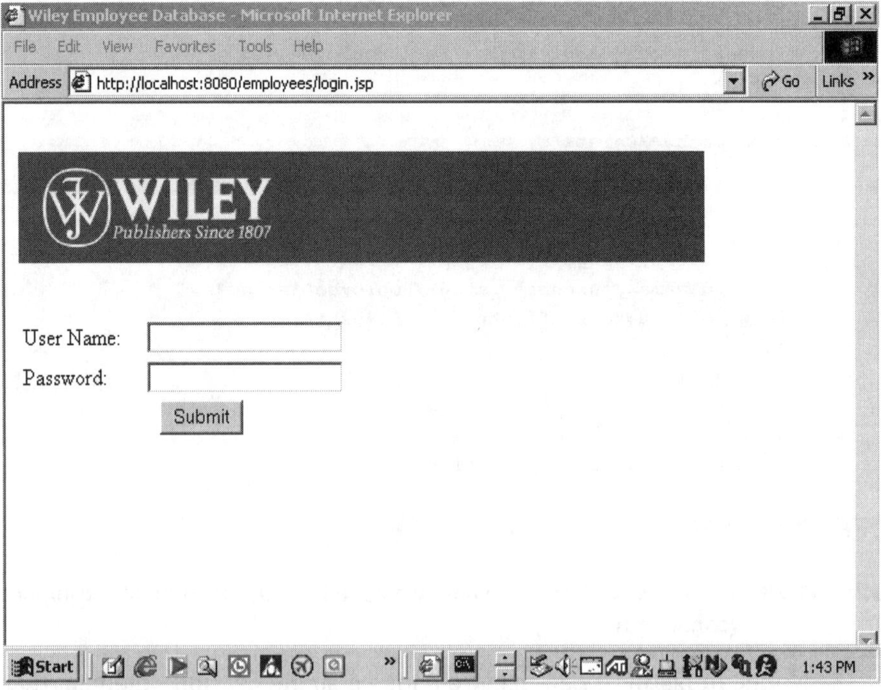

Figure 11.1 The Login View.

Now go ahead and enter a username and password that exist in the database. For our purposes, I am using the values *abrickey* and *$word*. If you logged in correctly, you should see a page similar to Figure 11.2, the Employee List View.

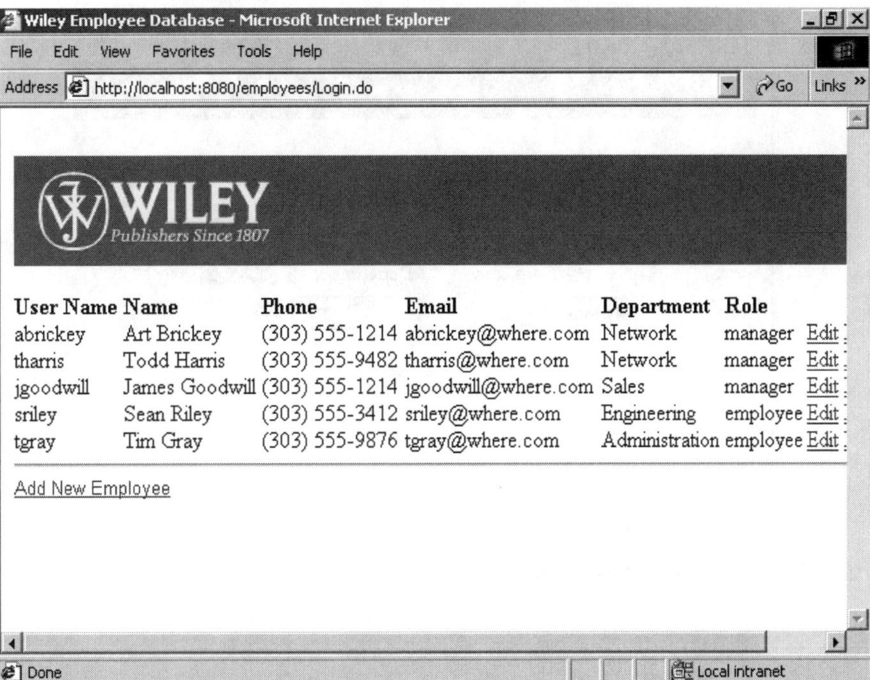

Figure 11.2 The Employee List View.

Now select the Edit link next to a user that you want to edit. I am selecting the user tharris. You should now see the Edit Employee View, which should look similar to Figure 11.3.

Change one of the attributes of the employee, and click the Submit button. You should now see the Employee List View with the changes you made.

Now select the Add New Employee link. You should see an empty HTML form, similar to Figure 11.4, which represents the possible attributes of an employee.

At this point, enter a new employee, and click the Submit button. If everything went according to plan, you should see the Employee List View with the new employee displayed.

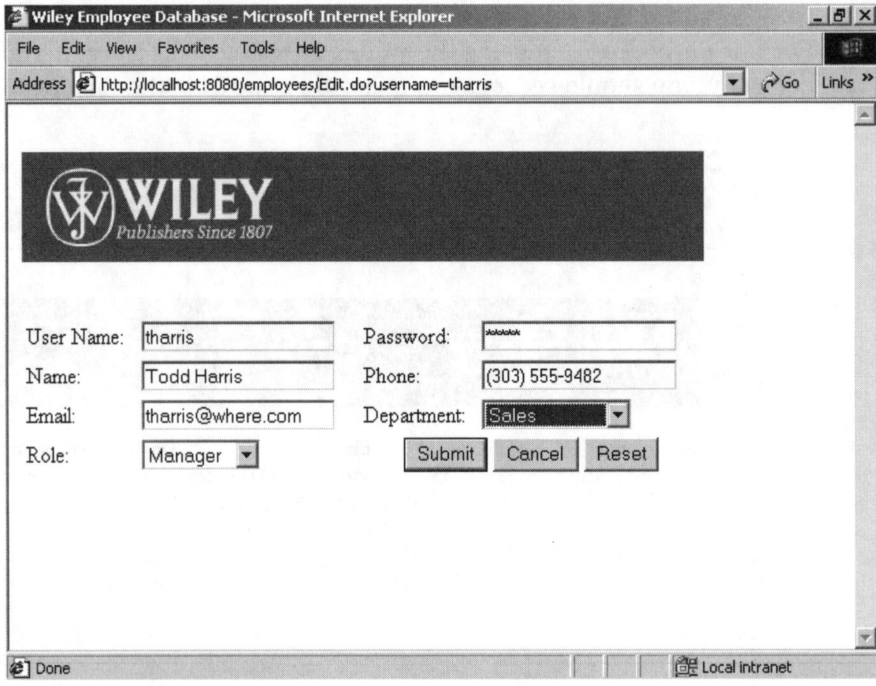

Figure 11.3 The Edit Employee View.

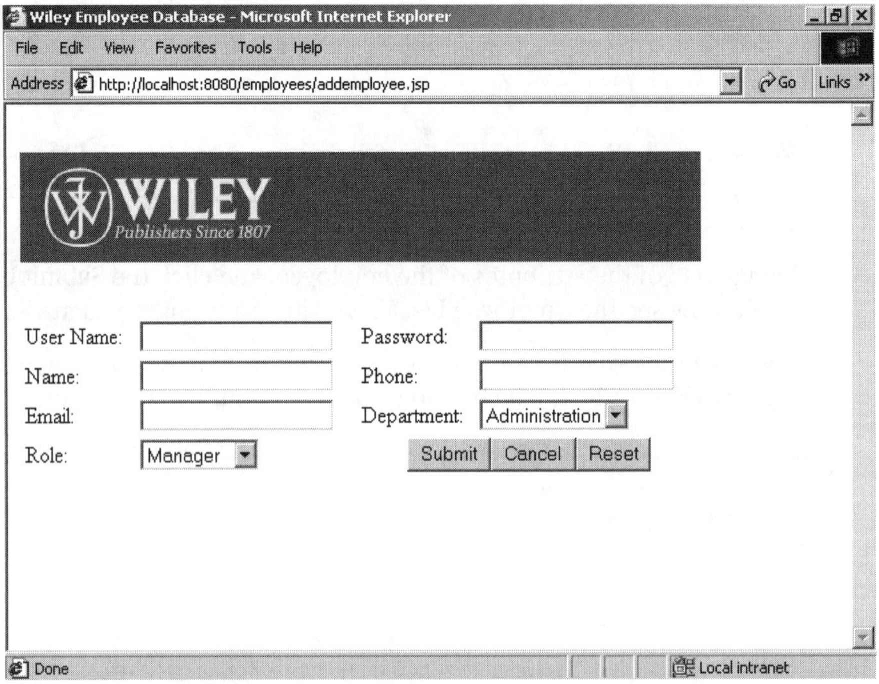

Figure 11.4 The Add Employee View.

Summary

In the next chapter, we discuss the struts-config.xml file. You will learn how to deploy all of the major Struts components—DataSources, FormBeans, Global Forwards, and ActionMappings—as well as RequestProcessors, application resources, and Plugins. In addition, we examine the subordinate components available as subelements of the major Struts components

CHAPTER 12

The struts-config.xml File

At the heart of the Jakarta Struts project is the struts-config.xml file, in which you describe all of your Struts components. In this chapter, we show you how to configure the major Struts components, including: DataSources, FormBeans, Global Forwards, ActionMappings, RequestProcessors, application resources, and Plugins. We also describe each of the subordinate components available as subelements of the major Struts components.

Listing 12.1 shows a stripped-down version of the struts-config.xml file. As you can see, this file contains all four of the major components of a Struts configuration file.

```
<struts-config>

  <data-sources>
    <data-source>
    </data-source>
  </data-sources>

  <form-beans>
    <form-bean />
  </form-beans>

  <global-forwards>
```

Listing 12.1 A stripped-down version struts-config.xml file. (continues)

```
    <forward />
  </global-forwards>

  <action-mappings>
    <action/>
  </action-mappings>

  <controller />

  <message-resource />

  <plug-in />


</struts-config>
```

Listing 12.1 A stripped-down version struts-config.xml file. (continued)

NOTE

It is very important to note the order of each of the elements in Listing 12.1. This is the order in which they must appear in the struts-config.xml file. If the order deviates from that shown previously, Struts will throw an exception upon startup.

The Struts Subelements

In this section, we discuss the four subelements available to the four major Struts components. Not all of these elements are used by all four major components, but they are available to further describe each component.

The <icon /> Subelement

The <icon /> subelement contains a <small-icon /> and <large-icon /> subelement that can be used to graphically represent its parent element in a Struts development tool. The syntax of the <icon /> subelement is shown here:

```
<icon>
  <small-icon>
    path to somegraphicsfile (16x16 pixels)
  </small-icon>
  <large-icon>
    somelargergraphicsfile (32x32 pixels)
  </large-icon>
</icon>
```

Table 12.1 describes the subelements of an <icon /> element.

Table 12.1 The Subelements of an <icon /> Entry

PROPERTY	DESCRIPTION
small-icon	Contains a path relative to the location of the Struts configuration file; it names a graphics file that contains a 16x16 pixel iconic image.
large-icon	Contains a path relative to the location of the Struts configuration file; it names a graphics file that contains a 32x32 pixel iconic image.

The following code snippet contains an example of how we can use these <icon /> subelements:

```
<icon>
  <small-icon>
    /images/smalllogo.gif
  </small-icon>
  <large-icon>
    /images/largelogo.gif
  </large-icon>
</icon>
```

NOTE

The images referenced in these subelements are made strictly for Struts development and configuration tools. They are not intended for client-side display.

The <display-name /> Subelement

The <display-name /> subelement contains a short textual description of its parent element that can be used in a Struts development tool. The syntax of the <display-name /> subelement is shown here:

```
<display-name>
  short textual discription of its parent element
</display-name>
```

The <description /> Subelement

The <description /> subelement contains a full-length textual description of its parent element that can be used in a Struts development tool. The syntax of the <description /> subelement is shown here:

```
<description>
  full-length textual discription of its parent element
</description>
```

The <set-property /> Subelement

The <set-property /> subelement is used to set the value of additional JavaBean properties of objects described by the <set-property /> subelement's parent. The <set-property /> subelement is commonly used to specify GenericDataSource properties, extended ActionMappings, and extended global forwards. The syntax of the <set-property /> subelement is shown here:

```
<set-property
  property="name of bean property"
  value="value of bean property" />
```

Table 12.2 describes the attributes of a <set-property /> element.

Table 12.2 The Attributes of a <set-property /> Subelement

PROPERTY	DESCRIPTION
property	The property of the JavaBeans property whose setter method will be called. (Required)
value	The large-icon String representation of the value to which this property will be set, following suitable type conversion. (Required)

The following code snippet illustrates how to use the <set-property /> subelement:

```
<set-property
  property="driverClass"
  value="org.gjt.mm.mysql.Driver" />
```

NOTE

The <set-property /> subelement contains no body. It is configured using only its two attributes.

Adding a Struts DataSource

The first component that we are going to configure is a DataSource. When describing a DataSource instance, you must use the <data-sources /> element.

This element will contain *n*-number of <data-source /> subelements, which actually describe each DataSource instance. The syntax of the <data-sources /> element containing a single <data-source /> subelement is shown in the following code snippet:

```
<data-sources>
  <data-source>
    <set-property property="driverClass"
      value="fully qualified path of JDBC driver"/>
    <set-property property="url"
      value="data source URL"/>
      value="the minimum number of connections to open"/>
    <set-property property="password"
      value="the password used to create connections"/>
    <set-property property="user"
      value="the username used to create connections"/>
  </data-source>
</data-sources>
```

As you can see from this code snippet, the <data-source /> subelement is described completely using <set-property /> subelements. Each one of the properties listed in the <set-property /> elements maps to a single <data-source /> attribute. This means that the <data-source /> subelement could just as easily have been configured using its attributes only. I chose this method simply to give an example of how the <set-property /> subelement can be used. Table 12.3 describes the attributes of a <data-source /> entry.

Table 12.3 The Attributes of a <data-source /> Entry (continues)

ATTRIBUTE	DESCRIPTION
key	A unique key that the DataSource instance will be bound to in the ServletContext. If this property is not used, then the key will be defaulted to Action.DATA_SOURCE_KEY. If you intend to use more than one DataSource in your application, then you need to include a key for each one. (Optional)
driverClass	The fully qualified JDBC driver class that will be used to connect to the URL named in the url property. (Required)
url	The URL of the database that we are connecting to. (Required)
maxCount	The maximum number of connections that will be open at any given time. The default value is 2. (Optional)
minCount	The minimum number of connections that will be open at any given time. The default value is 1. (Optional)
user	The username that will be used to connect to the database. (Required)

Table 12.3 The Attributes of a <data-source /> Entry (continued)

ATTRIBUTE	DESCRIPTION
password	The password that will be used to connect to the database. (Required)
description	A text description of the DataSource. The description attribute contains no default value. (Optional)
readOnly	If set to true, defaults the state of newly created connections to read-only. The default value is false. (Optional)
loginTimeout	Specifies the maximum number of seconds to wait for the creation of a connection. The default value is driver-dependent. (Optional)
autoCommit	If set to true (the default), forces a commit after every executed statement. (Optional)

Here's an example of using the <set-property /> subelement:

```
<data-sources>
  <data-source>
    <set-property property="key"
      value="WILEY_DATA_SOURCE" />
    <set-property property="driverClass"
      value="org.gjt.mm.mysql.Driver" />
    <set-property property="url"
      value="jdbc:mysql://localhost/wileyusers" />
    <set-property property="maxCount"
      value="5"/>
    <set-property property="minCount"
      value="1"/>
    <set-property property="user"
      value="sa"/>
    <set-property property="password"
      value="yourpassword"/>
  </data-source>
</data-sources>
```

Adding FormBean Definitions

The <form-bean /> subelement is used to describe an instance of a FormBean that will be later bound to an Action. The syntax of the <form-bean /> subelement is shown here:

```
<form-beans>
  <form-bean name="name used to uniquely identify a FormBean"
    type="fully qualified class name of FormBean" />
</form-beans>
```

NOTE

All <form-bean /> subelements must be nested within a single <form-beans /> element. The <form-beans /> element is used only as a container for <form-bean /> subelements.

Table 12.4 describes the attributes of an <form-bean /> subelement.

Table 12.4 The Attributes of a <form-bean /> Subelement

ATTRIBUTE	DESCRIPTION
name	Contains the unique identifier for this bean. This value is used in an <action–mappings /> element to bind a FormBean to an Action. (Required)
type	Specifies the fully qualified class name of the FormBean class. (Required)

Here's an example that uses the <form-bean /> subelement:

```
<form-beans>

  <form-bean name="lookupForm"
    type="wiley.LookupForm" />
</form-beans>
```

NOTE

The <form-bean /> subelement contains no body. It is configured using only its two attributes.

Adding Global Forwards

The <global-forwards /> subelement is used to define *n*-number of <forward /> subelements that are available to any Action in the Struts application. It acts as a container for public <forward /> subelements.

The <forward /> subelement is used to describe a mapping of a logical name to a context-relative URI path. A <forward /> is used to identify the target of an Action class when it returns its results. This target is most often used to present the results of the Action that names it. The syntax of the <global-forwards /> subelement, including a sample nested <forward /> element, is shown here:

```
<global-forwards>
  <forward name="unique target identifier"
```

```
    path="context-relative path to targetted resource "/>
</global-forwards>
```

NOTE

All <forward /> subelements that are to be made available to the entire application must be nested within a single <global-forwards /> element.

Table 12.5 describes the attributes of a <forward /> subelement.

Table 12.5 The Attributes of a <forward /> Subelement

ATTRIBUTE	DESCRIPTION
name	Contains the unique identifier for this target. This attribute is used by an Action class to identify its targeted resource. (Required)
path	Provides the context-relative path of the targeted resource. (Required)
redirect	If set to true, causes the ActionServlet to use the HttpServletResponse.sendRedirect() method, as opposed to the RequestDispatcher.forward() method, when sending the Action results to the targeted resource. The default value is false. (Optional)

NOTE

If the redirect attribute is set to true-—which means the HttpServletResponse. sendRedirect() method will be used—the values stored in the original HttpServletRequest will be lost.

Here's an example of using the <global-forwards /> subelement:

```
<global-forwards>
  <forward name="success" path="/welcome.jsp"/>
  <forward name="failure" path="/index.jsp"/>
</global-forwards>
```

NOTE

The <forward /> subelement contains no body. It is configured using only its two attributes.

Adding Actions

The <action-mappings /> subelement is used to define *n*-number of <action /> subelements, and acts as a container for those subelements. In this section, we focus on the actual configuration of individual <action /> subelements.

The <action /> subelement is used to describe an Action instance to the ActionServlet. It represents the information that uniquely defines an instance of a particular action class. The syntax of the <action-mappings /> subelement, including a sample <action /> subelement, is shown here:

```
<action-mappings>

  <action
    path="context-relative path mapping action to a request"
    type="fully qualified class name of the Action class"
    name="the name of the form bean bound to this Action">
    <forward name="forwardname1" path="context-relative path"/>
    <forward name="forwardname2" path="context-relative path"/>
  </action>

</action-mappings>
```

NOTE

You will notice that the <action /> element above contains two <forward /> subelements. These subelements are defined in exactly the same way as the <forward /> elements nested inside a <global-forwards /> element, except that they are local to the defined <action /> subelement. These <forward /> subelements can be referenced only by their parent <action />.

Table 12.6 describes the attributes of an <action /> subelement.

Table 12.6 The Attributes of an <action /> Subelement (continues)

ATTRIBUTE	DESCRIPTION
path	Represents the context-relative path of the submitted request. The path must start with a / character. (Required)
type	Gives the fully qualified class name of the Action class being described by this ActionMapping. The type attribute is valid only if no include or forward attribute is specified. (Optional)
name	Identifies the name of the form bean, if any, that is coupled with the Action being defined. (Optional)

Table 12.6 The Attributes of an <action /> Subelement (continued)

ATTRIBUTE	DESCRIPTION
scope	Specifies the scope of the form bean that is bound to the described Action. The default value is session. (Optional)
input	Gives the context-relative path of the input form to which control should be returned if a validation error is encountered. The input attribute is where control will be returned if ActionErrors are returned from the ActionForm or Action objects. (Optional)
className	Specifies the fully qualified class name of the ActionMapping implementation class to use when invoking this Action class. If the className attribute is not included, then the ActionMapping defined in the ActionServlet's mapping initialization parameter is used. (Optional)
forward	Specifies the context-relative path of the servlet or JSP resource that will process this request. Use this attribute if you do not want an Action to service the request to this path. The forward attribute is valid only if no include or type attribute is specified. (Optional)
include	Specifies the context-relative path of the servlet or JSP resource that will process this request. Use this attribute if you do not want an Action to service the request to this path. The include attribute is valid only if no forward or type attribute is specified. (Optional)
validate	If set to true (the default), causes the ActionForm.validate() method to be called on the form bean associated with the Action being described. If the validate attribute is set to false, then the ActionForm.validate() method is not called. (Optional)

Here's an example of using the <action-mappings /> subelement:

```
<action-mappings>

  <action path="/lookupAction"
    type="wiley.LookupAction"
    name="LookupForm"
    scope="request"
    validate="true"
    input="/index.jsp">
    <forward name="success" path="/quote.jsp"/>
    <forward name="faliue" path="/index.jsp"/>
  </action>

</action-mappings>
```

Adding a RequestProcessor

We use the <controller /> subelement to define a RequestProcessor, which is used to modify the default behavior of the Struts Controller. The syntax of the <controller /> subelement is shown here:

```
<controller processorClass="fully qualified class name" />
```

Table 12.7 describes the attributes of a <controller /> subelement.

Table 12.7 The Attributes of a <controller /> Subelement

ATTRIBUTE	DESCRIPTION
processorClass	Gives the fully qualified Java class name of the user define extension of the RequestProcessor class to be used in place of the default org.apache.struts.action.RequestProcessor. (Optional)
bufferSize	Defines the size of the input buffer used for file uploads. The default value is 4096 bytes. (Optional)
contentType	Defines the default response content-type. The default value is text/html. (Optional)
debug	Defines the debug level for the current application. The default value is 0. (Optional)
locale	If set to true (the default), stores a Locale object in the user's session, if it is not already present. (Optional)
maxFileSize	Specifies the maximum size (in bytes) of a file to be uploaded. The value of the maxFileSize attribute can be expressed by a "K", "M", or "G"—kilobytes, megabytes, or gigabytes, respectively. The default value is 250M. (Optional)
multipartClass	Specifies the fully qualified class name of a multipart request handler class to be used instead of the default org.apache.struts.upload.DiskMultipartRequestHandler. (Optional)
nocache	If set to true, adds HTTP headers that turn off caching for each response. The default value is false. (Optional)
tempDir	Specifies a temporary directory used to store files being uploaded. The default directory is determined by the JSP/servlet container.

Here's an example of how we can use the <controller /> subelement:

```
<controller processorClass="wiley.WileyRequestProcessor" />
```

Adding Message Resources

The <message-resources /> subelement is used to define the collection of messages for this application. The syntax of the <message-resources /> subelement is shown here:

```
<message-resources
  parameter="wiley.ApplicationResources"/>
```

Table 12.8 describes the attributes of an <message-resources /> subelement.

Table 12.8 The Attributes of an <message-resources /> Subelement

ATTRIBUTE	DESCRIPTION
parameter	Gives the resource bundle referencing the application's resource bundle. (Required)
className	Defines the default message resource implementation for the current application. The default value is org.apache.struts.config.MessageResourcesConfig. (Optional)
factory	Defines the fully qualified class name of the MessageResourcesFactory class that should be used for this application. The default value is org.apache.struts.util.PropertyMessageResourcesFactory. (Optional)
key	Defines the ServletContext attribute key under which this message resources bundle is bound. The default is the value defined by the String constant Action.MESSAGES_KEY. (Optional)
null	If set to true, causes the message resource implementation to return a null string for unknown message keys. The default value is true. (Optional)

The following code snippet contains an example of using the <message-resources /> subelement:

```
<message-resources
  parameter="wiley.ApplicationResources"/>
```

Adding a Plug-in

We use the <plugin /> subelement to define the fully qualified class name of a Struts plug-in, which will perform application-specific functionality during application startup and shutdown. The syntax of the <plugin /> subelement is shown here:

```
<plug-in className="fully qualified plugin classname" />
```

The <plugin /> subelement supports a single attribute className, which names the fully qualified class name of the Plugin implementation. Here's an example of using the <plugin /> subelement:

```
<plug-in
  className="wiley.WileyPlugin" />
```

CHAPTER 13

The Bean Tag Library

At this point, we begin our discussions of the Jakarta Struts tag libraries. In this chapter, we examine the Jakarta Struts Bean tag library. The Bean tag library provides a group of tags that encapsulate the logic necessary to access and manipulate JavaBeans, HTTP cookies, and HTTP headers using scripting variables. There are currently 11 custom tags in the Bean tag library.

Installing the Bean Tags

To use the Bean tag library in a Web application, you must complete the following steps, replacing the value *webappname* with the name of the Web application that will be using this library:

1. Copy the TLD packaged with this tag library, struts-bean.tld, to the <*TOMCAT_HOME*>/webapps/*webappname*/WEB-INF/ directory.
2. Make sure that the struts.jar file is in the <*TOMCAT_HOME*>/webapps/*webappname*/WEB-INF/lib directory.
3. Add the following <taglib> subelement to the web.xml file of the Web application:

```
<taglib>
  <taglib-uri>/WEB-INF/struts-bean.tld</taglib-uri>
  <taglib-location>/WEB-INF/struts-bean.tld</taglib-location>
</taglib>
```

You must add the following taglib directive to each JSP that will leverage the Bean tag library:

```
<%@ taglib uri="/WEB-INF/struts-bean.tld" prefix="bean" %>
```

This directive identifies the URI defined in the previously listed <taglib> element and states that all Bean tags should be prefixed with the string bean.

<bean:cookie />

The <bean:cookie /> tag is used to retrieve the value of an HTTP cookie. It can be used to retrieve single or multiple cookie values. The retrieved cookie(s) are stored in a page scoped attribute of type Cookie (or Cookie[] if there is more than one HTTP cookie). If the named cookie is not found and no default value is specified, then a request-time exception is thrown.

The <bean:cookie /> tag has no body and supports four attributes, described in Table 13.1.

Table 13.1 <bean:cookie /> Tag Attributes

ATTRIBUTE	DESCRIPTION
id	Specifies the ID of the scripting variable to be added to the request as a Cookie object. (Required)
name	Identifies the name of the HTTP cookie being retrieved. (Required)
multiple	If not null, will cause a Cookie[] containing all of the values for the named HTTP cookie to be returned, as opposed to a single Cookie object. If the multiple attribute is not null and there is only a single HTTP cookie, then the first [0] element of the Cookie[] will contain the retrieved value. (Optional)
value	Specifies the default value to return to store in the javax.servlet.http.Cookie object if no cookie is found. (Optional)

Here's an example of using the <bean:cookie /> tag:

```
<bean:cookie id="userId"
  name="userCookie"
  value="UNKNOWN_USER"/>
```

In this example, we are looking for a HTTP cookie named userCookie. If the userId cookie exists in the request, then a javax.servlet.http.Cookie object containing the retrieved value is created and stored in the page. Otherwise, a javax.servlet.http.Cookie object containing the string specified in the value attribute—UNKNOWN_USER in this example—is created and stored in the page.

<bean:define />

The <bean:define /> tag is used to retrieve the value of a named bean property and define it as a scripting variable, which will be stored in the scope specified by the toScope attribute. The retrieved object will perform type conversion on the returned property value unless it is a Java primitive type, in which case it is wrapped in the appropriate wrapper class (for example, int is wrapped by java.lang.Integer).

This <bean:define /> tag has a body type of JSP and supports seven attributes, described in Table 13.2.

Table 13.2 <bean:define /> Tag Attributes

ATTRIBUTE	DESCRIPTION
id	Specifies the scripting variable that will be created and stored in a scoped attribute that will be made available with the value of the indicated property. (Required)
name	Specifies the attribute name of the bean whose property is retrieved to define a new scoped attribute. You must include the name attribute, unless you specify a value attribute. (Optional)
property	Identifies the property of the bean, specified by the name attribute, that is being retrieved. If the property attribute is not specified, then the bean identified by the name attribute is given a new reference to the object identified by the id attribute. (Optional)
scope	Identifies the scope of the bean specified by the name attribute. If the scope attribute is not specified, then the tag will search for the bean in the scopes—in the order of page, request, session, and application. (Optional)
toScope	Identifies the scope of the newly defined bean. The default scope is page. (Optional)
type	Provides the fully qualified class name of the value to be exposed as the id attribute. The default type is java.lang.String if a value attribute is specified; otherwise, the object will be of type java.lang.Object. (Optional)
value	Contains a string value to which the exposed bean should be set. You must include the value attribute unless you specify the name attribute. (Optional)

An example of using the <bean:define /> tag is shown here:

```
<jsp:useBean
  id="user"
```

```
    scope="page"
    class="com.wiley.User"/>

  <bean:define
    id="name"
    name="user"
    property="firstName"/>

  Welcome: <%= name %>
```

In this example, we have user, a page-level object of type com.wiley.User. We then use the <bean:define /> tag to retrieve the user property firstName and store this value in the scripting variable named name. We conclude this snippet by printing the contents of the newly created name object.

<bean:header />

The <bean:header /> tag functions exactly like <bean:cookie />, except that it retrieves its values from the named request header. Once the tag has the header values, it creates a java.lang.String or java.lang.String[] attribute, and stores it in the PageContext.

If the named header cannot be located and no default value is given, then a request-time exception will be thrown. The <bean:header /> tag has a body type of JSP and supports four attributes, described in Table 13.3.

Table 13.3 <bean:header /> Tag Attributes

ATTRIBUTE	DESCRIPTION
id	Represents the name of the scripting variable that will be exposed as a page scoped attribute. (Required)
name	Identifies the name of the HTTP header being retrieved. (Required)
multiple	If not null, causes a String[] containing all of the header values for the named HTTP header to be returned, as opposed to a single header. If the multiple attribute is not null and there is only a single HTTP header, then the first or [0] element of the String[] will contain the retrieved value. (Optional)
value	Specifies the default value to return and store in the name object, if the named header is not found. (Optional)

An example of using the <bean:header /> tag is shown here:

```
<bean:header id="headId"
  name="Cache-Control"
  value="Cache-Control Not Found" />
```

In this example, we are looking for a HTTP header, Cache-Control. If the Cache-Control header exists, then a String object containing the retrieved value is created and stored in the page; otherwise, a String object containing the String named in the value attribute—Cache-Control Not Found in this example—is created and stored in the page.

<bean:include />

The <bean:include /> tag is used to evaluate and retrieve the results of a Web application resource. The tag makes the response data available as an object of type String. The tag functions much like the <jsp:include> standard action, except that the response is stored in a page scoped object attribute, as opposed to being written to the output stream.

The resource being evaluated by the <bean:include /> tag can be identified using three different attributes: forward, href, and page.

The <bean:include /> tag has no body and supports six attributes, described in Table 13.4.

Table 13.4 <bean:include /> Tag Attributes

ATTRIBUTE	DESCRIPTION
id	Specifies the page-level variable used to store the result of the evaluated URI condition. (Required)
anchor	Specifies an HTML anchor tag that will be added to the generated URI. You do not need to include the # character when identifying the anchor. (Optional)
forward	Used to name a global <forward /> subelement, which will be used to look up a reference to the application-relative or context-relative URI identified by the <forward /> element's path attribute. (Optional)
href	Used to include resources external to the hosting application. (Optional)
page	Used to include the value of an application-relative URI. (Optional)
transaction	If true, causes the transaction token, if available, to be included in the URI being requested. The default value is false. (Optional)

Here's an example of how we can use the <bean:include /> tag:

```
<bean:include id="navbar" page="/navbar.jsp"/>
```

In this example, the context-relative resource navbar.jsp is evaluated, and its response is placed in the page-level attribute navbar. The type of page-level attribute is java.lang.String.

<bean:message />

The <bean:message /> tag is a very useful tag that we can employ to retrieve keyed values from a previously defined resource bundle. It also supports the ability to include parameters that can be substituted for defined placeholders in the retrieved string. The <bean:message /> tag has no body and supports 11 attributes, described in Table 13.5.

NOTE

We used this tag throughout Chapter 6, "Internationalizing Your Struts Applications."

Table 13.5 <bean:message /> Tag Attributes

ATTRIBUTE	DESCRIPTION
arg0	Contains the first parametric replacement value. (Optional)
arg1	Contains the second parametric replacement value. (Optional)
arg2	Contains the third parametric replacement value. (Optional)
arg3	Contains the fourth parametric replacement value. (Optional)
arg4	Contains the fifth parametric replacement value. (Optional)
bundle	Specifies the name of the bean under which messages are stored. This bean is stored in the ServletContext. If the bundle is not included, the default value of the Action.MESSAGES_KEY is used. This attribute is an optional request-time attribute. If you use the ActionServlet to manage your resource bundles, you can ignore this attribute. (Optional)
key	Identifies the unique key that is used to retrieve a message from a previously defined resource bundle. (Optional)
locale	Specifies the session bean that references the requesting client's locale. If the bundle is not included, the default value of Action.LOCALE_KEY is used. (Optional)
name	Specifies the name of the object whose data member is being retrieved. If the property attribute is not specified, then the value of this bean itself will be used as the message resource key. (Optional)
property	Specifies the name of the property to be accessed on the bean identified by the name attribute. If this attribute is not specified, then the value of the bean identified by the name attribute will be used as the message resource key. (Optional)
scope	Identifies the scope of the bean specified by name attribute. If the scope attribute is not specified, then the tag will search for the bean in the scopes—in the order of page, request, session, and application. (Optional)

The following code snippet contains a simple example of using the <bean:message /> tag:

```
<html>
  <head>
    <title><bean:message key="app.title"/></title>
  </head>
  <body>

  </body>
</html>
```

In this example, we are retrieving the value stored in the resource bundle that is referenced by the key app.title. This retrieved value will be substituted for the occurrence of this <bean:message /> tag. The result is a JSP that will have an HTML <title> that matches the locale of the requesting client.

<bean:page />

The <bean:page /> tag is used to retrieve the value of an identified implicit JSP object, which it stores in the page context of the current JSP. The retrieved object will be stored in the page scoped scripting variable named by the id attribute. The <bean:page /> tag has no body and supports two attributes, as shown in Table 13.6.

Table 13.6 <bean:page /> Tag Attributes

ATTRIBUTE	DESCRIPTION
id	Identifies the name of the scripting variable that is being made available with the value of the specified page context property. (Required)
property	Specifies the implicit object being retrieved from the current page context. The property attribute must be set to one of these implicit object values: application, config, request, response, or session. (Required)

This code snippet contains a simple example of using the <bean:page /> tag:

```
<bean:page id="sessionVar" property="session"/>
```

In this example, we are retrieving the implicit session object and storing this reference in the scripting variable sessionVar.

<bean:parameter />

The <bean:parameter /> tag is used to retrieve the value of a request parameter identified by the name attribute. The retrieved value will be used to define a page scoped attribute of type java.lang.String, or String[] if the multiple attribute is not null. The <bean:parameter /> tag has no body and supports four attributes, as shown in Table 13.7.

Table 13.7 <bean:parameter /> Tag Attributes

ATTRIBUTE	DESCRIPTION
id	Represents the name of the scripting variable that will be exposed as a page scoped attribute. (Required)
name	Identifies the name of the request parameter being retrieved. (Required)
multiple	If not null, causes a String[] containing all of the parameter values for the named request parameter to be returned, as opposed to a single parameter. If the multiple attribute is not null and there is only a single parameter value, then the first or [0] element of the String[] will contain the retrieved value. (Optional)
value	Specifies the default value to return and store in the name object if the named parameter is not found. (Optional)

An example of using the <bean:parameter /> tag is shown here:

```
<bean:parameter id="userId"
  name="username"
  value="User Not Found" />
```

In this example, we are looking for the request parameter username. If the username parameter exists in the request, then a String object containing the retrieved value is created and stored in the page; otherwise, a String object containing the String named in the value attribute value—User Not Found in this example—is created and stored in the page.

<bean:resource />

The <bean:resource /> tag is used to retrieve the value of a Web application resource identified by the name attribute; the tag makes the resource available as either a java.io.InputStream or a java.lang.String object, based on the value of the input attribute. The <bean:resource /> tag has no body and supports three attributes, described in Table 13.8.

Table 13.8 <bean:resource /> Tag Attributes

ATTRIBUTE	DESCRIPTION
id	Identifies the name of the page scoped scripting variable that will contain the retrieved value of the named Web application resource. (Required)
name	Identifies the application-relative name of the Web application resource being retrieved. The resource name must begin with a / character. (Required)
input	If not null, causes the retrieved resource to be returned as an InputStream as opposed to a String. (Optional)

<bean:size />

The <bean:size /> tag is used to retrieve the number of elements contained in a reference to an array, collection, or map. The results of the <bean:size /> tag's evaluation is a scripting variable of type java.lang.Integer that contains the number of elements in that collection. You can specify the collection as a run-time expression, as a bean, or as a property of the bean named by the bean attribute. The <bean:size /> tag has no body and supports five attributes, as shown in Table 13.9.

Table 13.9 <bean:size /> Tag Attributes

ATTRIBUTE	DESCRIPTION
id	Contains the scripting variable used to store the result of the evaluation. (Required)
collection	Identifies the runtime expression that evaluates to an array, a collection, or a map. (Optional)
name	Identifies the bean that contains the collection that will be counted. If the property attribute is specified, then the collection is assumed to be a data member of the bean; otherwise, the bean itself is assumed to be a collection. (Optional)
property	Specifies the name of the property to be accessed on the bean identified by the name attribute whose getter method will return the collection to be counted. (Optional)
scope	Identifies the scope of the bean specified by the name attribute. If the scope attribute is not specified, then the tag will search for the bean in the scopes, in the order of page, request, session, and application. (Optional)

An example of using the <bean:size /> tag is shown here:

```
<bean:size id="count"
  name="users" />
```

In this example, we are counting the collection users and storing the results in the scripting variable count.

<bean:struts />

The <bean:struts /> tag is used to copy a specified Struts internal component into a paged scoped scripting variable. The Struts components that can be retrieved include a FormBean, a forward, or a mapping object. The <bean:struts /> tag has no body and supports four attributes, as shown in Table 13.10.

Table 13.10 <bean:struts /> Tag Attributes

ATTRIBUTE	DESCRIPTION
id	Specifies the scripting variable used to store the retrieved Struts component. (Required)
formBean	Specifies the Struts ActionFormBean object to be copied into the named scripting variable. (Optional)
forward	Specifies the Struts ActionFormBean object to be copied into the named scripting variable. (Optional)
mapping	Contains the path of the Struts ActionMapping object to be copied into the named scripting variable. (Optional)

NOTE

The forward and mapping attributes for the <bean:struts /> tag are mutually exclusive: you can only use one of the attributes for any single <bean:struts /> tag instance.

Here's an example of how we can use the <bean:struts /> tag:

```
<bean:struts id="userForm"
  formBean="UserForm"/>
```

In this example, we retrieve a UserForm FormBean, as it is described by the struts-config.xml file, and store a reference to it in the scripting variable userForm.

<bean:write />

The <bean:write /> tag is used to retrieve and print the value of a named bean property. If the format attribute is encountered, then the value being written will be formatted based upon the format string represented by the format attribute. The <bean:write /> tag has no body and supports nine attributes, described in Table 13.11.

Table 13.11 <bean:write /> Tag Attributes

ATTRIBUTE	DESCRIPTION
bundle	Represents the condition to be evaluated by the <bean:if> tag. If the <bean:if> tag is being included from the expression language tag library, then the value represented by the test attribute must evaluate to a Boolean primitive or a java.lang.Boolean. If the <bean:if> tag is being included from the runtime tag library, then the value represented by the test attribute must evaluate to a java.lang.Boolean. (Required)
filter	If set to true, causes the retrieved value to be filtered for HTML reserved characters. If an HTML-specific character is found, it will be replaced by its encoded counterpart. The default value of this attribute is false. (Optional)
format	Specifies the format string to use when converting the retrieved value to a String. (Optional)
formatKey	Specifies the key to search for a format string that is stored in an application resource bundle. (Optional)
ignore	If set to true and the named bean does not exist, causes the tag to skip its processing and ignore its evaluation. The default value is false, which causes a runtime exception to be thrown, consistent with the other tags in this tag library. (Optional)
locale	Identifies the session bean that references the current Locale object. The default value is Action.LOCALE_KEY. (Optional)
name	Identifies the attribute name of the bean property that is being retrieved and printed. If the property attribute is not included, then the value of the bean itself will be printed. (Optional)
property	Identifies the name of the bean property being accessed. (Optional)
scope	Identifies the scope of the bean specified by the name attribute. If the scope attribute is not specified, then the tag will search for the bean in the scopes—in the order of page, request, session, and application. (Optional)

An example of using the <bean:write /> tag is shown here:

```
<bean:write name="employee"
  property="username" />
```

In this example, we retrieve and print the username property of the employee scripting variable. Here, because the scope attribute is not set, the tag will search for the bean in the scopes—in the order of page, request, session, and application.

CHAPTER 14

The HTML Tag Library

In this chapter, we discuss the Jakarta Struts HTML tag library. This taglib contains tags used to create Struts input forms, as well as other tags you will find helpful when creating HTML-based user interfaces.

Installing the HTML Tags

To use the HTML tag library in a Web application, you must complete the following steps. Be sure to replace the value *webappname* with the name of the Web application that will be using this library.

1. Copy the TLD packaged with this tag library, struts-html.tld, to the <*TOMCAT_HOME*>/webapps/*webappname*/WEB-INF directory.
2. Make sure that the struts.jar file is in the <*TOMCAT_HOME*>/webapps/*webappname*/WEB-INF/lib directory.
3. Add the following <taglib> subelement to the web.xml file of the Web application:

```
<taglib>
  <taglib-uri>/WEB-INF/struts-html.tld</taglib-uri>
  <taglib-location>/WEB-INF/struts-html.tld</taglib-location>
</taglib>
```

You must add the following taglib directive to each JSP that will leverage the HTML tag library:

```
<%@ taglib uri="/WEB-INF/struts-html.tld" prefix="html" %>
```

This directive identifies the URI defined in the previously listed <taglib> element, and states that all HTML tags should be prefixed with the string html.

<html:base />

The <html:base /> tag is used to insert an HTML <base> element, including an href pointing to the absolute location of the hosting JSP page. This allows you to use relative URL references, rather than a URL that is relative to the most recent requested resource. The <html:base /> tag has no body and supports a single attribute target, which represents the target attribute of the HTML <base> tag. To use the <html:base /> tag, you simply need to insert the tag, as shown in the following code snippet, at the top of your JSP:

```
<html:base/>
```

<html:button />

The <html:button /> tag is used to render an HTML <input> element with an input type of button. The <html:button /> has a body type of JSP, and supports the attributes described in Table 14.1.

NOTE

The <html:button /> tag must be nested inside the body of an <html:form /> tag.

Table 14.1 <html:button /> Tag Attributes (continues)

ATTRIBUTE	DESCRIPTION
property	Identifies the name of the input field being processed. (Required)
accessKey	Identifies a keyboard character to be used to immediately move focus to the HTML element defined by this tag. (Optional)
alt	Defines an alternate text string for this element. (Optional)
altKey	Defines a resources key (to be retrieved from a resource bundle) that references an alternate text string for this element. (Optional)
disabled	If set to true, causes this HTML input element to be disabled. (Optional) The default value is false.
indexed	If set to true, then the name of the HTML tag will be rendered as propertyName[indexnumber]. The [] characters surrounding the index will be generated for every iteration and taken from its ancestor, the <logic:iterate /> tag. The indexed attribute is valid only when the tag using it is nested with a <logic:iterate /> tag. (Optional) The default value is false.

Table 14.1 <html:button /> Tag Attributes (continues)

ATTRIBUTE	DESCRIPTION
onblur	Specifies a JavaScript function that will be executed when the containing element loses its focus. (Optional)
onchange	Specifies a JavaScript function that will be executed when this element loses input focus and its value has changed. (Optional)
onclick	Specifies a JavaScript function that will be executed when this element receives a mouse click. (Optional)
ondbclick	Specifies a JavaScript function that will be executed when this element receives a mouse double-click. (Optional)
onfocus	Specifies a JavaScript function that will be executed when this element receives input focus. (Optional)
onkeydown	Specifies a JavaScript function that will be executed when this element has focus and a key is pressed. (Optional)
onkeypress	Specifies a JavaScript function that will be executed when this element has focus and a key is pressed and released. (Optional)
onkeyup	Specifies a JavaScript function that will be executed when this element has focus and a key is released. (Optional)
onmousedown	Specifies a JavaScript function that will be executed when this element is under the mouse pointer and a mouse button is pressed. (Optional)
onmousemove	Specifies a JavaScript function that will be executed when this element is under the mouse pointer and the pointer is moved. (Optional)
onmouseout	Specifies a JavaScript function that will be executed when this element is under the mouse pointer, but the pointer is then moved outside the element. (Optional)
onmouseover	Specifies a JavaScript function that will be executed when this element is not under the mouse pointer, but the pointer is then moved inside the element. (Optional)
onmouseup	Specifies a JavaScript function that will be executed when this element is under the mouse pointer and a mouse button is released. (Optional)
style	Specifies a Cascading Style Sheet style to apply to this HTML element. (Optional)
styleClass	Specifies a Cascading Style Sheet class to apply to this HTML element. (Optional)
styleId	Specifies an HTML identifier to be associated with this HTML element. (Optional)
tabindex	Identifies the tab order of this element in relation to the other elements of the containing Form. (Optional)

Table 14.1 <html:button /> Tag Attributes (continued)

ATTRIBUTE	DESCRIPTION
title	Specifies the advisory title for this HTML element. (Required)
titleKey	Specifies a resources key (to be retrieved from a resource bundle) that references a title string for this element. (Optional)
value	Specifies the label to be placed on this button. The body of this tag can also be used for the button label. (Optional)

An example of using the <html:button /> tag is shown here:

```
<tr>
  <td>
    <html:button property="itemId">Add</html:button>
  </td>
</tr>
```

When this snippet is evaluated, it will result in an HTML snippet similar to the following:

```
<tr>
  <td>
    <input type="button" name="itemId" value="Add">
  </td>
</tr>
```

In this example, we are creating a simple HTML <button> that will use its body as the label of the button. It will also be named using the value of the property attribute.

<html:cancel />

The <html:cancel /> tag is used to render an HTML <input> element with an input type of cancel. The<html:cancel /> has a body type of JSP and supports 26 attributes, as shown in Table 14.2.

NOTE

The <html:cancel /> tag must be nested inside the body of an <html:form /> tag.

Table 14.2 <html:cancel /> Tag Attributes (continues)

ATTRIBUTE	DESCRIPTION
accessKey	Identifies a keyboard character to be used to immediately move focus to the HTML element defined by this tag. (Optional)

Table 14.2 <html:cancel /> Tag Attributes (continues)

ATTRIBUTE	DESCRIPTION
alt	Defines an alternate text string for this element. (Optional)
altKey	Defines a resources key (to be retrieved from a resource bundle) that references an alternate text string for this element. (Optional)
disabled	If set to true, causes this HTML input element to be disabled. The default value is false. (Optional)
indexed	If set to true, then the name of the HTML tag will be rendered as propertyName[indexnumber]. The [] characters surrounding the index will be generated for every iteration and taken from its ancestor, the <logic:iterate /> tag. The indexed attribute is valid only when the tag using it is nested with a <logic:iterate /> tag. The default value is false. (Optional)
onblur	Specifies a JavaScript function that will be executed when the containing element loses its focus. (Optional)
onchange	Specifies a JavaScript function that will be executed when this element loses input focus and its value has changed. (Optional)
onclick	Specifies a JavaScript function that will be executed when this element receives a mouse click. (Optional)
ondbclick	Specifies a JavaScript function that will be executed when this element receives a mouse double-click. (Optional)
onfocus	Specifies a JavaScript function that will be executed when this element receives input focus. (Optional)
onkeydown	Specifies a JavaScript function that will be executed when this element has focus and a key is pressed. (Optional)
onkeypress	Specifies a JavaScript function that will be executed when this element has focus and a key is pressed and released. (Optional)
onkeyup	Specifies a JavaScript function that will be executed when this element has focus and a key is released. (Optional)
onmousedown	Specifies a JavaScript function that will be executed when this element is under the mouse pointer and a mouse button is pressed. (Optional)
onmousemove	Specifies a JavaScript function that will be executed when this element is under the mouse pointer and the pointer is moved. (Optional)
onmouseout	Specifies a JavaScript function that will be executed when this element is under the mouse pointer, but the pointer is then moved outside the element. (Optional)
onmouseover	Specifies a JavaScript function that will be executed when this element is not under the mouse pointer, but the pointer is then moved inside the element. (Optional)

Table 14.2 <html:cancel /> Tag Attributes (continued)

ATTRIBUTE	DESCRIPTION
onmouseup	Specifies a JavaScript function that will be executed when this element is under the mouse pointer and a mouse button is released. (Optional)
property	Identifies the name of the input field being processed. (Optional)
style	Specifies a Cascading Style Sheet style to apply to this HTML element. (Optional)
styleClass	Specifies a Cascading Style Sheet class to apply to this HTML element. (Optional)
styleId	Specifies an HTML identifier to be associated with this HTML element. (Optional)
tabindex	Identifies the tab order of this element in relation to the other elements of the containing Form. (Optional)
title	Specifies the advisory title for this HTML element. (Required)
titleKey	Specifies a resources key (to be retrieved from a resource bundle) that references a title string for this element. (Optional)
value	Specifies the label to be placed on this button. The body of this tag can also be used for the button label. (Optional)

An example of using the <html:cancel /> tag is shown here:

```
<tr>
  <td>
    <html:cancel />
  </td>
</tr>
```

When this snippet is evaluated, it will result in an HTML snippet similar to the following:

```
<tr>
  <td>
    <input type="submit"
      name="org.apache.struts.taglib.html.CANCEL"
      value="Cancel">
  </td>
</tr>
```

In this example, we are creating a simple HTML cancel button. You will note that this element has a unique name, org.apache.struts.taglib.html.CANCEL. This name tells the Struts framework that this is a special button that causes the browser to go back to the input path associated with the <html:form /> action attribute.

<html:checkbox />

The <html:checkbox /> tag is used to render an HTML <input> element with an input type of checkbox. The<html:checkbox /> has a body type of JSP and supports 26 attributes, described in Table 14.3.

NOTE

The <html:checkbox /> tag must be nested inside the body of an <html:form /> tag. Another thing to note about this tag is that in order to correctly recognize deselected checkboxes, the ActionForm bean associated with the parent form must include a reset() method that sets the property corresponding to this checkbox to false.

Table 14.3 <html:checkbox /> Tag Attributes (continues)

ATTRIBUTE	DESCRIPTION
accessKey	Identifies a keyboard character to be used to immediately move focus to the HTML element defined by this tag. (Optional)
alt	Defines an alternate text string for this element. (Optional)
altKey	Defines a resources key (to be retrieved from a resource bundle) that references an alternate text string for this element. (Optional)
disabled	If set to true, causes this HTML input element to be disabled. The default value is false. (Optional)
indexed	If set to true, then the name of the HTML tag will be rendered as propertyName[indexnumber]. The [] characters surrounding the index will be generated for every iteration and taken from its ancestor, the <logic:iterate /> tag. The indexed attribute is valid only when the tag using it is nested with a <logic:iterate /> tag. (Optional)
onblur	Specifies a JavaScript function that will be executed when the containing element loses its focus. (Optional)
onchange	Specifies a JavaScript function that will be executed when this element loses input focus and its value has changed. (Optional)
onclick	Specifies a JavaScript function that will be executed when this element receives a mouse click. (Optional)
ondbclick	Specifies a JavaScript function that will be executed when this element receives a mouse double-click. (Optional)
onfocus	Specifies a JavaScript function that will be executed when this element receives input focus. (Optional)

Table 14.3 <html:checkbox /> Tag Attributes (continued)

ATTRIBUTE	DESCRIPTION
onkeydown	Specifies a JavaScript function that will be executed when this element has focus and a key is pressed. (Optional)
onkeypress	Specifies a JavaScript function that will be executed when this element has focus and a key is pressed and released. (Optional)
onkeyup	Specifies a JavaScript function that will be executed when this element has focus and a key is released. (Optional)
onmousedown	Specifies a JavaScript function that will be executed when this element is under the mouse pointer and a mouse button is pressed. (Optional)
onmousemove	Specifies a JavaScript function that will be executed when this element is under the mouse pointer and the pointer is moved. (Optional)
onmouseout	Specifies a JavaScript function that will be executed when this element is under the mouse pointer, but the pointer is then moved outside the element. (Optional)
onmouseover	Specifies a JavaScript function that will be executed when this element is not under the mouse pointer, but the pointer is then moved inside the element. (Optional)
onmouseup	Specifies a JavaScript function that will be executed when this element is under the mouse pointer and a mouse button is released. (Optional)
property	Identifies the name of the input field being processed. (Optional)
style	Specifies a Cascading Style Sheet style to apply to this HTML element. (Optional)
styleClass	Specifies a Cascading Style Sheet class to apply to this HTML element. (Optional)
styleId	Specifies an HTML identifier to be associated with this HTML element. (Optional)
tabindex	Identifies the tab order of this element in relation to the other elements of the containing Form. (Optional)
title	Specifies the advisory title for this HTML element. (Required)
titleKey	Specifies a resources key (to be retrieved from a resource bundle) that references a title string for this element. (Optional)
value	Specifies the label to be placed on the request if this checkbox is selected. The default value is on. (Optional)

NOTE

The body of this tag can also be used as the element label.

An example of using the <html:checkbox /> tag is shown here:

```
<tr>
  <td>
    <html:checkbox property="deleteItem">
      Delete
    </html:checkbox>
  </td>
</tr>
```

When this snippet is evaluated, it will result in an HTML snippet similar to the following:

```
<tr>
  <td>
    <input type="checkbox"
      name="deleteItem"
      value="on">
    Delete
  </td>
</tr>
```

NOTE

This example assumes that there is an ActionForm bean, named by the <action> element associated with this form, with a property of deleteItem.

In this example, we are creating a simple HTML checkbox, with a name of deleteItem and a label of Delete. This will result in the creation of a checkbox with the value of the ActionForm's deleteItem property.

<html:errors />

The <html:errors /> tag is used to display the ActionError objects stored in an ActionErrors collection. The <html:errors /> tag has a body type of JSP and supports four attributes, described in Table 14.4.

Table 14.4 <html:errors /> Tag Attributes (continues)

ATTRIBUTE	DESCRIPTION
bundle	Specifies a MessageResources key of the resource bundle defined in the struts-config <message-resource> element. The default key is ApplicationResources. (Optional)

Table 14.4 <html:errors /> Tag Attributes (continued)

ATTRIBUTE	DESCRIPTION
locale	Specifies the session attribute containing the Locale instance of the current request. This Locale is then used to select Locale-specific text messages. (Optional)
name	Specifies the name of the request scope object that references the ActionErrors collection being displayed. The default value is Action.ERROR_KEY. (Optional)
property	Specifies which error messages should be displayed, based on each property contained in the ActionErrors collection. The default value indicates that all error messages should be displayed. (Optional)

To use the <html:errors /> tag, you simply need to insert the tag as shown in the following code snippet:

```
<html:errors />
```

We saw this tag used in Chapter 7, "Managing Errors."

<html:form />

The <html:form /> tag is used to create an HTML form. The form implicitly interacts with the named ActionForm bean to prepopulate the input fields values with the matching data members of the named bean. The <html:form /> tag has a body type of JSP and supports 13 attributes, described in Table 14.5.

Table 14.5 <html:form /> Tag Attributes (continues)

ATTRIBUTE	DESCRIPTION
action	Identifies the URL to which this form will be submitted. This value is also used to select an ActionMapping described by an <action> element in the struts-config.xml file. (Required)
enctype	Identifies the content encoding of the request submitted by this form. If you are using the file tag, then this attribute must be set to multipart/form-data. If this value is not indicated, then the default value is determined by the client browser. (Optional)
focus	Identifies the input field name to which initial focus will be assigned. (Required)

Table 14.5 <html:form /> Tag Attributes (continued)

ATTRIBUTE	DESCRIPTION
method	Identifies the HTTP request method used when submitting the form request (GET|POST). The default method is POST. (Optional)
name	Identifies the ActionForm bean whose properties will be used to populate the input field values rendered by this tag. If the named ActionForm bean is not found, then a new ActionForm bean will be created. (Required)
onreset	Specifies a JavaScript function that will be executed if the form is reset. (Optional)
onresubmit	Specifies a JavaScript function that will be executed if the form is submitted. (Optional)
scope	Specifies the scope of the form bean associated with this input form. (Optional)
style	Specifies a Cascading Style Sheet style to apply to this HTML element. (Optional)
styleClass	Specifies a Cascading Style Sheet class to apply to this HTML element. (Optional)
styleId	Specifies an HTML identifier to be associated with this HTML element. (Optional)
target	Specifies the frame window target to which this form is submitted. (Optional)
type	Provides the fully qualified class name of the ActionForm bean to be created, if no such bean is found in the named scope. (Optional)

An example of using the <html:form /> tag is shown here:

```
<html:form action="Search.do"
  name="searchForm"
  type="com.wiley.SearchForm" >

  <table width="45%" border="0">
    <tr>
      <td>Search String:</td>
      <td><html:text property="searchString" /></td>
    </tr>
    <tr>
      <td colspan="2" align="center"><html:submit /></td>
    </tr>
  </table>

</html:form>
```

In this example, we are creating an HTML form that will execute the Struts action associated with the path Search. It will look for an ActionForm bean named searchForm. If the searchForm bean is not found, the form will create it. Once it has a reference to this bean, it will then make all of its properties available to its nested HTML tags.

<html:hidden />

The <html:hidden /> tag is used to render an HTML <input> element with an input type of hidden. The<html:hidden /> has a body type of JSP and supports eight attributes, described in Table 14.6.

NOTE

The <html:hidden /> tag must be nested inside the body of an <html:form /> tag.

Table 14.6 <html:hidden /> Tag Attributes

ATTRIBUTE	DESCRIPTION
property	Identifies the ActionForm property used to set this element. (Required)
alt	Defines an alternate text string for this element. (Optional)
altKey	Defines a resources key (to be retrieved from a resource bundle) that references an alternate text string for this element. (Optional)
indexed	If set to true, then the name of the HTML tag will be rendered as propertyName[indexnumber]. The [] characters surrounding the index will be generated for every iteration and taken from its ancestor, the <logic:iterate /> tag. The indexed attribute is valid only when the tag using it is nested with a <logic:iterate /> tag. The default value is false. (Optional)
name	Specifies an ActionForm bean used to set the initial value of this element. If the name attribute is not indicated, then the ActionForm bean associated with the form tag containing this tag is used. (Optional)
title	Specifies the advisory title for this HTML element. (Optional)
titleKey	Specifies a resources key (to be retrieved from a resource bundle) that references a title advisory string for this element. (Optional)
value	Specifies the value that this element will be initialized with. (Optional)

An example of using the <html:hidden /> tag is shown here:

```
<html:hidden property="itemId" />
```

When this snippet is evaluated, it will result in an HTML snippet similar to the following:

```
<input type="hidden" name="itemId" value="54774">
```

NOTE

This example assumes that there is an ActionForm bean, named by the <action> element associated with this form, with a property of itemId.

In this example, we are creating a simple <html:hidden /> tag with a single attribute property, which is set to the value itemId. When this tag instance is evaluated, it will generate an HTML <hidden> element, with a name of itemId and a value of 54774, which was retrieved from the form's ActionForm bean's itemId property.

<html:html />

The <html:html /> tag is used to render the top-level <html> element. The <html:html /> tag has a body type of JSP and supports two attributes, as shown in Table 14.7.

Table 14.7 <html:html /> Tag Attributes

ATTRIBUTE	DESCRIPTION
locale	If set to true, then the Locale object named by the HTTP Accept-Language header will be used to set the language preferences. The default value is false. (Optional)
xhtml	If set to true, causes an xml:lang attribute to be rendered as an attribute of the generated <html> element. The default value is false. (Optional)

To use the <html:html /> tag, you simply need to surround the body of your JSP with opening and closing <html:html /> tags, as shown in the following code snippet:

```
<html:html>

     JSP body

</html:html>
```

<html:image />

The <html:image /> tag is used to render an HTML <input> element with an input type of image. The image URL generated for this image is calculated using the value identified by the src or page attributes. You must specify one of the src or page attributes. The <html:image /> has a body type of JSP and supports 34 attributes, described in Table 14.8.

NOTE

The <html:image /> tag must be nested inside the body of an <html:form /> tag.

Table 14.8 <html:image /> Tag Attributes (continues)

ATTRIBUTE	DESCRIPTION
accessKey	Identifies a keyboard character to be used to immediately move focus to the HTML element defined by this tag. (Optional)
align	Defines the image alignment of this image. (Optional)
alt	Defines an alternate text string for this element. (Optional)
altKey	Defines a resources key (to be retrieved from a resource bundle) that references an alternate text string for this element. (Optional)
border	Defines the width, in pixels, of the image border. (Optional)
bundle	Specifies a MessageResources key of the resource bundle defined in the struts-config <message-resource> element. The default key is ApplicationResources. (Optional)
disabled	If set to true, causes this HTML input element to be disabled. The default value is false. (Optional)
indexed	If set to true, then the name of the HTML tag will be rendered as propertyName[indexnumber]. The [] characters surrounding the index will be generated for every iteration and taken from its ancestor, the <logic:iterate /> tag. The indexed attribute is valid only when the tag using it is nested with a <logic:iterate /> tag. The default value is false. (Optional)
locale	Specifies the session attribute containing the Locale instance of the current request. This Locale is then used to select Locale-specific text messages. (Optional)
onblur	Specifies a JavaScript function that will be executed when the containing element loses its focus. (Optional)
onchange	Specifies a JavaScript function that will be executed when this element loses input focus and its value has changed. (Optional)

Table 14.8 <html:image /> Tag Attributes (continues)

ATTRIBUTE	DESCRIPTION
onclick	Specifies a JavaScript function that will be executed when this element receives a mouse click. (Optional)
ondbclick	Specifies a JavaScript function that will be executed when this element receives a mouse double-click. (Optional)
onfocus	Specifies a JavaScript function that will be executed when this element receives input focus. (Optional)
onkeydown	Specifies a JavaScript function that will be executed when this element has focus and a key is pressed. (Optional)
onkeypress	Specifies a JavaScript function that will be executed when this element has focus and a key is pressed and released. (Optional)
onkeyup	Specifies a JavaScript function that will be executed when this element has focus and a key is released. (Optional)
onmousedown	Specifies a JavaScript function that will be executed when this element is under the mouse pointer and a mouse button is pressed. (Optional)
onmousemove	Specifies a JavaScript function that will be executed when this element is under the mouse pointer and the pointer is moved. (Optional)
onmouseout	Specifies a JavaScript function that will be executed when this element is under the mouse pointer, but the pointer is then moved outside the element. (Optional)
onmouseover	Specifies a JavaScript function that will be executed when this element is not under the mouse pointer, but the pointer is then moved inside the element. (Optional)
onmouseup	Specifies a JavaScript function that will be executed when this element is under the mouse pointer and a mouse button is released. (Optional)
page	Provides the application-relative path of the image source used by this input tag. (Optional)
pageKey	Specifies a resources key (to be retrieved from a resource bundle) that references an application-relative path of the image source used by this input tag. (Optional)
property	Identifies the parameter names of the image tag. The parameter names will appear as property.x and property.y, with the x and y characters representing the coordinates of the mouse click for the image. (Optional)
src	Specifies a URL that references the location of the image source used by this input tag. (Optional)

Table 14.8 <html:image /> Tag Attributes (continued)

ATTRIBUTE	DESCRIPTION
srcKey	Specifies a resources key (to be retrieved from a resource bundle) that references a URL pointing to the location of the image source used by this input tag. (Optional)
style	Specifies a Cascading Style Sheet style to apply to this HTML element. (Optional)
styleClass	Specifies a Cascading Style Sheet class to apply to this HTML element. (Optional)
styleId	Specifies an HTML identifier to be associated with this HTML element. (Optional)
tabindex	Identifies the tab order of this element in relation to the other elements of the containing Form. (Optional)
title	Specifies the advisory title for this HTML element. (Required)
titleKey	Specifies a resources key (to be retrieved from a resource bundle) that references a title string for this element. (Optional)
value	Specifies the label to be placed on this button. (Optional)

An example of using the <html:image /> tag is shown here:

```
<html:image property="add" src="images/add.gif" />
```

When this snippet is evaluated, it will result in an HTML snippet similar to the following:

```
<input type="image" name="add" src="images/add.gif">
```

In this example, we are creating a simple <html:image /> tag with an attribute property (which is used to name the tag's request parameter) and an src element (which references the location of the image to be used by this tag). When this tag instance is evaluated, it will generate an HTML <input> element of type image that executes the action associated with its parent's action attribute.

<html:img />

The <html:img /> tag is used to render an HTML <img> element. The image URL generated for this image is calculated using the value identified by the src or page attributes. You must specify one of the src or page attributes. The <html:image /> has a body type of JSP and supports 35 attributes, described in Table 14.9.

Table 14.9 <html:img /> Tag Attributes (continues)

ATTRIBUTE	DESCRIPTION
accessKey	Identifies a keyboard character to be used to immediately move focus to the HTML element defined by this tag. (Optional)
align	Defines the image alignment of this image. (Optional)
alt	Defines an alternate text string for this element. (Optional)
altKey	Defines a resources key (to be retrieved from a resource bundle) that references an alternate text string for this element. (Optional)
border	Defines the width, in pixels, of the image border. (Optional)
bundle	Specifies a MessageResources key of the resource bundle defined in the struts-config <message-resource> element. The default key is ApplicationResources. (Optional)
disabled	If set to true, causes this HTML input element to be disabled. The default value is false. (Optional)
height	Indicates the height of the image, in pixels. (Optional)
hspave	Specifies the amount of horizontal space, in pixels, between the image and the text. (Optional)
mageName	Defines a JavaScript name that can be referenced by JavaScript methods. (Optional)
ismap	Specifies a server-side map that this image references, if applicable. (Optional)
locale	Specifies the session attribute containing the Locale instance of the current request. This Locale is then used to select Locale-specific text messages. (Optional)
lowsrc	Specifies an image for clients with low-resolution graphics cards. (Optional)
name	Identifies a scripting variable containing a java.util.Map object of parameters and values to be appended to the src attribute, enabling the dynamic augmentation of the image src. (Optional)
property	Identifies a data member of the bean named by the name attribute that contains the java.util.Map object of parameters. (Optional)
scope	Identifies the scope of the bean specified by the name attribute. If the scope attribute is not specified, then the tag will search for the bean in the scopes–in the order of page, request, session, and application. (Optional)
onkeydown	Specifies a JavaScript function that will be executed when this element has focus and a key is pressed. (Optional)
onkeypress	Specifies a JavaScript function that will be executed when this element has focus and a key is pressed and released. (Optional)

Table 14.9 <html:img /> Tag Attributes (continued)

ATTRIBUTE	DESCRIPTION
onkeyup	Specifies a JavaScript function that will be executed when this element has focus and a key is released. (Optional)
paramId	Specifies a request parameter that will be added to the generated src URL when the hosting JSP is requested. (Optional)
page	Specifies the application-relative path of the image source used by this input tag. (Optional)
pageKey	Specifies a resources key (to be retrieved from a resource bundle) that references an application-relative path of the image source used by this input tag. (Optional)
paramName	Identifies the name of a scripting variable of type java.lang.String that referenced the value for the request parameter identified by paramId attribute. (Optional)
paramProperty	Identifies a data member of the bean named by the paramName attribute that will be dynamically added to this src URL. (Optional)
paramScope	Identifies the scope of the bean specified by the paramName attribute. If the paramScope attribute is not specified, then the tag will search for the bean in the scopes—in the order of page, request, session, and application. (Optional)
src	Specifies a URL that references the location of the image source used by this tag. (Optional)
srcKey	Specifies a resources key (to be retrieved from a resource bundle) that references a URL pointing to the location of the image source used by this tag. (Optional)
style	Specifies a Cascading Style Sheet style to apply to this tag's HTML element. (Optional)
styleClass	Specifies a Cascading Style Sheet class to apply to this tag's HTML element. (Optional)
styleId	Specifies an HTML identifier to be associated with this tag's HTML element. (Optional)
title	Specifies the advisory title for this HTML element. (Required)
titleKey	Specifies a resources key (to be retrieved from a resource bundle) that references a title string for this element. (Optional)
usemap	Specifies a coordinate map used when hyperlinking a hot-spot of this image. (Optional)
vspace	Indicates the amount of vertical spacing between the identified image and its surrounding text. (Optional)
width	Indicates the width of the image being displayed. (Optional)

An example of using the <html:img /> tag is shown here:

```
<html:img page="/images/code.gif" alt="Add to Basket"/>
```

When this snippet is evaluated, it will result in an HTML snippet similar to the following:

```
<img src="/webappname/images/add.gif"
  alt="Add to Basket">
```

In this example, we are creating a simple <html:img /> tag with two attributes: page (which references the location of the image to display) and alt (which defines an alternate string that will be displayed when the image cannot be found).

<html:link />

The <html:link /> tag is used to generate an HTML hyperlink. The URL for the generated link can be calculated using either the forward, href, or page attributes. The <html:link /> tag has a body type of JSP and supports 35 attributes, described in Table 14.10.

Table 14.10 <html:link /> Tag Attributes (continues)

ATTRIBUTE	DESCRIPTION
accessKey	Identifies a keyboard character to be used to immediately move focus to the HTML element defined by this tag. (Optional)
anchor	Used to append an HTML anchor to the end of a generated hyperlink. (Optional)
forward	Identifies the name of the global forward element that will receive control of the forwarded request. (Optional)
href	Specifies the URL of the resource to forward the current request to. (Optional)
name	Identifies a scripting variable referencing a java.util.Map object, whose collection of key/value pairs is used as the HTTP request parameter augmenting the redirected request. (Optional)
indexed	If set to true, then the name of the HTML tag will be rendered as propertyName[indexnumber]. The [] characters surrounding the index will be generated for every iteration and taken from its ancestor, the <logic:iterate /> tag. The indexed attribute is valid only when the tag using it is nested with a <logic:iterate /> tag. The default value is false. (Optional)

Table 14.10 <html:link /> Tag Attributes (continues)

ATTRIBUTE	DESCRIPTION
indexId	Specifies a JSP scripting variable, exposed by the <logic:iterate /> tag, that will hold the current index of the current object in the named collection. (Optional)
linkName	Specifies an anchor to be defined within the hosting page, so that you can reference it with hyperlinks hosted in the same document. (Optional)
onblur	Specifies a JavaScript function that will be executed when the containing element loses its focus. (Optional)
onchange	Specifies a JavaScript function that will be executed when this element loses input focus and its value has changed. (Optional)
onclick	Specifies a JavaScript function that will be executed when this element receives a mouse click. (Optional)
ondbclick	Specifies a JavaScript function that will be executed when this element receives a mouse double-click. (Optional)
onfocus	Specifies a JavaScript function that will be executed when this element receives input focus. (Optional)
onkeydown	Specifies a JavaScript function that will be executed when this element has focus and a key is pressed. (Optional)
onkeypress	Specifies a JavaScript function that will be executed when this element has focus and a key is pressed and released. (Optional)
onkeyup	Specifies a JavaScript function that will be executed when this element has focus and a key is released. (Optional)
onmousedown	Specifies a JavaScript function that will be executed when this element is under the mouse pointer and a mouse button is pressed. (Optional)
onmousemove	Specifies a JavaScript function that will be executed when this element is under the mouse pointer and the pointer is moved. (Optional)
onmouseout	Specifies a JavaScript function that will be executed when this element is under the mouse pointer, but the pointer is then moved outside the element. (Optional)
onmouseover	Specifies a JavaScript function that will be executed when this element is not under the mouse pointer, but the pointer is then moved inside the element. (Optional)
onmouseup	Specifies a JavaScript function that will be executed when this element is under the mouse pointer and a mouse button is released. (Optional)
page	Specifies an application-relative path of the image source used by this input tag. (Optional)

Table 14.10 <html:link /> Tag Attributes (continued)

ATTRIBUTE	DESCRIPTION
pageKey	Specifies a resources key (to be retrieved from a resource bundle) that references an application-relative path of the image source used by this input tag. (Optional)
paramName	Identifies the name of a scripting variable of type java.lang.String that references the value to be used for the request parameter identified by the paramId attribute. (Optional)
paramProperty	Used to identify a data member of the bean named by the paramName attribute that will be dynamically added to this src URL. (Optional)
paramScope	Specifies the scope of the bean specified by the paramName attribute. If the paramScope attribute is not specified, then the tag will search for the bean in the scopes—in the order of page, request, session, and application. (Optional)
property	Used to identify a data member of the bean named by the name attribute that contains the java.util.Map object of parameters. (Optional)
scope	Identifies the scope of the bean specified by the name attribute. If the scope attribute is not specified, then the tag will search for the bean in the scopes—in the order of page, request, session, and application. (Optional)
style	Specifies a Cascading Style Sheet style to apply to this HTML element. (Optional)
styleClass	Specifies a Cascading Style Sheet class to apply to this HTML element. (Optional)
styleId	Specifies an HTML identifier to be associated with this HTML element. (Optional)
tabindex	Identifies the tab order of this element in relation to the other elements of the containing Form. (Optional)
title	Specifies the advisory title for this HTML element. (Required)
titleKey	Specifies a resources key (to be retrieved from a resource bundle) that references a title string for this element. (Optional)
transaction	If set to true, indicates that the current transaction control token should be included in the generated URL. The default value is false. (Optional)

An example of using the <html:link /> tag is shown here:

```
<%
  String userName = "Bob";
  pageContext.setAttribute("userName", userName);
%>

<html:link page="/Edit.do"
```

```
    paramId="user" paramName="userName">
    Edit User
  </html:link>
```

When this snippet is evaluated, it will result in an HTML snippet similar to the following:

```
<a href="/webappname/Edit.do?user=Bob">Edit User</a>
```

In this example, we are creating a simple <html:link /> tag with three attributes: page, which references the action that will be executed when this link is selected; paramId, which defines a request parameter that will be appended to the request string; and paramName, which will retrieve the value of the userName variable and set it to the value of the user request parameter.

<html:multibox />

The <html:multibox /> tag is used to generate an HTML <input> element of type checkbox. The <html:multibox /> has a body type of JSP and supports 26 attributes, described in Table 14.11.

Table 14.11 <html:multibox /> Tag Attributes (continues)

ATTRIBUTE	DESCRIPTION
accessKey	Identifies a keyboard character to be used to immediately move focus to the HTML element defined by this tag. (Optional)
alt	Defines an alternate text string for this element. (Optional)
altKey	Defines a resources key (to be retrieved from a resource bundle) that references an alternate text string for this element. (Optional)
disabled	If set to true, causes this HTML input element to be disabled. The default value is false. (Optional)
name	Identifies a scripting variable referencing a java.util.Map object, whose collection of key/value pairs is used as the HTTP request parameter augmenting the redirected request. (Optional)
onblur	Specifies a JavaScript function that will be executed when the containing element loses its focus. (Optional)
onchange	Specifies a JavaScript function that will be executed when this element loses input focus and its value has changed. (Optional)
onclick	Specifies a JavaScript function that will be executed when this element receives a mouse click. (Optional)
ondbclick	Specifies a JavaScript function that will be executed when this element receives a mouse double-click. (Optional)

Table 14.11 <html:multibox /> Tag Attributes (continued)

ATTRIBUTE	DESCRIPTION
onfocus	Specifies a JavaScript function that will be executed when this element receives input focus. (Optional)
onkeydown	Specifies a JavaScript function that will be executed when this element has focus and a key is pressed. (Optional)
onkeypress	Specifies a JavaScript function that will be executed when this element has focus and a key is pressed and released. (Optional)
onkeyup	Specifies a JavaScript function that will be executed when this element has focus and a key is released. (Optional)
onmousedown	Specifies a JavaScript function that will be executed when this element is under the mouse pointer and a mouse button is pressed. (Optional)
onmousemove	Specifies a JavaScript function that will be executed when this element is under the mouse pointer and the pointer is moved. (Optional)
onmouseout	Specifies a JavaScript function that will be executed when this element is under the mouse pointer but the pointer is then moved outside the element. (Optional)
onmouseover	Specifies a JavaScript function that will be executed when this element is not under the mouse pointer but the pointer is then moved inside the element. (Optional)
onmouseup	Specifies a JavaScript function that will be executed when this element is under the mouse pointer and a mouse button is released. (Optional)
property	Used to identify a data member of the bean named by the name attribute that contains the java.util.Map object of parameters. (Optional)
style	Specifies a Cascading Style Sheet style to apply to this HTML element. (Optional)
styleClass	Specifies a Cascading Style Sheet class to apply to this HTML element. (Optional)
styleId	Specifies an HTML identifier to be associated with this HTML element. (Optional)
tabindex	Identifies the tab order of this element in relation to the other elements of the containing Form. (Optional)
title	Specifies the advisory title for this HTML element. (Required)
titleKey	Specifies a resources key (to be retrieved from a resource bundle) that references a title string for this element. (Optional)
value	Represents the value that will be submitted if this checkbox is selected. (Optional)

An example of using the <html:multibox /> tag is shown here:

NOTE

For this example, it is assumed that the parent <html:form /> contains a reference to an ActionForm that contains a String array with the values Bob, Robert, Bobby, and Roberto.

```
<tr>
  <td align="left">
    Bob
    <html:multibox property="nameArray">
      Bob
    </html:multibox>
  </td>
  <td align="left">
    Robert
    <html:multibox property="nameArray">
      Robert
    </html:multibox>
  </td>
  <td align="left">
    Bobby
    <html:multibox property="nameArray">
      Bobby
    </html:multibox>
  </td>
  <td align="left">
    Roberto
    <html:multibox property="nameArray">
      Roberto
    </html:multibox>
  </td>
</tr>
```

NOTE

The body of this tag can also be used as the element label.

When this snippet is evaluated, it will result in an HTML snippet similar to the following:

```
<tr>
  <td align="left">
    Bob
    <input type="checkbox" name="nameArray"
      value="Bob" checked="checked">
  </td>
  <td align="left">
    Robert
```

```
        <input type="checkbox" name="nameArray"
          value="Robert" checked="checked">
      </td>
      <td align="left">
        Bobby
        <input type="checkbox" name="nameArray"
          value="Bobby" checked="checked">
      </td>
    <tr>
      <td align="left">
        Ralph
        <input type="checkbox" name="nameArray" value="Ralph">
      </td>
    </tr>
```

In this example, we are creating a series of <html:multibox /> tags with a single attribute property, which is used to associate the tag with an array of Strings. The values of the associated array will be compared, in index order, to the String in the body of the tag. If the current String in the array matches the body of the tag, then the checkbox generated by the tag will be marked as checked. In this example, all checkboxes have a match, excluding the checkbox with the value Ralph.

<html:select />

The <html:select /> tag is used to render an HTML <input> element with an input type of select. The <html:select /> has a body type of JSP and supports 28 attributes, described in Table 14.12.

NOTE

The <html:select /> tag must be nested inside the body of an <html:form /> tag.

Table 14.12 <html:select /> Tag Attributes (continues)

ATTRIBUTE	DESCRIPTION
property	Specifies a request parameter that will be included with the current request, set to the value of the selection. (Required)
accessKey	Identifies a keyboard character to be used to immediately move focus to the HTML element defined by this tag. (Optional)
alt	Defines an alternate text string for this element. (Optional)
altKey	Defines a resources key (to be retrieved from a resource bundle) that references an alternate text string for this element. (Optional)

Table 14.12 <html:select /> Tag Attributes (continues)

ATTRIBUTE	DESCRIPTION
disabled	If set to true, causes this HTML input element to be disabled. The default value is false. (Optional)
indexed	If set to true, then the name of the HTML tag will be rendered as propertyName[indexnumber]. The [] characters surrounding the index will be generated for every iteration and taken from its ancestor, the <logic:iterate /> tag. The indexed attribute is valid only when the tag using it is nested with a <logic:iterate /> tag. The default value is false. (Optional)
multiple	If set to true, creates a <select> list support for multiple selections. The default value is false. (Optional)
onblur	Specifies a JavaScript function that will be executed when the containing element loses its focus. (Optional)
onchange	Specifies a JavaScript function that will be executed when this element loses input focus and its value has changed. (Optional)
onclick	Specifies a JavaScript function that will be executed when this element receives a mouse click. (Optional)
ondbclick	Specifies a JavaScript function that will be executed when this element receives a mouse double-click. (Optional)
onfocus	Specifies a JavaScript function that will be executed when this element receives input focus. (Optional)
onkeydown	Specifies a JavaScript function that will be executed when this element has focus and a key is pressed. (Optional)
onkeypress	Specifies a JavaScript function that will be executed when this element has focus and a key is pressed and released. (Optional)
onkeyup	Specifies a JavaScript function that will be executed when this element has focus and a key is released. (Optional)
onmousedown	Specifies a JavaScript function that will be executed when this element is under the mouse pointer and a mouse button is pressed. (Optional)
onmousemove	Specifies a JavaScript function that will be executed when this element is under the mouse pointer and the pointer is moved. (Optional)
onmouseout	Specifies a JavaScript function that will be executed when this element is under the mouse pointer, but the pointer is then moved outside the element. (Optional)
onmouseover	Specifies a JavaScript function that will be executed when this element is not under the mouse pointer, but the pointer is then moved inside the element. (Optional)

Table 14.12 <html:select /> Tag Attributes (continued)

ATTRIBUTE	DESCRIPTION
onmouseup	Specifies a JavaScript function that will be executed when this element is under the mouse pointer and a mouse button is released. (Optional)
style	Specifies a Cascading Style Sheet style to apply to this HTML element. (Optional)
styleClass	Specifies a Cascading Style Sheet class to apply to this HTML element. (Optional)
styleId	Specifies an HTML identifier to be associated with this HTML element. (Optional)
tabindex	Identifies the tab order of this element in relation to the other elements of the containing Form. (Optional)
size	Indicates the number of options to display at once. (Optional)
title	Specifies the advisory title for this HTML element. (Required)
titleKey	Specifies a resources key (to be retrieved from a resource bundle) that references a title string for this element. (Optional)
value	Specifies the value to test for when setting the currently selected option. (Optional)

An example of using the <html:select /> tag is shown here:

NOTE

For this example, it is assumed that the parent <html:form /> contains a reference to an ActionForm that contains the String property, userName, set to the value Bob.

```
<tr>
  <td>
    <html:select property="userName">
      <html:option value="Robert">Robert</html:option>
      <html:option value="Bob">Bob</html:option>
      <html:option value="Roberto">Roberto</html:option>
      <html:option value="Bobby">Bobby</html:option>
    </html:select>
  </td>
</tr>
```

When this snippet is evaluated, it will result in an HTML snippet similar to the following:

```
<tr>
  <td>
    <select name="userName">
```

```
        <option value="Robert">Robert</option>
        <option value="Bob" selected="selected">Bob</option>
        <option value="Roberto">Roberto</option>
        <option value="Bobby">Bobby</option>
      </select>
    </td>
  </tr>
```

In this example, we are creating a <html:select /> tag with a single attribute property, which maps to the ActionForm bean property userName. This property is used to determine the currently selected <option> of the <select> element, which will be demonstrated in the <html:option /> and <html:options /> tags.

<html:option />

The <html:option /> tag is used to generate an HTML <input> element of type <option>, which represents a single option element nested inside a parent <select> element. This <html:option /> tag has a body type of JSP and supports seven attributes, described in Table 14.13.

NOTE

This tag is valid only when nested within an <html:select /> tag.

Table 14.13 <html:option /> Tag Attributes (continues)

ATTRIBUTE	DESCRIPTION
value	Represents the value that will be submitted if this checkbox is selected. (Required)
bundle	Specifies a MessageResources key of the resource bundle defined in the struts-config <message-resource> element. The default key is ApplicationResources. (Optional)
disabled	If set to true, causes this HTML input element to be disabled. The default value is false. (Optional)
key	Defines a resources key (to be retrieved from a resource bundle) that references a text string to be displayed to the user as this element's text value. (Optional)
locale	Specifies the session attribute containing the Locale instance of the current request. This Locale is then used to select Locale-specific text messages. (Optional)

Table 14.13 <html:option /> Tag Attributes (continued)

ATTRIBUTE	DESCRIPTION
style	Specifies a Cascading Style Sheet style to apply to this HTML element. (Optional)
styleClass	Specifies a Cascading Style Sheet class to apply to this HTML element. (Optional)

An example of using the <html:option /> tag is shown here:

NOTE

For this example, it is assumed that the parent <html:form /> contains a reference to an ActionForm that contains the String property, userName, set to the value Bob.

```
<tr>
  <td>
    <html:select property="userName">
      <html:option value="Robert">Robert</html:option>
      <html:option value="Bob">Bob</html:option>
      <html:option value="Roberto">Roberto</html:option>
      <html:option value="Bobby">Bobby</html:option>
    </html:select>
  </td>
</tr>
```

NOTE

The body of this tag can also be used as the element label.

When this snippet is evaluated, it will result in an HTML snippet similar to the following:

```
<tr>
  <td>
    <select name="userName">
      <option value="Robert">Robert</option>
      <option value="Bob" selected="selected">Bob</option>
      <option value="Roberto">Roberto</option>
      <option value="Bobby">Bobby</option>
  </td>
</tr>
```

In this example, we are creating a collection of <html:option /> tags with a single attribute value. These value attributes are compared to the value of the ActionForm bean property named by the <html:select /> attribute property. If the current String referenced by the named beans property equals one of the

<html:option /> tag's value attributes, then the matching <option> element will be marked as selected, as shown in the second <html:option /> tag.

<html:options />

The <html:options /> tag is used, as a child to of the <html:select /> tag, to generate a list of HTML <option> elements. The <html:options /> tag has a body type of JSP and supports eight attributes, described in Table 14.14.

NOTE

The <html:options /> tag must be nested inside an <html:select /> tag. The <html:options /> tag can also be used *n*-number of times within an <html:select /> element.

Table 14.14 <html:options /> Tag Attributes

ATTRIBUTE	DESCRIPTION
collection	Specifies a JSP scripting variable that references a collection of beans, with each bean containing the properties property and labelProperty, which are used as the tag attribute value's property and labelProperty, respectively. (Required)
filter	If set to true (the default), causes the tag to replace all HTML-sensitive characters with their encoded equivalents. (Optional)
labelName	Specifies a scripting variable that references a collection of labels to be displayed to the user for the options in this option list. The object referenced by the labelName attribute can point to the collection directly or to an object that contains a data member referencing the collection. (Optional)
labelProperty	Specifies the property of the object identified by the labelName attribute that references the collection of option labels. (Optional)
name	Identifies a scripting variable referencing a Collection object that contains a collection of option values. (Optional)
property	Used to identify a data member of the bean named by the name attribute that contains a collection of option values. (Optional)
style	Specifies a Cascading Style Sheet style to apply to this HTML element. (Optional)
styleClass	Specifies a Cascading Style Sheet class to apply to this HTML element. (Optional)

An example of using the <html:options /> tag is shown here:

NOTE

For this example, it is assumed that the parent <html:form /> contains a reference to an ActionForm that contains a String array, userList, with the values Bob and Bobby.

```
<%
  String users[] =
   { "Bob", "Robert", "Roberto", "Bobby"};

  pageContext.setAttribute("users", users);
%>

<html:form action="select-user.do" method="POST">

  <table border="0" width="100%">

    <tr>
      <td
        <html:select property="userList" size="4"
          multiple="true">
          <html:options name="users"
            labelName="users"/>
        </html:select>
      </td>
    </tr>
  </table>
  <html:submit>Save</html:submit>
<html:form>
```

When this snippet is evaluated, it will result in an HTML snippet similar to the following:

```
<form name="userForm" method="POST"
  action="/applicationname/select-user.do">

  <table border="0" width="100%">

    <tr>
      <td>
        <select name="userList"
          multiple="multiple" size="10">
          <option value="Bob" selected="selected">Bob</option>
          <option value="Robert">Robert</option>
          <option value="Roberto">Roberto</option>
          <option value="Bobby" selected="selected">
            Bobby
          </option>
        </select>
      </td>
    </tr>
  </table>
```

```
    <input type="submit" name="submit" value="Submit">

  </form>
```

In this example, we are creating a single <html:options /> with its name and labelName attributes set to users. This causes the <option> element to be generated using the user scripting variable, which references an array of Strings, as the value and labels for each option in the <select> element. While the users list is being iterated over, the name attribute is compared to the value of the ActionForm bean property named by the <html:select /> attribute property. If the current String referenced by the named beans property equals one of the <html:option /> tag's value attributes, then the matching <option> element will be marked as selected, as shown in the first and fourth <html:option /> tags.

<html:password />

The <html:password /> tag is used to render an HTML <input> element with an input type of password. The <html:password /> has a body type of JSP and supports 28 attributes, described in Table 14.15.

NOTE

The <html:password /> tag must be nested inside the body of a <html:form /> tag.

Table 14.15 <html:password /> Tag Attributes (continues)

ATTRIBUTE	DESCRIPTION
accessKey	Identifies a keyboard character to be used to immediately move focus to the HTML element defined by this tag. (Optional)
alt	Defines an alternate text string for this element. (Optional)
altKey	Defines a resources key (to be retrieved from a resource bundle) that references an alternate text string for this element. (Optional)
disabled	If set to true, causes this HTML input element to be disabled. The default value is false. (Optional)
indexed	If set to true, then the name of the HTML tag will be rendered as propertyName[indexnumber]. The [] characters surrounding the index will be generated for every iteration and taken from its ancestor, the <logic:iterate /> tag. The indexed attribute is valid only when the tag using it is nested with a <logic:iterate /> tag. The default value is false. (Optional)

Table 14.15 <html:password /> Tag Attributes (continues)

ATTRIBUTE	DESCRIPTION
maxlength	Determines the maximum number of input characters allowed in this input field. The default is no limit. (Optional)
onblur	Specifies a JavaScript function that will be executed when the containing element loses its focus. (Optional)
onchange	Specifies a JavaScript function that will be executed when this element loses input focus and its value has changed. (Optional)
onclick	Specifies a JavaScript function that will be executed when this element receives a mouse click. (Optional)
ondbclick	Specifies a JavaScript function that will be executed when this element receives a mouse double-click. (Optional)
onfocus	Specifies a JavaScript function that will be executed when this element receives input focus. (Optional)
onkeydown	Specifies a JavaScript function that will be executed when this element has focus and a key is pressed. (Optional)
onkeypress	Specifies a JavaScript function that will be executed when this element has focus and a key is pressed and released. (Optional)
onkeyup	Specifies a JavaScript function that will be executed when this element has focus and a key is released. (Optional)
onmousedown	Specifies a JavaScript function that will be executed when this element is under the mouse pointer and a mouse button is pressed. (Optional)
onmousemove	Specifies a JavaScript function that will be executed when this element is under the mouse pointer and the pointer is moved. (Optional)
onmouseout	Specifies a JavaScript function that will be executed when this element is under the mouse pointer, but the pointer is then moved outside the element. (Optional)
onmouseover	Specifies a JavaScript function that will be executed when this element is not under the mouse pointer, but the pointer is then moved inside the element. (Optional)
onmouseup	Specifies a JavaScript function that will be executed when this element is under the mouse pointer and a mouse button is released. (Optional)
property	Identifies the name of the input field being processed. (Optional)
readonly	If set to true, sets the input field generated by this tag to uneditable. The default value is false. (Optional)
style	Specifies a Cascading Style Sheet style to apply to this HTML element. (Optional)

Table 14.15 <html:password /> Tag Attributes (continued)

ATTRIBUTE	DESCRIPTION
styleClass	Specifies a Cascading Style Sheet class to apply to this HTML element. (Optional)
styleId	Specifies an HTML identifier to be associated with this HTML element. (Optional)
tabindex	Identifies the tab order of this element in relation to the other elements of the containing Form. (Optional)
title	Specifies the advisory title for this HTML element. (Required)
titleKey	Specifies a resources key (to be retrieved from a resource bundle) that references a title string for this element. (Optional)
value	Specifies the value of this input element. If the ActionForm bean associated with the parent <html:form /> tag has a property that matches the value attribute, then the value of the ActionForm bean property will be used as the value of this attribute. (Optional)

An example of using the <html:password /> tag is shown here:

```
<html:password property="password" />
```

When this snippet is evaluated, it will result in an HTML snippet similar to the following:

```
<input type="password" name="password" value="">
```

NOTE

If the ActionForm bean associated with this tag's parent <html:form /> tag contains a property named password, then the current value of this property would be placed in the value attribute of the <input> element.

In this example, we are creating a simple <html:password /> tag with a single attribute property, which is set to the value password. When this tag instance is evaluated, it will generate an HTML <input> element of type password, with a name password.

<html:radio />

The <html:radio /> tag is used to render an HTML <input> element with an input type of radio. The <html:radio /> has a body type of JSP and supports 22 attributes, described in Table 14.16.

NOTE

The <html:radio /> tag must be nested inside the body of a <html:form /> tag.

Table 14.16 <html:radio /> Tag Attributes (continues)

ATTRIBUTE	DESCRIPTION
property	Identifies the property of the ActionForm bean associated with this input element. (Required)
value	Specifies the value of this input element. (Required)
accessKey	Identifies a keyboard character to be used to immediately move focus to the HTML element defined by this tag. (Optional)
alt	Defines an alternate text string for this element. (Optional)
altKey	Defines a resources key (to be retrieved from a resource bundle) that references an alternate text string for this element. (Optional)
disabled	If set to true, causes this HTML input element to be disabled. The default value is false. (Optional)
indexed	If set to true, then the name of the HTML tag will be rendered as propertyName[indexnumber]. The [] characters surrounding the index will be generated for every iteration and taken from its ancestor, the <logic:iterate /> tag. The indexed attribute is valid only when the tag using it is nested with a <logic:iterate /> tag. The default value is false. (Optional)
onblur	Specifies a JavaScript function that will be executed when the containing element loses its focus. (Optional)
onchange	Specifies a JavaScript function that will be executed when this element loses input focus and its value has changed. (Optional)
onclick	Specifies a JavaScript function that will be executed when this element receives a mouse click. (Optional)
ondbclick	Specifies a JavaScript function that will be executed when this element receives a mouse double-click. (Optional)
onfocus	Specifies a JavaScript function that will be executed when this element receives input focus. (Optional)
onkeydown	Specifies a JavaScript function that will be executed when this element has focus and a key is pressed. (Optional)
onkeypress	Specifies a JavaScript function that will be executed when this element has focus and a key is pressed and released. (Optional)
onkeyup	Specifies a JavaScript function that will be executed when this element has focus and a key is released. (Optional)

Table 14.16 <html:radio /> Tag Attributes (continued)

ATTRIBUTE	DESCRIPTION
onmousedown	Specifies a JavaScript function that will be executed when this element is under the mouse pointer and a mouse button is pressed. (Optional)
style	Specifies a Cascading Style Sheet style to apply to this HTML element. (Optional)
styleClass	Specifies a Cascading Style Sheet class to apply to this HTML element. (Optional)
styleId	Specifies an HTML identifier to be associated with this HTML element. (Optional)
tabindex	Identifies the tab order of this element in relation to the other elements of the containing Form. (Optional)
title	Specifies the advisory title for this HTML element. (Required)
titleKey	Specifies a resources key (to be retrieved from a resource bundle) that references a title string for this element. (Optional)

An example of using the <html:radio /> tag is shown here:

NOTE

This example assumes that the ActionForm bean associated with this tag's parent <html:form /> tag contains a property named id set to the value 123.

```
<html:radio property="id" value="123" />
<html:radio property="id" value="200" />
<html:radio property="id" value="504" />
```

NOTE

The body of this tag can also be used as the element label.

When this snippet is evaluated, it will result in an HTML snippet similar to the following:

```
<input type="radio" name="id" value="123"
  checked="checked">
<input type="radio" name="id" value="200">
<input type="radio" name="id" value="504">
```

In this example, we are creating three <html:radio /> tags, each with two attributes: property (which is set to the value id) and value (which represents the value of the radio button). When these tags are evaluated, they will generate HTML <input> elements of type radio and compare each of their values to the id property of the ActionForm bean associated with this form. If a match is found, then that radio button will be marked as checked.

<html:reset />

The <html:reset /> tag is used to render an HTML <input> element with an input type of reset. The <html:reset /> has a body type of JSP and supports 24 attributes, described in Table 14.17.

NOTE

The <html:reset /> tag must be nested inside the body of an <html:form /> tag.

Table 14.17 <html:reset /> Tag Attributes (continues)

ATTRIBUTE	DESCRIPTION
accessKey	Identifies a keyboard character to be used to immediately move focus to the HTML element defined by this tag. (Optional)
alt	Defines an alternate text string for this element. (Optional)
altKey	Defines a resources key (to be retrieved from a resource bundle) that references an alternate text string for this element. (Optional)
disabled	If set to true, causes this HTML input element to be disabled. The default value is false. (Optional)
onblur	Specifies a JavaScript function that will be executed when the containing element loses its focus. (Optional)
onchange	Specifies a JavaScript function that will be executed when this element loses input focus and its value has changed. (Optional)
onclick	Specifies a JavaScript function that will be executed when this element receives a mouse click. (Optional)
ondbclick	Specifies a JavaScript function that will be executed when this element receives a mouse double-click. (Optional)
onfocus	Specifies a JavaScript function that will be executed when this element receives input focus. (Optional)
onkeydown	Specifies a JavaScript function that will be executed when this element has focus and a key is pressed. (Optional)
onkeypress	Specifies a JavaScript function that will be executed when this element has focus and a key is pressed and released. (Optional)
onkeyup	Specifies a JavaScript function that will be executed when this element has focus and a key is released. (Optional)

Table 14.17 <html:reset /> Tag Attributes (continued)

ATTRIBUTE	DESCRIPTION
onmousedown	Specifies a JavaScript function that will be executed when this element is under the mouse pointer and a mouse button is pressed. (Optional)
onmousemove	Specifies a JavaScript function that will be executed when this element is under the mouse pointer and the pointer is moved. (Optional)
onmouseout	Specifies a JavaScript function that will be executed when this element is under the mouse pointer, but the pointer is then moved outside the element. (Optional)
onmouseover	Specifies a JavaScript function that will be executed when this element is not under the mouse pointer, but the pointer is then moved inside the element. (Optional)
onmouseup	Specifies a JavaScript function that will be executed when this element is under the mouse pointer and a mouse button is released. (Optional)
style	Specifies a Cascading Style Sheet style to apply to this HTML element. (Optional)
styleClass	Specifies a Cascading Style Sheet class to apply to this HTML element. (Optional)
styleId	Specifies an HTML identifier to be associated with this HTML element. (Optional)
tabindex	Identifies the tab order of this element in relation to the other elements of the containing Form. (Optional)
title	Specifies the advisory title for this HTML element. (Optional)
titleKey	Specifies a resources key (to be retrieved from a resource bundle) that references a title string for this element. (Optional)
value	Specifies the label to be placed on this button. You should note that the body of this tag can also be used as the button label. The default value is Reset. (Optional)

An example of using the <html:reset /> tag is shown here:

```
<html:reset>Reset</html:reset>
```

When this snippet is evaluated, it will result in an HTML snippet similar to the following:

```
<input type="reset" name="reset" value="Reset">
```

In this example, we are simply creating an <input> element of type reset.

<html:rewrite />

The <html:rewrite /> tag is used to create a request URI based on the identical policies as with the <html:link /> tag, but without the <a> element. The <html: rewrite /> tag has no body and supports 12 attributes, described in Table 14.18.

NOTE

The <html:rewrite /> tag is especially useful when used to generate a String constant that is expected to be used by a JavaScript function.

Table 14.18 <html:rewrite> Tag Attributes

ATTRIBUTE	DESCRIPTION
anchor	Used to append an HTML anchor to the end of a generated hyperlink. (Optional)
forward	Identifies the name of the global forward element that will receive control of the forwarded request. (Optional)
href	Specifies the URL of the resource to forward the current request to. (Optional)
name	Identifies a scripting variable referencing a java.util.Map object, whose collection of key/value pairs is used as the HTTP request parameter augmenting the redirected request. (Optional)
page	Specifies an application-relative path of the image source used by this input tag. (Optional)
paramId	Specifies a request parameter that will be added to the generated src URL when the hosting JSP is requested. (Optional)
paramName	Identifies the name of a scripting variable of type java.lang.String that references the value to be used for the request parameter identified by the paramId attribute. (Optional)
paramProperty	Used to identify a data member of the bean named by the paramName attribute that will be dynamically added to this src URL. (Optional)
paramScope	Defines the scope of the bean specified by the paramName attribute. If the paramScope attribute is not specified, then the tag will search for the bean in the scopes—in the order of page, request, session, and application. (Optional)
property	Used to identify a data member of the bean named by the name attribute that contains the java.util.Map object of parameters. (Optional)
scope	Defines the scope of the bean specified by the name attribute. If the scope attribute is not specified, then the tag will search for the bean in the scopes—in the order of page, request, session, and application. (Optional)
transaction	If set to true, indicates that the current transaction control token should be included in the generated URL. The default value is false. (Optional)

An example of using the <html:rewrite /> tag is shown here:

```
<%
  String userName = "Bob";
  pageContext.setAttribute("userName", userName);
%>

<html:rewrite page="/Edit.do"
  paramId="user" paramName="userName" />
```

When this snippet is evaluated, it will result in an HTML snippet similar to the following:

```
/struts-exercise-taglib/html-link.do?user=Bob
```

In this example, we are creating a simple <html:rewrite /> tag with three attributes: page, paramId, and paramName. The page attribute references the action that is used as the path of the URL, the paramId defines a request parameter that will be appended to the request string, and the paramName attribute will retrieve the value of the userName variable and set it to the value of the user request parameter.

<html:submit />

The <html:submit /> tag is used to render an HTML <input> element with an input type of submit, which results in a submit button. The <html:submit /> tag has a body type of JSP and supports 26 attributes, described in Table 14.19.

NOTE

The <html:submit /> tag must be nested inside the body of an <html:form /> tag.

Table 14.19 <html:submit /> Tag Attributes (continues)

ATTRIBUTE	DESCRIPTION
accessKey	Identifies a keyboard character to be used to immediately move focus to the HTML element defined by this tag. (Optional)
alt	Defines an alternate text string for this element. (Optional)
altKey	Defines a resources key (to be retrieved from a resource bundle) that references an alternate text string for this element. (Optional)
disabled	If set to true, causes this HTML input element to be disabled. The default value is false. (Optional)
indexed	If set to true, then the name of the HTML tag will be rendered as propertyName[indexnumber]. The [] characters surrounding the index will

Table 14.19 <html:submit /> Tag Attributes (continues)

ATTRIBUTE	DESCRIPTION
	be generated for every iteration and taken from its ancestor, the <logic:iterate /> tag. The indexed attribute is valid only when the tag using it is nested with a <logic:iterate /> tag. The default value is false. (Optional)
onblur	Specifies a JavaScript function that will be executed when the containing element loses its focus. (Optional)
onchange	Specifies a JavaScript function that will be executed when this element loses input focus and its value has changed. (Optional)
onclick	Specifies a JavaScript function that will be executed when this element receives a mouse click. (Optional)
ondbclick	Specifies a JavaScript function that will be executed when this element receives a mouse double-click. (Optional)
onfocus	Specifies a JavaScript function that will be executed when this element receives input focus. (Optional)
onkeydown	Specifies a JavaScript function that will be executed when this element has focus and a key is pressed. (Optional)
onkeypress	Specifies a JavaScript function that will be executed when this element has focus and a key is pressed and released. (Optional)
onkeyup	Specifies a JavaScript function that will be executed when this element has focus and a key is released. (Optional)
onmousedown	Specifies a JavaScript function that will be executed when this element is under the mouse pointer and a mouse button is pressed. (Optional)
onmousemove	Specifies a JavaScript function that will be executed when this element is under the mouse pointer and the pointer is moved. (Optional)
onmouseout	Specifies a JavaScript function that will be executed when this element is under the mouse pointer, but the pointer is then moved outside the element. (Optional)
onmouseover	Specifies a JavaScript function that will be executed when this element is not under the mouse pointer, but the pointer is then moved inside the element. (Optional)
onmouseup	Specifies a JavaScript function that will be executed when this element is under the mouse pointer and a mouse button is released. (Optional)
property	Specifies a request parameter that will be included with the current request, set to the value of the selection. (Optional)
style	Specifies a Cascading Style Sheet style to apply to this HTML element. (Optional)

Table 14.19 <html:submit /> Tag Attributes (continued)

ATTRIBUTE	DESCRIPTION
styleClass	Specifies a Cascading Style Sheet class to apply to this HTML element. (Optional)
styleId	Specifies an HTML identifier to be associated with this HTML element. (Optional)
tabindex	Identifies the tab order of this element in relation to the other elements of the containing Form. (Optional)
title	Specifies the advisory title for this HTML element. (Optional)
titleKey	Specifies a resources key (to be retrieved from a resource bundle) that references a title string for this element. (Optional)
value	Specifies the label to be placed on this button. You should note that the body of this tag can also be used as the button label. The default value is Submit. (Optional)

An example of using the <html:submit /> tag is shown here:

```
<html:submit>Submit Query</html:submit>
```

When this snippet is evaluated, it will result in an HTML snippet similar to the following:

```
<input type="submit" name="submit" value="Submit Query">
```

In this example, we are simply creating an <input> element of type submit that uses its body as the button label.

<html:text />

The <html:text /> tag is used to render an HTML <input> element with an input type of text. The <html:text /> has a body type of JSP and supports 29 attributes, described in Table 14.20.

NOTE

The <html:text /> tag must be nested inside the body of a <html:form /> tag.

Table 14.20 <html:text /> Tag Attributes (continues)

ATTRIBUTE	DESCRIPTION
accessKey	Identifies a keyboard character to be used to immediately move focus to the HTML element defined by this tag. (Optional)

Table 14.20 <html:text /> Tag Attributes (continues)

ATTRIBUTE	DESCRIPTIO
alt	Defines an alternate text string for this element. (Optional)
altKey	Defines a resources key (to be retrieved from a resource bundle) that references an alternate text string for this element. (Optional)
disabled	If set to true, causes this HTML input element to be disabled. The default value is false. (Optional)
indexed	If set to true, then the name of the HTML tag will be rendered as propertyName[indexnumber]. The [] characters surrounding the index will be generated for every iteration and taken from its ancestor, the <logic:iterate /> tag. The indexed attribute is valid only when the tag using it is nested with a <logic:iterate /> tag. The default value is false. (Optional)
maxlength	Determines the maximum number of input characters allowed in this input field. The default is no limit. (Optional)
onblur	Specifies a JavaScript function that will be executed when the containing element loses its focus. (Optional)
onchange	Specifies a JavaScript function that will be executed when this element loses input focus and its value has changed. (Optional)
onclick	Specifies a JavaScript function that will be executed when this element receives a mouse click. (Optional)
ondbclick	Specifies a JavaScript function that will be executed when this element receives a mouse double-click. (Optional)
onfocus	Specifies a JavaScript function that will be executed when this element receives input focus. (Optional)
onkeydown	Specifies a JavaScript function that will be executed when this element has focus and a key is pressed. (Optional)
onkeypress	Specifies a JavaScript function that will be executed when this element has focus and a key is pressed and released. (Optional)
onkeyup	Specifies a JavaScript function that will be executed when this element has focus and a key is released. (Optional)
onmousedown	Specifies a JavaScript function that will be executed when this element is under the mouse pointer and a mouse button is pressed. (Optional)
onmousemove	Specifies a JavaScript function that will be executed when this element is under the mouse pointer and the pointer is moved. (Optional)
onmouseout	Specifies a JavaScript function that will be executed when this element is under the mouse pointer, but the pointer is then moved outside the element. (Optional)

Table 14.20 <html:text /> Tag Attributes (continued)

ATTRIBUTE	DESCRIPTION
onmouseover	Specifies a JavaScript function that will be executed when this element is not under the mouse pointer, but the pointer is then moved inside the element. (Optional)
onmouseup	Specifies a JavaScript function that will be executed when this element is under the mouse pointer and a mouse button is released. (Optional)
property	Identifies the name of the input field being processed. (Optional)
readonly	If set to true, will set the input field generated by this tag to uneditable. The default value is false. (Optional)
size	Indicates the number of character positions to display. (Optional)
style	Specifies a Cascading Style Sheet style to apply to this HTML element. (Optional)
styleClass	Specifies a Cascading Style Sheet class to apply to this HTML element. (Optional)
styleId	Specifies an HTML identifier to be associated with this HTML element. (Optional)
tabindex	Identifies the tab order of this element in relation to the other elements of the containing Form. (Optional)
title	Specifies the advisory title for this HTML element. (Required)
titleKey	Specifies a resources key (to be retrieved from a resource bundle) that references a title string for this element. (Optional)
value	Specifies the value of this input element. If the ActionForm bean associated with the parent <html:form /> tag has a property that matches the value attribute, then the value of the ActionForm bean property will be used as the value of this attribute. (Optional)

An example of using the <html:text /> tag is shown here:

```
<html:text property="username" />
```

When this snippet is evaluated, it will result in an HTML snippet similar to the following:

```
<input type="text" name="username" value="">
```

NOTE

If the ActionForm bean associated with this tag's parent <html:form /> tag contains a property named username, then the current value of this property will be placed in the value attribute of the <input> element.

In this example, we are creating a simple <html:text /> tag with a single attribute property, which is set to the value text. When this tag instance is evaluated, it will generate an HTML <input> element of type text element, with a name username.

<html:textarea />

The <html:textarea /> tag is used to render an HTML <input> element with an input type of textarea. The <html:textarea /> has a body type of JSP and supports 29 attributes, described in Table 14.21.

NOTE

The <html:textarea /> tag must be nested inside the body of a <html:form /> tag.

Table 14.21 <html:textarea /> Tag Attributes (continues)

ATTRIBUTE	DESCRIPTION
accessKey	Identifies a keyboard character to be used to immediately move focus to the HTML element defined by this tag. (Optional)
alt	Defines an alternate text string for this element. (Optional)
altKey	Defines a resources key (to be retrieved from a resource bundle) that references an alternate text string for this element. (Optional)
cols	Indicates the number of columns to display in the generated textarea. (Optional)
disabled	If set to true, causes this HTML input element to be disabled. The default value is false. (Optional)
indexed	If set to true, then the name of the HTML tag will be rendered as propertyName[indexnumber]. The [] characters surrounding the index will be generated for every iteration and taken from its ancestor, the <logic:iterate /> tag. The indexed attribute is valid only when the tag using it is nested with a <logic:iterate /> tag. The default value is false. (Optional)
onblur	Specifies a JavaScript function that will be executed when the containing element loses its focus. (Optional)
onchange	Specifies a JavaScript function that will be executed when this element loses input focus and its value has changed. (Optional)
onclick	Specifies a JavaScript function that will be executed when this element receives a mouse click. (Optional)
ondbclick	Specifies a JavaScript function that will be executed when this element receives a mouse double-click. (Optional)

Table 14.21 <html:textarea /> Tag Attributes (continues)

ATTRIBUTE	DESCRIPTION
onfocus	Specifies a JavaScript function that will be executed when this element receives input focus. (Optional)
onkeydown	Specifies a JavaScript function that will be executed when this element has focus and a key is pressed. (Optional)
onkeypress	Specifies a JavaScript function that will be executed when this element has focus and a key is pressed and released. (Optional)
onkeyup	Specifies a JavaScript function that will be executed when this element has focus and a key is released. (Optional)
onmousedown	Specifies a JavaScript function that will be executed when this element is under the mouse pointer and a mouse button is pressed. (Optional)
onmousemove	Specifies a JavaScript function that will be executed when this element is under the mouse pointer and the pointer is moved. (Optional)
onmouseout	Specifies a JavaScript function that will be executed when this element is under the mouse pointer, but the pointer is then moved outside the element. (Optional)
onmouseover	Specifies a JavaScript function that will be executed when this element is not under the mouse pointer, but the pointer is then moved inside the element. (Optional)
onmouseup	Specifies a JavaScript function that will be executed when this element is under the mouse pointer and a mouse button is released. (Optional)
property	Identifies the name of the input field being processed and the name of the bean property that maps to this input element. (Optional)
readonly	If set to true, sets the input field generated by this tag to uneditable. The default value is false. (Optional)
rows	Indicates the number of rows to display in the textarea. (Optional)
style	Specifies a Cascading Style Sheet style to apply to this HTML element. (Optional)
styleClass	Specifies a Cascading Style Sheet class to apply to this HTML element. (Optional)
styleId	Specifies an HTML identifier to be associated with this HTML element. (Optional)
tabindex	Identifies the tab order of this element in relation to the other elements of the containing Form. (Optional)
title	Specifies the advisory title for this HTML element. (Required)
titleKey	Specifies a resources key (to be retrieved from a resource bundle) that references a title string for this element. (Optional)

Table 14.21 <html:textarea /> Tag Attributes (continued)

ATTRIBUTE	DESCRIPTION
value	Specifies the value of this input element. If the ActionForm bean associated with the parent <html:form /> tag has a property that matches the value attribute, then the value of the ActionForm bean property will be used as the value of this attribute. (Optional)

An example of using the <html:textarea /> tag is shown here:

NOTE

This example assumes that the ActionForm bean associated with this tag's parent <html:form /> tag contains a property named summary set to the value *This is a summary*.

```
<tr>
  <td>
    <html:textarea property="summary" />
  </td>
</tr>
```

When this snippet is evaluated, it will result in an HTML snippet similar to the following:

```
<tr>
  <td>
    <textarea name="summary">This is a summary</textarea>
  </td>
</tr>
```

In this example, we are creating a simple <html:textarea /> tag with a single attribute property, which is set to the value summary. When this tag instance is evaluated, it will generate an HTML <input> element of type textarea element; its body will be the value retrieved from the ActionForm bean's summary property.

CHAPTER 15

The Logic Tag Library

The focus of the Logic tag library is on decision-making and object evaluation. This taglib contains 14 tags that can be used in a Struts application. In this chapter, we introduce you to each of these tags and show you how to use them.

Installing the Logic Tags

To use the Logic tag library in a Web application, you must complete the following steps. Be sure to replace the value *webappname* with the name of the Web application that will be using this library:

1. Copy the TLD packaged with this tag library, struts-logic.tld, to the <*TOMCAT_HOME*>/webapps/*webappname*/WEB-INF/ directory.
2. Make sure that the struts.jar file is in the <*TOMCAT_HOME*>/webapps/*webappname*/WEB-INF/lib directory.
3. Add the following <taglib> subelement to the web.xml file of the Web application:

```
<taglib>
  <taglib-uri>/WEB-INF/struts-logic.tld</taglib-uri>
  <taglib-location>/WEB-INF/struts-logic.tld</taglib-location>
</taglib>
```

You must add the following taglib directive to each JSP that will leverage the Logic tag library:

```
<%@ taglib uri="/WEB-INF/struts-logic.tld" prefix="logic" %>
```

This directive identifies the URI defined in the previously listed <taglib> element, and states that all Logic tags should be prefixed with the string logic.

<logic:empty />

The <logic:empty /> tag evaluates its body if either the scripting variable identified by the name attribute or a property of the named scripting variable is equal to null or an empty string. The <logic:empty /> tag has a body type of JSP and supports three attributes, described in Table 15.1.

Table 15.1 <logic:empty /> Tag Attributes

ATTRIBUTE	DESCRIPTION
name	Identifies the scripting variable being tested. If the property attribute is included in the tag instance, then the property of the named scripting variable is tested; otherwise, the named scripting variable itself is tested. (Required)
property	Identifies the data member of the scripting variable to be tested. (Optional)
scope	Defines the scope of the bean specified by the name attribute. If the scope attribute is not specified, then the tag will search for the bean in the scopes—in the order of page, request, session, and application. (Optional)

An example of using the <logic:empty /> tag is shown here:

```
<logic:empty name="user">
  <forward name="login" />
</logic:empty>
```

In this example, we test the scripting variable user. If this variable is null or an empty string, then the body will be evaluated, which will result in the user being forwarded to the global forward login.

<logic:notEmpty />

The <logic:notEmpty /> tag evaluates its body if either the named scripting variable or property of the named scripting variable is not equal to null or an empty string. The <logic:notEmpty /> tag has a body type of JSP and supports three attributes, described in Table 15.2.

Table 15.2 <logic:notEmpty /> Tag Attributes

ATTRIBUTE	DESCRIPTION
name	Specifies a scripting variable to be used as the variable being tested. (Required)
property	Specifies the data member of the scripting variable to be tested. (Optional)
scope	Defines the scope of the bean specified by the name attribute. If the scope attribute is not specified, then the tag will search for the bean in the scopes–in the order of page, request, session, and application. (Optional)

An example of using the <logic:notEmpty /> tag is shown here:

```
<logic:notEmpty name="user">
  Welcome to our Struts application.
</logic:notEmpty>
```

In this example, we test the scripting variable user. If this variable is not null and does not contain an empty string, then the body will be evaluated, which will result in the body of the tag being evaluated.

<logic:equal />

The <logic:equal /> tag evaluates its body if the variable specified by any one of the attributes cookie, header, name, parameter, or property equals the constant value specified by the value attribute. The <logic:equal /> tag has a body type of JSP and supports seven attributes, described in Table 15.3.

Table 15.3 <logic:equal /> Tag Attributes (continues)

ATTRIBUTE	DESCRIPTION
value	Identifies the constant value to which the scripting variable will be compared. (Required)
cookie	Specifies an HTTP cookie to be used as the variable being compared to the value attribute. (Optional)
header	Specifies an HTTP header to be used as the variable being compared to the value attribute. (Optional)
name	Specifies a scripting variable to be used as the variable being compared to the value attribute. (Required)
property	Specifies the data member of the scripting variable to be tested. (Optional)

Table 15.3 <logic:equal /> Tag Attributes (continued)

ATTRIBUTE	DESCRIPTION
parameter	Specifies an HTTP parameter to be used as the variable being compared to the value attribute. (Optional)
scope	Defines the scope of the bean specified by the name attribute. If the scope attribute is not specified, then the tag will search for the bean in the scopes–in the order of page, request, session, and application. (Optional)

An example of using the <logic:equal /> tag is shown here:

```
<logic:equal name="user"
  property="age"
  value="<%= requiredAge %>">
  You are exactly the right age.
</logic:equal>
```

In this example, we test the age data member of the scripting variable user. If this data member equals the value stored in the requiredAge scripting variable, then the tag's body will be evaluated.

<logic:notEqual />

The <logic:notEqual /> tag evaluates its body if the variable specified by any one of the attributes cookie, header, name, parameter, or property is not equal to the constant value specified by the value attribute. The <logic:notEqual /> tag has a body type of JSP and supports seven attributes, described in Table 15.4.

Table 15.4 <logic:notEqual /> Tag Attributes (continues)

ATTRIBUTE	DESCRIPTION
value	Identifies the constant value to which the scripting variable will be compared. (Required)
cookie	Specifies an HTTP cookie to be used as the variable being compared to the value attribute. (Optional)
header	Specifies an HTTP header to be used as the variable being compared to the value attribute. (Optional)
name	Specifies a scripting variable to be used as the variable being compared to the value attribute. (Required)
property	Specifies the data member of the scripting variable to be tested. (Optional)

Table 15.4 <logic:notEqual /> Tag Attributes (continued)

ATTRIBUTE	DESCRIPTION
parameter	Specifies an HTTP parameter to be used as the variable being compared to the value attribute. (Optional)
scope	Defines the scope of the bean specified by the name attribute. If the scope attribute is not specified, then the tag will search for the bean in the scopes–in the order of page, request, session, and application. (Optional)

An example of using the <logic:notEqual /> tag is shown here:

```
<logic:notEqual name="user"
  property="age"
  value="<%= requiredAge %>">
  You are not the right age.
</logic:notEqual>
```

In this example, we test the age data member of the scripting variable user. If this data member equals the value stored in the requiredAge scripting variable, then the tag's body will be evaluated.

<logic:forward />

The <logic:forward /> tag is used to forward control of the current request to a previously identified global forward element. The <logic:forward /> tag has no body and supports a single attribute name, which identifies the name of the global element that will receive control of the request. An example of using the <logic:forward /> tag is shown here:

```
<logic:forward name="login" />
```

In this example, we forward the current request to the global forward login. This resource must be defined in the <global-forwards /> section of the struts-config.xml file.

```
<global-forwards>
  <forward name="login" path="/login.jsp"/>
</global-forwards>
```

<logic:redirect />

The <logic:redirect /> tag uses the HttpServletResponse.sendRedirect() method to redirect the current request to a resource identified by either the forward, href, or page attributes. The <logic:redirect /> tag has no body and supports 12 attributes, described in Table 15.5.

Table 15.5 <logic:redirect /> Tag Attributes

ATTRIBUTE	DESCRIPTION
anchor	Used to append an HTML anchor to the end of a generated resource. (Optional)
forward	Identifies the name of a global forward element that will receive control of the forwarded request. (Optional)
href	Specifies the URL of the resource to forward the current request to. (Optional)
name	Identifies a scripting variable referencing a java.util.Map object whose collection of key/value pairs is used as HTTP request parameters augmenting the redirected request. (Optional)
property	Identifies a bean property of the bean named by the name attribute that contains a java.util.Map reference whose collection of key/value pairs is used as HTTP request parameters augmenting the redirected request. (Optional)
scope	Defines the scope of the bean specified by the name attribute. If the scope attribute is not specified, then the tag will search for the bean in the scopes–in the order of page, request, session, and application. (Optional)
transaction	If set to true, indicates that the current transaction control token should be included in the generated URL. The default value is false. (Optional)
page	Specifies a context-relative path to a resource that will receive control of the current request. You must prepend the named resource with the / character. (Optional)
paramId	Identifies the name of a request parameter that will be added to the generated URL. The corresponding value of this parameter is defined by the paramName attribute. (Optional)
paramName	Specifies a JSP scripting variable, containing a String reference, that represents the value for the request parameter named by the paramId attribute. (Optional)
paramProperty	Identifies a bean property of the bean named by the paramName attribute; the property will be used as the value of the parameter identified by the paramId attribute. (Optional)
paramScope	Specifies the scope of the bean specified by the paramName attribute. If the paramScope attribute is not specified, then the tag will search for the bean in the scopes–in the order of page, request, session, and application. (Optional)

An example of using the <logic:redirect /> tag is shown here:

```
<logic:redirect name="login"
  paramId="companyId" paramName="company" />
```

In this example, we perform a redirect to the global forward login. This resource must be defined in the <global-forwards /> section of the struts-config.xml file. The <logic:redirect /> tag differs from the <logic:forward /> tag in that the <logic:redirect /> tag allows you to dynamically augment the request with parameters.

<logic:greaterEqual />

The <logic:greaterEqual /> tag evaluates its body if the variable specified by any one of the attributes cookie, header, name, parameter, or property is greater than or equal to the constant value specified by the value attribute. The <logic:greaterEqual /> tag has a body type of JSP and supports seven attributes, described in Table 15.6.

Table 15.6 <logic:greaterEqual /> Tag Attributes

ATTRIBUTE	DESCRIPTION
value	Identifies the constant value to which the scripting variable will be compared. (Required)
cookie	Specifies an HTTP cookie to be used as the variable being compared to the value attribute. (Optional)
header	Specifies an HTTP header to be used as the variable being compared to the value attribute. (Optional)
name	Specifies a scripting variable to be used as the variable being compared to the value attribute. (Required)
property	Specifies the data member of the scripting variable to be tested. (Optional)
parameter	Specifies an HTTP parameter to be used as the variable being compared to the value attribute. (Optional)
scope	Specifies the scope of the bean specified by the name attribute. If the scope attribute is not specified, then the tag will search for the bean in the scopes–in the order of page, request, session, and application. (Optional)

An example of using the <logic:greaterEqual /> tag is shown here:

```
<logic:greaterEqual name="user" property="age"
  value="<%= minAge %>">
  You are old enough.
</logic:greaterEqual>
```

In this example, we test the age data member of the scripting variable user. If this data member is greater than or equal to the value stored in the scripting variable minAge, then the tag's body will be evaluated.

<logic:greaterThan />

The <logic:greaterThan /> tag evaluates its body if the variable specified by any one of the attributes cookie, header, name, parameter, or property is greater than the constant value specified by the value attribute. The <logic:greater Than /> tag has a body type of JSP and supports seven attributes, described in Table 15.7.

Table 15.7 <logic:greaterThan /> Tag Attributes

ATTRIBUTE	DESCRIPTION
value	Identifies the constant value to which the scripting variable will be compared. (Required)
cookie	Specifies an HTTP cookie to be used as the variable being compared to the value attribute. (Optional)
header	Specifies an HTTP header to be used as the variable being compared to the value attribute. (Optional)
name	Specifies a scripting variable to be used as the variable being compared to the value attribute. (Required)
property	Specifies the data member of the scripting variable to be tested. (Optional)
parameter	Specifies an HTTP parameter to be used as the variable being compared to the value attribute. (Optional)
scope	Defines the scope of the bean specified by the name attribute. If the scope attribute is not specified, then the tag will search for the bean in the scopes–in the order of page, request, session, and application. (Optional)

An example of using the <logic:greaterThan /> tag is shown here:

```
<logic:greaterThan name="user" property="age"
  value="<%= minAge %>">
  You are over the minimum age <%= minAge %>.
</logic:greaterThan>
```

In this example, we test the age data member of the scripting variable user. If this data member is greater than the value stored in the scripting variable minAge, then the tag's body will be evaluated.

<logic:iterate />

The <logic:iterate /> tag is used to iterate over a named collection—which contains a Collection, Enumerator, Iterator, Map, or Array—and evaluates its body for each Object in the collection. We can identify the collection being iterated over by using a request-time expression or a scripting variable. The <logic:iterate /> tag has a body type of JSP and supports nine attributes, described in Table 15.8.

Table 15.8 <logic:iterate /> Tag Attributes

ATTRIBUTE	DESCRIPTION
id	Specifies a JSP scripting variable, exposed by the <logic:iterate /> tag, that will hold the current object in the named collection. (Required)
collection	Used to identify a collection using a request-time expression. (Optional)
name	Specifies a scripting variable that represents the collection to be iterated over. (Optional)
property	Specifies the data member of the scripting variable, identified by the name attribute, that contains a reference to a collection. (Optional)
scope	Defines the scope of the bean specified by the name attribute. If the scope attribute is not specified, then the tag will search for the bean in the scopes–in the order of page, request, session, and application. (Optional)
type	Provides the fully qualified class name of the element being exposed from the collection. This object is referenced by the id attribute. (Optional)
indexId	Specifies a JSP scripting variable, exposed by the <logic:iterate /> tag, that will hold the current index of the current object in the named collection. (Optional)
length	Identifies the maximum number of collection entries to be iterated over. The length attribute can be either an integer or a scripting variable of type java.lang.Integer. If the length attribute is not included, then the entire collection will be iterated over. (Optional)
offset	Indicates where iteration should begin. If this value is not specified, then the beginning of the collection is used. (Optional)

An example of using the <logic:iterate /> tag is shown here:

```
<logic:iterate id="employee" name="employees">
  <tr align="left">
    <td>
      <bean:write name="employee" property="username" />
```

```
        </td>
        <td>
          <bean:write name="employee" property="name" />
        </td>
        <td>
          <bean:write name="employee" property="phone" />
        </td>
      </tr>
    </logic:iterate>
```

In this example, we are iterating over the collection referenced by the employee's scripting variable. As the <logic:iterate /> tag iterates over the named collection, it exposes each object in the collection in the employee scripting variable. The result of this iteration is an HTML table row for each object in the named collection.

<logic:lessEqual />

The <logic:lessEqual /> tag evaluates its body if the variable specified by any one of the attributes cookie, header, name, parameter, or property is less than or equal to the constant value specified by the value attribute. The <logic:less Equal /> tag has a body type of JSP and supports seven attributes, described in Table 15.9.

Table 15.9 <logic:lessEqual /> Tag Attributes

ATTRIBUTE	DESCRIPTION
value	Identifies the constant value to which the scripting variable will be compared. (Required)
cookie	Specifies an HTTP cookie to be used as the variable being compared to the value attribute. (Optional)
header	Specifies an HTTP header to be used as the variable being compared to the value attribute. (Optional)
name	Specifies a scripting variable to be used as the variable being compared to the value attribute. (Required)
property	Specifies the data member of the scripting variable to be tested. (Optional)
parameter	Specifies an HTTP parameter to be used as the variable being compared to the value attribute. (Optional)
scope	Specifies the scope of the bean specified by the name attribute. If the scope attribute is not specified, then the tag will search for the bean in the scopes—in the order of page, request, session, and application. (Optional)

An example of using the <logic:lessEqual /> tag is shown here:

```
<logic:lessEqual name="user" property="age"
  value="<%= maxAge %>">
  You are young enough.
</logic:lessEqual>
```

In this example, we test the age data member of the scripting variable user. If this data member is less than or equal to the value stored in the scripting variable minAge, then the tag's body will be evaluated.

<logic:lessThan />

The <logic:lessThan /> tag evaluates its body if the variable specified by any one of the attributes cookie, header, name, parameter, or property is less than the constant value specified by the value attribute. The <logic:lessThan /> tag has a body type of JSP and supports seven attributes, described in Table 15.10.

Table 15.10 <logic:lessThan /> Tag Attributes

ATTRIBUTE	DESCRIPTION
value	Identifies the constant value to which the scripting variable will be compared. (Required)
cookie	Specifies an HTTP cookie to be used as the variable being compared to the value attribute. (Optional)
header	Specifies an HTTP header to be used as the variable being compared to the value attribute. (Optional)
name	Specifies a scripting variable to be used as the variable being compared to the value attribute. (Required)
property	Specifies the data member of the scripting variable to be tested. (Optional)
parameter	Specifies an HTTP parameter to be used as the variable being compared to the value attribute. (Optional)
scope	Defines the scope of the bean specified by the name attribute. If the scope attribute is not specified, then the tag will search for the bean in the scopes—in the order of page, request, session, and application. (Optional)

An example of using the <logic:lessThan /> tag is shown here:

```
<logic:lessThan name="user" property="age"
  value="<%= maxAge %>">
  You are under the maximum age <%= maxAge %>.
</logic:lessThan>
```

In this example, we test the age data member of the scripting variable user. If this data member is less than the value stored in the scripting variable maxAge, then the tag's body will be evaluated.

<logic:match />

The <logic:match /> tag evaluates its body if the variable specified by any one of the attributes cookie, header, name, parameter, or property attributes contains the specified constant value. The <logic:match /> tag has a body type of JSP and supports eight attributes, described in Table 15.11.

Table 15.11 <logic:match /> Tag Attributes

ATTRIBUTE	DESCRIPTION
value	Identifies the constant value to which the scripting variable will be compared. (Required)
location	Specifies where the match should occur in the named variable. The possible values are *start* and *end.* If the location attribute is not specified, then the value can occur anywhere in the variable. (Optional)
cookie	Specifies an HTTP cookie to be used as the variable being compared to the value attribute. (Optional)
header	Specifies an HTTP header to be used as the variable being compared to the value attribute. (Optional)
name	Specifies a scripting variable to be used as the variable being compared to the value attribute. (Required)
property	Specifies the data member of the scripting variable to be tested. (Optional)
parameter	Specifies an HTTP parameter to be used as the variable being compared to the value attribute. (Optional)
scope	Defines the scope of the bean specified by the name attribute. If the scope attribute is not specified, then the tag will search for the bean in the scopes–in the order of page, request, session, and application. (Optional)

An example of using the <logic:match /> tag is shown here:

```
<logic:match name="sentence" value="Bob">
  The string Bob occurs in the sentence.
</logic:match>
```

In this example, we test the scripting variable sentence. If it contains the text Bob, then the tag's body will be evaluated.

<logic:notMatch />

The <logic:notMatch /> tag evaluates its body if the variable specified by any one of the attributes cookie, header, name, parameter, or property does not contain the constant specified by the value attribute. The <logic:notMatch /> tag has a body type of JSP and supports eight attributes, described in Table 15.12.

Table 15.12 <logic:notMatch /> Tag Attributes

ATTRIBUTE	DESCRIPTION
value	Identifies the constant value to which the scripting variable will be compared. (Required)
location	Specifies where the match should occur in the named variable. The possible values are *start* and *end*. If the location attribute is not specified, then the value can occur anywhere in the variable. (Optional)
cookie	Specifies an HTTP cookie to be used as the variable being compared to the value attribute. (Optional)
header	Specifies an HTTP header to be used as the variable being compared to the value attribute. (Optional)
name	Specifies a scripting variable to be used as the variable being compared to the value attribute. (Required)
property	Specifies the data member of the scripting variable to be tested. (Optional)
parameter	Specifies an HTTP parameter to be used as the variable being compared to the value attribute. (Optional)
scope	Defines the scope of the bean specified by the name attribute. If the scope attribute is not specified, then the tag will search for the bean in the scopes–in the order of page, request, session, and application. (Optional)

An example of using the <logic:notMatch /> tag is shown here:

```
<logic:notMatch name="sentence" value="Bob">
  The string Bob does not occur in the sentence.
</logic:notMatch >
```

In this example, we test the scripting variable sentence. If it does not contain the text Bob, then the tag's body will be evaluated.

<logic:present />

The <logic:present /> tag evaluates its body if the variable specified by any one of the cookie, header, name, parameter, or property attributes is present in the applicable scope. The <logic:present /> tag has a body type of JSP and supports eight attributes, described in Table 15.13.

Table 15.13 <logic:present /> Tag Attributes

ATTRIBUTE	DESCRIPTION
cookie	Specifies an HTTP cookie to be used as the variable being tested for existence. (Optional)
header	Specifies a case-insensitive HTTP header to be used as the variable being tested for existence. (Optional)
name	Defines a scripting variable to be used as the variable being tested for existence. (Optional)
property	Specifies the data member of the scripting variable to be tested. (Optional)
parameter	Specifies an HTTP parameter to be used as the variable being tested for existence. (Optional)
scope	Defines the scope of the bean specified by the name attribute. If the scope attribute is not specified, then the tag will search for the bean in the scopes—in the order of page, request, session, and application. (Optional)
role	Used to determine if the currently authenticated user belongs to one or more named roles. If more than one role is listed, then they must be separated by commas. (Optional)
user	Used to determine if the currently authenticated user has the specified name. (Optional)

An example of using the <logic:present /> tag is shown here:

```
<logic:present parameter="username">
  Welcome <%= username %>.
</logic:present >
```

In this example, we test for the existence of the request parameter username. If the username parameter is part of the request, then the tag's body will be evaluated.

<logic:notPresent />

The <logic:notPresent /> tag evaluates its body if the variable specified by any one of the cookie, header, name, parameter, or property attributes is not present in the applicable scope. The <logic:notPresent /> tag has a body type of JSP and supports eight attributes, described in Table 15.14.

Table 15.14 <logic:notPresent /> Tag Attributes

ATTRIBUTE	DESCRIPTION
cookie	Specifies an HTTP cookie to be used as the variable being tested for existence. (Optional)
header	Specifies a case-insensitive HTTP header to be used as the variable being tested for existence. (Optional)
name	Defines a scripting variable to be used as the variable being tested for existence. (Optional)
property	Specifies the data member of the scripting variable to be tested. (Optional)
parameter	Specifies an HTTP parameter to be used as the variable being tested for existence. (Optional)
scope	Defines the scope of the bean specified by the name attribute. If the scope attribute is not specified, then the tag will search for the bean in the scopes–in the order of page, request, session, and application. (Optional)
role	Used to determine if the currently authenticated user belongs to one or more named roles. If more than one role is listed, then they must be separated by commas. (Optional)
user	Used to determine if the currently authenticated user has the specified name. (Optional)

An example of using the <logic:notPresent /> tag is shown here:

```
<logic:notPresent name="username" scope="session">
  There is no username attribute in the session.
</logic:notPresent >
```

In this example, we test for the existence of the session attribute username. If the username parameter is not found in the HttpSession, then the tag's body will be evaluated.

CHAPTER 16

The Template Tag Library

The Struts Template tags provide a simple method of defining reusable templatized Views. It does this through the use of three custom tags that allow you to define JSP template files. These three tags are the <template:get />, <template:insert /> and <template:put /> tags. In this chapter, we define each of these tags and examine their use.

Installing the Template Tags

To use the Template tag library in a Web application, you must complete the following steps. Be sure to replace the value *webappname* with the name of the Web application that will be using this library.

1. Copy the TLD packaged with this tag library, struts-template.tld, to the <*TOMCAT_HOME*>/webapps/*webappname*/WEB-INF/lib directory.
2. Make sure that the struts.jar file is in the <*TOMCAT_HOME*>/webapps/*webappname*/WEB-INF/lib directory.
3. Add the following <taglib> subelement to the web.xml file of the Web application:

```
<taglib>
  <taglib-uri>/WEB-INF/struts-template.tld</taglib-uri>
  <taglib-location>
    /WEB-INF/struts-template.tld
  </taglib-location>
</taglib>
```

You must add the following taglib directive to each JSP that will leverage the Template tag library:

```
<%@ taglib uri="/WEB-INF/tlds/struts-template.tld"
  prefix="template" %>
```

This directive identifies the URI defined in the previously listed <taglib> element and states that all Template tags should be prefixed with the string template.

<template:get />

The <template:get /> tag is used to retrieve the contents of a bean stored in the request scope, with the intention of replacing the tag instance with the contents of the retrieved bean. It is used to define the actual template JSP that will be referenced by the <template:insert /> tag. The bean being retrieved is assumed to have been placed on the request by a <template:put /> tag. The <template:get /> tag has no body and supports three attributes, as shown in Table 16.1.

Table 16.1 <template:get /> Tag Attributes

ATTRIBUTE	DESCRIPTION
name	Identifies the name of the request attribute to be retrieved. The name attribute should match the name attribute of the <template:put /> tag. (Required)
role	Specifies the role in which the user must exist for this tag to be evaluated. If the user does not exist in the named role, then the tag is ignored. If no role is named, then the tag will be evaluated by default. (Optional)
flush	If set to true, results in the flushing of the response buffer prior to the inclusion of the specified request attribute. The default value is false. (Optional)

A sample code snippet, from a JSP named catalogTemplate.jsp, is shown here:

```
<%@ taglib uri="/WEB-INF/tlds/struts-template.tld"
  prefix="template" %>

<html>
  <body>
    <table>
      <tr valign="top">
        <td><template:get name="navbar"/></td>
```

```
          <td>
            <table>
              <tr><td><template:get name="header" /></td></tr>
              <tr><td><template:get name="body" /></td></tr>
              <tr><td><template:get name="footer" /></td></tr>
            </table>
          </td>
        </tr>
      </table>
    </body>
  </html>
```

This JSP defines a template with four parameterized tags: navbar, header, body, and footer. This JSP will first be evaluated, and the <template:get /> tag instances will be replaced by the named request attributes. Then, it will be inserted into a JSP that names it using the <template:insert /> tag. You will see an example of the <template:insert /> tag in the following section.

<template:insert />

The <template:insert /> tag is used to retrieve and insert the contents of the named URI. The <template:insert /> tag acts as the parent to one or more <template:put /> tags, which act as parameters to the named template JSP. The <template:insert /> tag has a body type of JSP and a single required attribute template that names the URI of the resource to include as the template. A sample code snippet using the <template:insert /> tag is shown here:

```
<%@ taglib uri="/WEB-INF/tlds/struts-template.tld"
  prefix="template" %>

<template:insert template="/catalogTemplate.jsp">

  <template:put name="navbar" content="/navbar.jsp" />
  <template:put name="header" content="/header.jsp" />
  <template:put name="body" content="/login.jsp" />
  <template:put name="footer" content="/footer.html" />

</template:insert>
```

This instance of the <template:insert /> tag will set four request attributes to the values of their content attributes, which in this case are a combination of JSPs and a single HTML document.

NOTE

The content attributes in this example could just as easily have been a static string that could be stored as the value in the request attribute.

<template:put />

The <template:put /> tag is used to store the content of a particular URL or text (URIs or text) into the request scope. This tag is the parent to one or more put tags. The put tags specify the content to be inserted into the template. The layout of the content is determined by get tags placed in the template. The <template: put /> tag has no body and supports four attributes, described in Table 16.2.

Table 16.2 <template:put /> Tag Attributes

ATTRIBUTE	DESCRIPTION
name	Identifies the name of the attribute to be stored in the request. The name attribute should match the name attribute of the <template:get /> tag being used to retrieve it. (Required)
role	Specifies the role in which the user must exist for this tag to be evaluated. If the user does not exist in the name role, then the tag is ignored. If no role is named, then the tag will be evaluated by default. (Optional)
content	Specifies the content that will be stored in the request. This value can be a URI or static text. If this value is not included, then the body of the tag will be used as the content and the direct attribute must be set to true. (Optional)
direct	If set to true, indicates that the content attribute or body is printed to the request; if set to false (the default), the content is included. (Optional)

NOTE

The <template:put /> tag must be nested within a <template:insert /> tag.

A sample code snippet using the <template:put /> tag is shown here:

```
<%@ taglib uri="/WEB-INF/tlds/struts-template.tld"
  prefix="template" %>

<template:insert template="/chapterTemplate.jsp">

  <template:put name="title" content="Templates"
    direct="true" />
  <template:put name="header" content="/header.html" />
  <template:put name="sidebar" content="/sidebar.jsp" />
  <template:put name="content" content="/introduction.html"/>
  <template:put name="footer" content="/footer.html" />

</template:insert>
```

Index

A

<action> element
  ActionMapping objects, 131
  error handling, 118–119
<action /> subelement, 243–244
Action class, 68. *See also* ActionMapping objects
  configuring, 84–86
  execute() method, 82–83
  extending, 83–84
  instance pooling, 75
ActionError class, 115–117
ActionErrors class, 117–118
ActionForms, 65–67, 98–101
  employees application, 183–185
ActionMapping objects, 129–131
  attributes, 130
  customizing, 131
  employees application, 170–172
  wileystruts application
    deploying ActionMapping extension, 133
    extending ActionMapping class, 132–133
    LookupAction modifications, 134–137
<action-mappings> element, 131
<action-mappings /> subelement, 243–244
ActionServlet class, 68, 77–79. *See also* ActionMapping objects
  configuring, 80–82
  extending, 79–80
  initialization parameters, 80–81
  process() method, 77–78
Add Employee transation (employees application)
  AddEmployeeAction, 204–208
  Add Employee JSP, 198–200
  deploying, 208–210
  EmployeeForm, 201–204
application object (JSPs), 44
applications. *See* employees application; wileystruts application

B

<bean:cookie /> tag, 250
<bean:define /> tag, 251–252
<bean:header /> tag, 252–253
<bean:include /> tag, 253
<bean:message /> tag, 108–109, 254–255
<bean:page /> tag, 255
<bean:parameter /> tag, 256
<bean:resource /> tag, 256–257
<bean:size /> tag, 257–258
<bean:struts /> tag, 258
<bean:write /> tag, 259–260
Bean tag library
  deploying, 108
  installing, 249–250
breakpoints, setting, 163

C

classes
  Action, 68
    configuring, 84–86
    execute() method, 68
    extending, 83–84
    instance pooling, 75

ActionError, 115–117
ActionErrors, 117–118
ActionForm, 65–67
ActionServlet, 68, 77–79
configuring, 80–82
extending, 79–80
initialization parameters, 80–81
process() method, 77–78
Embedded, 150
GenericServlet, 14–16
HttpServlet, 14–16
RequestProcessor, 90
configuring, 93
creating, 90–92
processPreprocess() method, 90–92
storing, 6
config object (JSPs), 44
ContextServlet example
code listing, 22–23
deploying, 24–26
<controller /> subelement, 245
Controller components, 5, 68
Action class, 68
configuring, 84–86
execute() method, 82–83
extending, 83–84
ActionServlet class, 68, 77–79
configuring, 80–82
extending, 79–80
initialization parameters, 80–81
process() method, 77–78
internationalization
defining resource bundles, 106–107
deploying resource bundles, 107
Plugins, 87
adding, 247
configuring, 89–90
creating, 87–89
destroy() method, 87
init() method, 87
RequestProcessor class, 90
configuring, 93
creating, 90–92
processPreprocess() method, 90–92
Counter bean example (JSPs), 48–51

D

databases. *See also* DataSouce
employees application
creating, 175–176
departments table, 174
employees table, 173
roles table, 174
DataSource
Basic implementation, 140
configuring, 238–240
Distributed implementation, 140
employees application, 179
Pooled implementation, 140
wileystruts application
getQuote() method modifications, 144–146
initializing DataSource, 142–143
sample database, 140–142
<data-sources /> element, 238–240
debugging
JBuilder
classpath setup, 160–162
project setup, 158–160
source paths, adding, 162
Tomcat, embedding into applications
application testing, 157–158
container hierarchy, 149–150
creating container structure, 150
Embedded class, 150
EmbeddedTomcat.java application, 151–156
wileystruts application, 163–164
declarations (JSP scripting), 36–37
Delete Employee transation (employees application)
DeleteEmployeeAction, 224–227
deploying, 227–229
departments table (employees application), 174
<description /> subelement, 237–238
destroy() method
Plugins, 87
servlets, 17
directives (JSPs)
defined, 34
include, 35
page, 34–35
taglib, 36
<display-name /> subelement, 237

E

Edit Employee transation (employees application)
deploying, 221–223
EditEmployeeAction, 217–221
Edit Employee JSP, 215–217
EmployeeForm, 217
GetEmployeeAction, 210–215
elements. *See also* subelements
<action>
ActionMapping objects, 131
error handling, 118–119
<action-mappings>, 131
<data-sources />, 238–240
<forward>, 96–97
Embedded class, 150
employees application
Add Employee transation
AddEmployeeAction, 204–208
Add Employee JSP, 198–200
deploying, 208–210
EmployeeForm, 201–204
adding employees, 231–232
database
creating, 175–176
departments table, 174
employees table, 173
roles table, 174
DataSource configuration, 179
defining, 165–172
ActionMapping objects, 170–172
copying jar files, 166
resource bundles, 167–168

tag libraries, 169–170
web.xml file, 166–167
Delete Employee transaction
DeleteEmployeeAction, 224–227
deploying, 227–229
Edit Employee transaction
deploying, 221–223
EditEmployeeAction, 217–221
Edit Employee JSP, 215–217
EmployeeForm, 217
GetEmployeeAction, 210–215
editing employees, 231–232
Employee object, 176–178
launching, 230
logging in, 230–231
Login transaction
deploying, 196–198
EmployeeListAction, 189–193
Employee List JSP, 193–196
LoginAction, 185–189
LoginForm, 183–185
Login JSP, 180–183
employees table (employees application), 173
error handling. *See also* debugging
<action> element, 118–119
ActionError class, 115–117
ActionErrors class, 117–118
JSPs (Java Server Pages), 38–40
stock symbol application, 75
wileystruts application
Action.perform() method, 123–124
ApplicationResources file modifications, 127
<html:errors /> tag, 121–123, 269–270
LookupAction code listing, 124–126
error pages (JSPs), 38–40
exception object (JSPs), 45
execute() method, 68
expressions (JSP scripting), 37–38

F

<form-bean /> subelement, 240–241
forms
ActionForm beans, 98–101
<html:form /> tag, 64–65, 98, 270–272
input tags
<html:password />, 101, 292–294
<html:submit />, 65, 102, 300–302
<html:text />, 64–65, 101, 302–307
request-time processing, 100
submitting, 102–103
validating, 100–101
<forward> element, 96–97
<forward /> subelement, 241–242

G-H

GenericServlet class, 14–16
<global-forwards /> subelement, 241–242

handling errors. *See also* debugging
<action> element, 118–119
ActionError class, 115–117
ActionErrors class, 117–118
JSPs (Java Server Pages), 38–40
stock symbol application, 75
wileystruts application
Action.perform() method, 123–124
ApplicationResources file modifications, 127
<html:errors /> tag, 121–123, 269–270
LookupAction code listing, 124–126
<html:base /> tag, 262
<html:button /> tag, 262–264
<html:cancel /> tag, 264–266
<html:checkbox /> tag, 267–269
<html:errors /> tag, 121–123, 269–270
<html:form /> tag, 64–65, 98, 270–272
<html:hidden /> tag, 272–273
<html:html /> tag, 273
<html:image /> tag, 274–276
<html:img /> tag, 276–279
<html:link /> tag, 279–282
<html:multibox /> tag, 282–285
<html:option /> tag, 288–290
<html:options /> tag, 290–292
<html:password /> tag, 101, 292–294
<html:radio /> tag, 294–297
<html:reset /> tag, 297–298
<html:rewrite /> tag, 299–300
<html:select /> tag, 285–288
<html:submit /> tag, 65, 102, 300–302
<html:text /> tag, 64–65, 101, 302–307
HTML tag library, installing, 261–262
HttpServlet class, 14–16

I

i18n. *See* internationalization
<icon /> subelement, 236–237
implicit objects (JSPs)
application, 44
config, 44
exception, 45
out, 40–41
page, 45
pageContext, 43
request, 42
response, 42
session, 43–44
include directive (JSPs), 35
Index View (stock symbol application), 63–67
init() method, 16, 87
input tags (forms)
<html:password />, 101, 292–294
<html:submit />, 65, 102, 300–302
<html:text />, 64–65, 101, 302–307
installing tag libraries
Bean tag library, 249–250
HTML tag library, 261–262
Logic tag library, 309–310
Template tag library, 325–326

interfaces, Servlet, 14
internationalization, 105
Controller components
defining resource bundles, 106–107
deploying resource bundles, 107
stock symbol application example, 109–114
View components
<bean:message /> tag, 108–109, 254–255
deploying bean tag library, 108

J

Jakarta struts. *See* struts
JavaBeans. *See also* Bean tag library
standard actions
Counter bean example, 48–51
<jsp:getProperty>, 48
<jsp:setProperty>, 47–48
<jsp:useBean>, 46–47
Java Server Pages. *See* JSPs
Java servlets. *See* servlets
javax.servlet.http package, 14
javax.servlet package, 13
JBuilder, debugging with
classpath setup, 160–162
project setup, 158–160
source paths, adding, 162
JDBC 2.0 extensions package, 139
JDBC DataSource. *See* DataSource
JDK, installing, 9
<jsp:forward> standard action, 53–56
<jsp:getProperty> standard action, 48
<jsp:include> standard action, 52–53
<jsp:param> standard action, 51–52
<jsp:plugin> standard action, 56–57
<jsp:setProperty> standard action, 47–48
<jsp:useBean> standard action, 46–47
JSPs (Java Server Pages)
defined, 32
deploying to struts applications, 96–97
directives
defined, 34
include, 35
page, 34–35
taglib, 36
error handling, 38–40
example, 32
gathering data with (forms), 97–98
ActionForm beans, 98–101
<html:form /> tag, 98
input tags, 101–102
implicit objects
application, 44
config, 44
exception, 45
out, 40–41
page, 45
pageContext, 43
request, 42
response, 42
session, 43–44
requests, 33
scripting
declarations, 36–37
expressions, 37–38
scriptlets, 38
standard actions
Counter bean example, 48–51
defined, 45
<jsp:forward>, 53–56
<jsp:getProperty>, 48
<jsp:include>, 52–53
<jsp:param>, 51–52
<jsp:plugin>, 56–57
<jsp:setProperty>, 47–48
<jsp:useBean>, 46–47

L

<large-icon /> subelement, 236–237
<logic:empty /> tag, 310
<logic:equal /> tag, 311–312
<logic:forward /> tag, 313
<logic:greaterEqual /> tag, 315
<logic:greaterThan /> tag, 316
<logic:iterate /> tag, 316–318
<logic:lessEqual /> tag, 318–319
<logic:lessThan /> tag, 319–320
<logic:match /> tag, 320
<logic:notEmpty /> tag, 310–311
<logic:notEqual /> tag, 312–313
<logic:notMatch /> tag, 321
<logic:notPresent /> tag, 323
<logic:present /> tag, 322
<logic:redirect /> tag, 313–315
Logic tag library, installing, 309–310
Login transaction (employees application)
deploying, 196–198
EmployeeListAction, 189–193
Employee List JSP, 193–196
LoginAction, 185–189
LoginForm, 183–185
Login JSP, 180–183

M-O

managing errors. *See also* debugging
<action> element, 118–119
ActionError class, 115–117
ActionErrors class, 117–118
JSPs (Java Server Pages), 38–40
stock symbol application, 75
wileystruts application
Action.perform() method, 123–124
ApplicationResources file modifications, 127
<html:errors /> tag, 121–123, 269–270
LookupAction code listing, 124–126
McClanahan, Craig, 1
<message-resources /> subelement, 246
Model components, employees application
departments table, 174
employees table, 173
MVC design patterns
overview, 2–3
struts implementation, 3–5
MySQL database (wileystruts application), 140–142

out object (JSPs), 40–41

P

pageContext object (JSPs), 43
page directive (JSPs), 34–35
page object (JSPs), 45
ParameterServlet example
  code listing, 28–29
  invoking (HTML form), 29–30
  running, 30–32
parsers, Xerces, 59–60
<plugin /> subelement, 247
Plugins, 87
  adding, 247
  configuring, 89–90
  creating, 87–89
  destroy() method, 87
  init() method, 87
process() method, 77–78
processPreprocess() method, 90–92

R

request object (JSPs), 42
RequestProcessor class, 90
  adding, 245
  configuring, 93
  creating, 90–92
  processPreprocess() method, 90–92
request-time processing (forms), 100
resource bundles
  defining, 106–107
  deploying, 107
  employees application, 167–168
response object (JSPs), 42
roles table (employees application), 174

S

scripting (JSPs)
  declarations, 36–37
  expressions, 37–38
  scriptlets, 38
scriptlets (JSPs), 38
service() method (servlets), 14–15, 16–17
ServletContext, 21–22
  ContextServlet example
    code listing, 22–23
    deploying, 24–26
  getAttribute() method, 22
  getAttributeNames() method, 22
  removeAttribute() method, 22
  setAttribute() method, 22
  Web application relationship, 22
Servlet interface, 14
servlets
  defined, 13
  deploying, 20–21
  executing, 14
  GenericServlet class, 14–16
  HttpServlet class, 14–16
  javax.servlet.http package, 14
  javax.servlet package, 13
  life cycle, 16–17
  ParameterServlet example
    code listing, 28–29
    invoking (HTML form), 29–30
    running, 30–32
  retrieving data with, 27
    getParameter() method, 27
    getParameterNames() method, 27
    getParameterValues() method, 27
  Servlet interface, 14
  SimpleServlet example
    code listing, 17–18
    doGet() method, 19–20
    doPost() method, 19–20
    init() method, 19
session object (JSPs), 43–44
<set-property /> subelement, 238, 239–240
SimpleServlet example
  code listing, 17–18
  deploying, 20–21
  doGet() method, 19–20
  doPost() method, 19–20
  init() method, 19
<small-icon /> subelement, 236–237
standard actions (JSPs)
  defined, 45
  <jsp:forward>, 53–56
  <jsp:getProperty>, 48
  <jsp:include>, 52–53
  <jsp:param>, 51–52
  <jsp:plugin>, 56–57
  <jsp:setProperty>, 47–48
  <jsp:useBean>, 46–47
stock symbol application, 163–164
  ActionForm class, 65–67
  ActionMapping extension
    creating, 132–133
    deploying, 133
    LookupAction modifications, 134–137
  Controller component, 69–72
  database, 140–142
  DataSource
    getQuote() method modifications, 144–146
    initializing, 142–143
    LookupAction modifications, 143–144
  deploying, 72–73
  development process, 62
  error handling, 75
    Action.perform() method, 123–124
    ApplicationResources file modifications, 127
    <html:errors /> tag, 121–123
    LookupAction code listing, 124–126
  internationalizing, 109–114
  running, 73–76
  Views
    creating, 62
    Index View, 63–67
    Quote View, 67–68
Struts. *See also* employees application; wileystruts application
  Controller components, 5, 68
    Action class, 68, 82–86
    ActionServlet class, 68, 77–82
    Plugins, 87–90
    RequestProcessor class, 90–93
  deploying, 60–61, 72–73
  design pattern debate, 2
  development process, 62

downloading, 59
installing, 60–61
JSPs (Java Server Pages)
deploying, 96–97
gathering data with, 97–103
project history, 1–2
View components, 62, 95–96
struts-config.xml file, 235–236
subelements. *See also* elements
<action />, 243–244
<action-mappings>, 243–244
<controller />, 245
<description />, 237–238
<display-name />, 237
<form-bean />, 240–241
<forward />, 241–242
<global-forwards />, 241–242
<icon />, 236–237
<large-icon />, 236–237
<message-resources />, 246
<plugin />, 247
<set-property />, 238, 239–240
<small-icon />, 236–237

T

taglib directive (JSPs), 36
tag libraries. *See also* tags
adding to applications, 169–170
deploying, 108
installing
Bean tag library, 249–250
HTML tag library, 261–262
Logic tag library, 309–310
Template tag library, 325–326
tags. *See also* tag libraries
<bean:cookie />, 250
<bean:define />, 251–252
<bean:header />, 252–253
<bean:include />, 253
<bean:message />, 108–109, 254–255
<bean:page />, 255
<bean:parameter />, 256
<bean:resource />, 256–257
<bean:size />, 257–258
<bean:struts />, 258
<bean:write />, 259–260
<html:base />, 262
<html:button />, 262–264
<html:cancel />, 264–266
<html:checkbox />, 267–269
<html:errors />, 121–123, 269–270
<html:form />, 64–65, 98, 270–272
<html:hidden />, 272–273
<html:html />, 273
<html:image />, 274–276
<html:img />, 276–279
<html:link />, 279–282
<html:multibox />, 282–285
<html:option />, 288–290
<html:options />, 290–292
<html:password />, 101, 292–294
<html:radio />, 294–297
<html:reset />, 297–298
<html:rewrite />, 299–300
<html:select />, 285–288
<html:submit />, 65, 102, 300–302
<html:text />, 64–65, 101, 302–307
<logic:empty />, 310
<logic:equal />, 311–312
<logic:forward />, 313
<logic:greaterEqual />, 315
<logic:greaterThan />, 316
<logic:iterate />, 316–318
<logic:lessEqual />, 318–319
<logic:lessThan />, 319–320
<logic:match />, 320
<logic:notEmpty />, 310–311
<logic:notEqual />, 312–313
<logic:notMatch />, 321
<logic:notPresent />, 323
<logic:present />, 322
<logic:redirect />, 313–315
<template:get />, 326–327
<template:insert />, 327
<template:put />, 328
<template:get /> tag, 326–327
<template:insert /> tag, 327
<template:put /> tag, 328
Tomcat
embedding into Java applications
application testing, 157–158
container hierarchy, 149–150
creating container structure, 150
Embedded class, 150
EmbeddedTomcat.java application, 151–156
installing, 9–10
requirements, 8
testing, 10–12
transactions (employees application)
Add Employee
AddEmployeeAction, 204–208
Add Employee JSP, 198–200
deploying, 208–210
EmployeeForm, 201–204
defined, 179
Delete Employee
DeleteEmployeeAction, 224–227
deploying, 227–229
Edit Employee
deploying, 221–223
EditEmployeeAction, 217–221
Edit Employee JSP, 215–217
EmployeeForm, 217
GetEmployeeAction, 210–215
Login
deploying, 196–198
EmployeeListAction, 189–193
Employee List JSP, 193–196
LoginAction, 185–189
loginForm, 183–185
Login JSP, 180–183

V

validating forms, 100–101
View components, 4, 95–96
  creating, 62
  employees application
    Add Employee JSP, 198–200
    Edit Employee JSP, 215–217
    Login JSP, 180–183
  forms
    ActionForm beans, 98–101
    <html:form /> tag, 64–65, 98, 270–272
    <html:password /> tag, 101, 292–294
    request-time processing, 100
    submitting, 102–103
    validating, 100–101
  internationalization
    <bean:message /> tag, 108–109, 254–255
    deploying bean tag library, 108
  JSPs (Java Server Pages)
    deploying, 96–97
    gathering data with, 97–103
  stock symbol application
    Index View, 63–67
    Quote View, 67–68

W-Z

WARs (Web Archive files), 8
web.xml files, creating, 166–167
Web applications. *See also* employees application; wileystruts application
  components, 5
  deployment descriptors, 6–8
  directory structure, 5–6
  packaging, 8
  ServletContext relationship, 22
Web Archive files (WARs), 8
wileystruts application
  ActionForm class, 65–67
  ActionMapping extension
    creating, 132–133
    deploying, 133
    LookupAction modifications, 134–137
  Controller component, 69–72
  database, 140–142
  DataSource
    getQuote() method modifications, 144–146
    initializing, 142–143
    LookupAction modifications, 143–144
  debugging, 163–164
  deploying, 72–73
  development process, 62
  error handling, 75
    Action.perform() method, 123–124
    ApplicationResources file modifications, 127
    <html:errors /> tag, 121–123, 269–270
    LookupAction code listing, 124–126
  internationalizing, 109–114
  running, 73–76
  Views
    creating, 62
    Index View, 63–67
    Quote View, 67–68

Xerces parser, 59–60